Mrs. Hill's Journal – Civil War Reminiscences

Sarah Jane Full Hill

Courtesy of the Hill family

The Lakeside Classics

MRS. HILL'S JOURNAL–CIVIL WAR REMINISCENCES

By Sarah Jane Full Hill

EDITED BY
MARK M. KRUG

The Lakeside Press

R. R. DONNELLEY & SONS COMPANY

CHICAGO

Christmas, 1980

PUBLISHERS' PREFACE

OUR selection for this year's *Lakeside Classic* is a never-before-published account of a family's involvement in the Civil War. We are told the story contains historically significant information as well as revealing perceptions about several important personalities of that period.

Mr. Marvin Chandler, a long-time friend of our Company, nominated his grandmother's recollections as appropriate *Classic* material. Many years earlier, Sarah Jane Full Hill had written her memoirs in response to urgings from her children. Her remarkable experiences were originally verbalized at story-telling time. In later years, however, after infirmities had curtailed Mrs. Hill's activities, her daughter suggested that the stories be recorded in the form of a continuous narrative. By so doing, Mrs. Hill found occupation for her keen, alert mind and provided her descendants (as well as *Lakeside Classic* readers) with a record of experiences which will probably never again be paralleled.

After our selection committee read Mrs. Hill's fascinating experiences, we asked Dr. Mark Krug, of the faculty at the University of Chicago, to vouch for the historical accuracy of Mrs. Hill's story. Dr. Krug, who has earned a reputation as an authority on the Civil War, told us that Mrs. Hill's memoirs are well written and afford new insights into the history of the Civil War and the people of that time.

Dr. Krug became so interested in what he felt to be an interesting and worthwhile book that he asked to be appointed as the editor.

This *Classic*—like the seventy-seven that have preceded—conforms to our objective of producing a book of highest quality using the best of contemporary technology. Design criteria were handled by Mobium Corporation for Design & Communication, the Company's new creative services subsidiary. Computerized composition was supplied by our Electronic Graphics Division. Web offset printing, automated binding and distribution were handled by our Crawfordsville, Indiana, Manufacturing Division. The map was researched and created through Donnelley's Cartographic Services.

In addition to introducing the *Classic* that follows, the Publishers' Preface also provides an opportunity for us to comment on various Company events that occurred during the first year of this new decade.

In spite of the recession and startup costs of three new divisions, overall sales and income again surpassed previous years, and sales passed the billion dollar mark for the first time. Growth in magazines and books slowed somewhat, but were more than offset by growth in other areas of business. As pointed out several years ago, the printing industry tends to lag the turns in the general economy so that we feel the full effects of a recession and the subsequent recovery some months after the generally agreed upon dates.

Three new divisions commenced production during the year and are in the early phases of start-up. The Harrisonburg, Virginia, Division produced its first book in July and will be in an excellent position to serve the eastern book publishers. The Lancaster, Pennsylvania, Gravure Division commenced its printing of *TV Guide* in August. Eventually, it will handle other publications as well. In September, our Spartanburg, South Carolina, Division started up its first gravure press. This division will be serving requirements of merchandisers for catalogs in the Southeast and East Coast areas. Bringing all three divisions on-stream in a single quarter presented a challenge without precedent in the expansion of the Company, and we are pleased to report that it is being accomplished according to plan in each case. We drew on talent throughout the Company in assembling the teams to manage these new divisions. The dedication and spirit with which they approached the job are greatly appreciated, as are the contributions they and their families are making to their new communities.

During the year, at various other divisions, space has been expanded and equipment added. The operations of our Interweb subsidiary in Los Angeles were consolidated in one location in the interest of greater efficiencies and economies. Abroad, Ben

Johnson and Company in York, England, expanded its plant and installed web offset presses to enter this new field. Already they have obtained a contract to print telephone directories for Her Majesty's Stationery Office, as well as other work.

We have also expanded our sales effort. Our goal always is to serve our customers well and to make it convenient and easy to do business with us. This has meant moving more sales people to the field to be close to their customers. Not long ago, certainly within the last 25 years, all of our sales people operated out of our headquarters in Chicago. Now we have sales locations throughout the country. In many cases, starting with a single representative, we have set up sales units in areas with high potential but virtually no existing business and have developed very substantial volumes of sales by being able to give the close, personal, dedicated attention each customer needs. This year we have set up such a unit in the United Kingdom and are enthused about the potential that can be realized there.

All this expansion has not gone on without an even greater advance in technology as it affects our Company and our industry. Some of the new technology is very costly to develop and adapt, at times obsoleting established methods and equipment. Again, to ignore these changes would, in the long run, be a disservice to our customers, our Company, our employees, and our stockholders. Examples are the satellite connection in use between Chicago and

New York, undoubtedly to be expanded; the use of Sci-Tex equipment in Lancaster to improve greatly our preliminary operations; and direct color engraving of gravure cylinders in Warsaw, eliminating a number of intermediate, time-consuming steps.

In several gravure divisions, new solvent recovery systems are in operation which keep virtually all of the evaporated solvent from the ink out of the atmosphere and capture it for re-use. The advances in electronic and computer technology challenge even the experts. Our Technical Advisory Committee is invaluable in helping us to keep abreast, and hopefully ahead. Besides scientists and engineers within the Company, it includes Dr. Albert V. Crewe, a Director of our Company, Dean of the Division of Physical Sciences at the University of Chicago, and former Director of the Argonne National Laboratory; Dr. William F. Miller, President of the Stanford Research Institute, formerly Provost and Professor of Computer Sciences at Stanford University; and Professor Arthur L. Schawlow, also of Stanford, and co-inventor of the laser.

Our accelerated expansion naturally has resulted in multiple promotions throughout the Company. Fortunately, we have had a vast talent to draw upon. At the upper level of General Management, John C. Dennis and John B. Schwemm were elected Senior Group Vice Presidents, new positions, and to the Board of the Company. Also elected to the Board was H. Blair White, partner in the law firm of Sidley & Austin, Chicago, replacing Howard J. Trienens, who was elected General Counsel of American Telephone & Telegraph Company, the oldest and one of the largest of our customers. C. Bouton McDougal and Harold B. Smith also retired from our Board after long and distinguished service, in accordance with our policy of tenure with regard to age. To all three, we are most grateful and greatly indebted.

At the beginning of the year our Board of Directors again increased our rate of dividends, by 14% to $1.14 per share. This was in the face of the unprecedented capital expansion program and the uncertainties of the year ahead. It was recognized that for the first time in decades insufficient funds would be generated from retained earnings, depreciation charges, and other internal sources. Over the last three years, our capital expenditures approximated $360,000,000. Short-term borrowings have been made, and it is quite possible that long-term debt will be incurred as well. However, not to meet the challenges and opportunities of our markets could have seriously affected our Company's future growth and prosperity.

The most pervasive problem in all areas of the business, including the planning of expansion, is inflation. We must position the business in a way that will allow us to take advantage of the available growth opportunities and yet protect the Company, its customers, employees, and shareholders from the most serious hazards of inflation. In planning our growth, we cannot create debt that would put the business in jeopardy in the event of a major economic collapse. On the other hand, debt is useful in providing the capital for expansion. Our policy has been to invest steadily to realize the market opportunities, always, however, within the context of maintaining a sound financial position.

Inflation is quite discouraging to our employees who through their devoted service and outstanding performance have every right to see their standard of living rise. There seems to be more realistic thinking as to the causes of inflation, but whether the Administration and the Congress have the courage to do what is necessary to curb inflation is, at this time, an open question.

In spite of the problems and challenges before us, we face the future with confidence and a measure of optimism. We hope our customers, our suppliers, employees, and other friends share in this feeling as well. To all, sincere wishes for a Merry Christmas and Happy New Year.

THE PUBLISHERS

Christmas, 1980

CONTENTS

List of Illustrations xix

Historical Introduction xxiii

Editor's Acknowledgments xlvii

Her Story 3

Index 337

List of The Lakeside Classics 347

ILLUSTRATIONS

Sarah Jane Full Hill . . . . *Frontispiece*
Eben Marvin Hill xxii
Captain Hill's Commission xxix
Map: The March of Captain Hill's Engineers
from St. Louis to Savannah 2
Carl Schurz and Franz Sigel 7
Jefferson Barracks 11
St. Louis Arsenal 11
Nathaniel Lyon 15
Centenary Church and Parsonage, St. Louis . 19
Sterling Price 23
Frank P. Blair, Jr. 27
Camp Benton, St. Louis 36
John C. Frémont 45
Death of General Lyon during the battle
of Wilson's Creek 53
The famous Hungarian Regiment
of General Frémont's bodyguards 57
St. Louis Mercantile Library Hall 61
Charge of General Smith's Division
during the capture of Fort Donelson 71
The gunboat attack on the water
batteries at Fort Donelson 72
Taylor's and McAllister's batteries
during the Battle at Fort Donelson 74

Views of New Madrid and Point Pleasant,
Missouri about 1862 80
Bombardment of Island No. 10
in the Mississippi River 86
Island No. 10 after the surrender 88
U.S. Hospital Ship *Red Rover* 95
Views of Steamers sunk by the Rebels
between Island No. 10 and
New Madrid, Missouri 110
The gunboat *New Era*, just built
at St. Louis, Missouri about 1861 155
William T. Sherman 169
St. Louis levee about 1871 173
Ulysses S. Grant 217
Andrew Johnson 281

Major Eben Marvin Hill

Courtesy of the Hill family

HISTORICAL INTRODUCTION

THE CIVIL WAR reminiscences of Mrs. Sarah Jane Full Hill should prove to be of interest to many general readers and to Civil War buffs and historians. Sarah Hill's wartime adventures, and she had many of them, make for interesting reading because she writes well, is perceptive and intelligent, and has keen and observant eyes for people and events. Her remarkable memory allows her to recall conversations with prominent people and her descriptions of life under war conditions are vivid and insightful.

Sarah Hill was born in England on December 15, 1838. She was twelve when she immigrated to America with her parents. The family settled in St. Louis. At the age of twenty, in 1858, three years before the outbreak of the Civil War, she married Eben Marvin Hill, a native of Highgate, a small village in Vermont. Her memoirs cover the period from 1861 when her husband became an officer in the Union's Corps of Engineers 'til the day that he came back home after the victory over the Confederacy. E.M., as Mrs. Hill affectionately called her husband, was a valiant officer and his regiment of engineers performed valuable service in the war, but his accomplishments were not any more remarkable than those of many thousands of other officers in the army of the North. But to Mrs. Hill, her husband was the central figure of her life, and her love and devotion to him shines brightly throughout the pages of this book. It is this devotion that impelled Sarah Hill to overcome the great hardships of travel under wartime conditions to be with E.M. at the front lines any time he was ill or wounded. Her reminiscences of these travels are fascinating.

With the facility of an experienced travel writer, Mrs. Hill gives us fresh and informative descriptions of travel on trains and steamboats filled beyond capacity by soldiers, army suppliers, speculators and camp followers. The trains and the Mississippi steamboats were overcrowded, dirty and the food was unbearable. Yet, when Sarah Hill decided to see her husband in an Army camp in Tennessee or in Mississippi, she endured all the hardships of travel with a remarkable tenacity. On one occasion when she received a message that her husband was desperately ill near Trenton, Tennessee, she embarked on a long journey with her seven year old son George in spite of a warning from her doctor that the child may die on the way. Luckily, both her husband and her son recovered.

E.M. and Sarah Hill lived in St. Louis, Missouri. The 1860 St. Louis City Directory has the following entry: "Eben M. Hill, builder, 293 Morgan Street." Hill worked for his wife's father who had a successful construction firm in the city. St. Louis, in 1860, was the largest city in Missouri and in the Middle

West. Geographically, it was located on the border between the North and the South, and it was of great strategic importance to both sides in the great civil controversy.

Sarah Hill had a vivid recollection of the long and bitter struggle between the pro-Confederate and the pro-Union forces in Missouri—a struggle which was to decide whether Missouri would join the Confederacy or remain in the Union. The outcome was of enormous importance to both sides.

Missouri, and particularly St. Louis, controlled a large portion of the shipping and war supply lines on the Mississippi. If the secessionists were to be successful in making this large border state a part of the Confederate States of America, there was a real danger that southern Illinois, the so-called "Little Egypt," where the great majority of the population were immigrants from Southern states, would also leave the Union. There was also a strong possibility that with Missouri joining the Confederacy, Kansas, where secessionists were strong and vocal, could also cut its ties to the Union. Since slavery was legal in Missouri and since slave owners controlled much of the rural part of the state, chances were slim that the state would stay in the Union.

President Lincoln was convinced that the holding of the border states, particularly Missouri, Kentucky and Maryland, was absolutely essential to the eventual victory of the Union. During the first year of the war, Lincoln stated on numerous occasions that the Union could not win without the 300,000 soldiers that the border states could (and indeed did) raise for the Union army. Lincoln felt that the Union needed the economic and political support of these strategically located states. When General John Frémont issued a proclamation which in effect freed the slaves in Missouri, Lincoln ordered him to rescind the order because as he wrote: "the emancipation of slaves will alarm our Southern Union friends, and turn them against us—perhaps ruin our rather fair prospect for Kentucky."

This conviction caused Lincoln to be extremely cautious on the issue of the emancipation of slaves because slavery existed and was legal in all the border states, including Missouri. Of the several border states, Missouri was by far the strongest and the richest. It had a population of 1,200,000 and St. Louis with 175,000 inhabitants was a great business, shipping and military center. The United States Arsenal in St. Louis had 60,000 muskets, a large number of cannons and field guns, 9,000 pounds of powder and 1,500,000 ball cartridges. These stores of ammunition were desperately needed by the Union army which lacked arms and was just in the process of formation.

After the election of Abraham Lincoln in November of 1860, the time when Mrs. Hill begins her narrative, the outcome of the civil strife in Missouri was in doubt. In the 1860 Presidential election, Senator Stephen Douglas of Illinois, the leader of the pro-Union Democrats, won the state by a small margin over John Bell of Tennessee, the head of the Constitutional Union party. Significantly, Abraham Lincoln carried St. Louis by a comfortable majority. The results reflected the deep differences among the people of Missouri on the crucial question of slavery. Bell muted the issue and emphasized his adherence to the Constitution of the United States. Douglas advocated plebiscites to determine if a state was to join the Union with or without slavery. Lincoln, on the other hand, was adamantly opposed to any further extension of slavery. Lincoln's victory in St. Louis clearly reflected the fact that while there were over 100,000 slaves in rural sections of Missouri, there were, in 1860, only 120 slaves in St. Louis. Even more important was the almost unanimous support that Lincoln received from the city's large German-American population.

To accentuate their political divisions, the people of Missouri gave few votes to John Breckinridge of Kentucky, the candidate of the Southern Democrats favoring secession, but they elected Claiborne Jackson, a pro-Confederate slave owner, Governor of Missouri. Nominally, Jackson ran on Douglas' ticket, but he made no bones about his conviction that the state should join the Confederacy. Jackson's support in the state was considerable. On December 31, 1860, the *Missouri Republican*, one of the most influential papers in the Middle West, carried an editorial calling on Congress to provide remedies for the just grievances of the South. In case Congress refused to pass appropriate laws, the newspaper urged that Missouri secede from the Union and join the Confederacy.

In those crucial days of turmoil and bitter controversy between the Union and the Confederate factions in Missouri, Sarah Hill and her husband did not hesitate because they were ardent Unionists. Eben Marvin Hill, a New Englander, was deeply devoted to one and undivided United States of America. His father, who still lived in Highgate, Vermont, near the Canadian border, came from a family which settled in New England in Colonial times, and whose antecedents fought in the American Revolution. The elder Hill was to see four of his sons serve in the Union army. Immediately after the start of hostilities, E.M. volunteered for service, and since he was a builder and an engineer by training, he enlisted in the Corps of Engineers. Sarah shed many tears, but she fully supported her husband's decision.

Mrs. Hill's Journal sheds important light on the role of the Germans, who constituted about a third of the population of St. Louis in those crucial early days of the Civil War, when Missouri was deciding on which side it would fight. German immigrants came to St. Louis and to the areas around Alton and Belleville, Illinois in the early 1850's because of the failure of the democratic revolutions in the Austro-Hungarian Empire and in various parts of Germany.

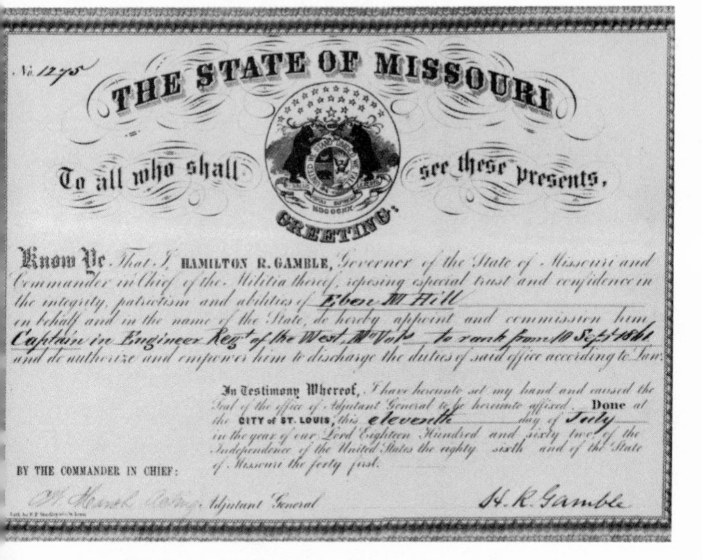

No. 1275

THE STATE OF MISSOURI

To all who shall see these presents, GREETING:

Know Ye, That I, HAMILTON R. GAMBLE, Governor of the State of Missouri and Commander in Chief of the Militia thereof, reposing especial trust and confidence in the integrity, patriotism and abilities of Eben M. Hill on behalf and in the name of the State, do hereby appoint and commission him Captain in Engineer Reg^t of the West, Mo Vols to rank from 10 Sept 1861 and do authorize and empower him to discharge the duties of said office according to Law.

In Testimony Whereof, I have hereunto set my hand and caused the Seal of the office of Adjutant General to be hereunto affixed. Done at the CITY of ST. LOUIS, this eleventh day of July in the year of our Lord Eighteen Hundred and sixty two, of the Independence of the United States the eighty sixth and of the State of Missouri the forty first.

BY THE COMMANDER IN CHIEF:

[illegible] Adjutant General

H. R. Gamble

Eben Marvin Hill's Commission as Captain in the Engineer Corps of the Missouri Volunteers.

Courtesy of the Hill family

Since they were victims and refugees from autocratic regimes which ruthlessly crushed what historians call the "Spring of Nations" rebellions, they became, almost without exception, bitter opponents of slavery, and threw their support to Lincoln and to the Republican party whose platform opposed the extension of slavery and re-affirmed the principle that "all men are created equal."

Mrs. Hill notes that "state after state in the South seceded and Missouri tried to, but St. Louis, which had a large German population that remained loyal to the Union, kept it from so doing." The German immigrants in St. Louis, quickly converted their Turnervereinen, the gymnastic societies, into military units of the Home Guards and kept the secessionists at bay. Their main objective was to defend the U.S. Arsenal which on direct orders of Jefferson Davis, the President of the Confederacy, was to be captured by pro-Confederate forces. President Lincoln was equally determined to keep the Arsenal in Union hands. To help him achieve this objective Lincoln had the full support of Carl Schurz and Franz Sigel, both veterans of the German rebellions and who now commanded two excellent Home Guard regiments.

The Union forces in St. Louis were under the command of Captain Nathaniel Lyon, a Connecticut Yankee and a West Point graduate. Lyon fought slave owners in Kansas, and he hated slavery and the South. After the fall of Fort Sumter, Lyon, with the help of Frank Blair, Jr., an influential Unionist politician, assembled a force of Union army volunteers and aided by the German Home Guards attacked and captured the United States Arsenal. The huge haul of ammunition was immediately taken for safekeeping to Springfield, Illinois on a boat supplied by the Governor of Illinois, Richard Yates, a close friend of Lincoln.

To secure the state for the Union, Lyon decided to capture Camp Jackson, a camp of state militia located on the edge of the city. Lyon suspected that General D. M. Frost, the commander of Camp Jackson, had designs to defect to the Confederacy. Some historians doubt whether this was Frost's intention. Allan Nevins, in his history of the Civil War, contends that General Frost opposed secession and advocated that Missouri adopt a position of armed neutrality in the conflict.

Mrs. Hill is a bit confused in her chronology of events, but she is basically correct when she writes, "This time it was known to the military authorities that they [the Confederates] were concentrating for an attack on the Arsenal and Jefferson Barracks—to capture the stores, ammunition and men—then they would hold St. Louis, and Missouri could join the Confederacy."

The outnumbered garrison of Camp Jackson surrendered to the attackers, but a bloody confrontation ensued between Lyon's forces and an unruly pro-slavery mob which pelted the Union soldiers with stones and bottles. The resentment against the German soldiers was expressed by repeated shouts, "Down with the Black Dutch." After pistol shots were fired from the crowd, the Union troops fired back. Twenty-eight people were killed or mortally wounded. Governor Jackson and the Missouri secessionists raised the cry of "No Coercion" and a bloody, cruel Civil War ensued in Missouri. It was a war that would last for four years.

There is an interesting sidelight to Mrs. Hill's story of events during the first weeks of the Civil War in St. Louis. On the day of the capture of the Arsenal by Captain Lyon and his forces, both Ulysses S. Grant and William Tecumseh Sherman, two men who later were to play such important roles in the Civil War, were on the streets of St. Louis. Grant was on a few days leave in St. Louis from his post in Alton, Illinois where he served as recruiting officer for Governor Richard Yates and Sherman was president of one of St. Louis street car line companies.

The battles between Unionist and Confederate units in Missouri see-sawed throughout the state. In July 1861, Lincoln sent General John C. Frémont, the famous explorer of the West, to take command of the Union's Department of the West, with headquarters in St. Louis with orders to keep Missouri and Kentucky in the Union. Three Confederate armies under the command of General Leonidas Polk were poised to invade Missouri. The Confederates failed, but in one of the bloody battles fought near Wilson's Creek, Nathaniel Lyon, by then a Brigadier General, was killed.

Missouri stayed in the Union because of the daring and bravery of Nathaniel Lyon and the steadfast support of the Union by Frank Blair, Jr., a Missouri lawyer and later a Union Army General. But what probably helped most was the staunch support of the Union by the German population in St. Louis.

In Forest Park in St. Louis there stands a statue of Franz Sigel. The inscription on the pedestal reads:

> "To remind future generations of the heroism of the German-American Patriots of St. Louis and Vicinity, in the Civil War of 1861–1865."

To remind us of the bitter division among the people of Missouri, there is another monument in Forest Park which was erected by the St. Louis Daughters of the Confederacy. The inscription on this monument reads as follows:

> "To the memory of the Soldiers and Sailors of the Southern Confederacy who fought to uphold the rights declared by the pen of Jefferson and achieved by the sword of Washington.
>
> With sublime self-sacrifice they battled to preserve the independence of the states which was won from Great Britain and to perpetuate the constitutional government which was established by the fathers.
>
> Actuated by the purest patriotism they performed deeds of prowess such as thralled the heart of mankind with admiration.

Full in the front of war they stood and displayed a courage so superb that it gave a new and brighter luster to the annals of valor.

History contains no chronicle more illustrious than the story of their achievements; and although worn out by ceaseless conflict and overwhelmed by numbers they were finally forced to yield.

Their glory "On brightest pages penned by poets and by sages, shall go sounding down the ages."

"We had sacred principles to maintain and rights to defend for which we were in duty bound to do our best, even if we perished in the endeavor." R. E. Lee

On her many trips to visit her husband in several army camps, Sarah Hill met many prominent people. Her recollections of these meetings are not only interesting but they also add to our knowledge of such known Civil War personalities as General Ulysses S. Grant; Confederate General Nathaniel B. Forrest; John Wilkes Booth, Lincoln's assassin; and Andrew Johnson, Civil War general, military governor of Tennessee and later Vice President and President of the United States.

In January, 1864, Mrs. Hill received a letter from Major Hill who was then stationed in a camp near Nashville, Tennessee. His regiment of the Missouri Corps of Engineers was engaged in building a railroad from Nashville to the Tennessee River in order to add another supply line for the Union army, which was advancing into the heartland of the South. This was of great importance since the tracks of the Louisville and Nashville Railroad were easily and frequently disrupted and sabotaged by raids of Confederate troops and pro-Southern guerrilla bands. Major Hill wrote his wife that he could arrange for her to stay with him in the camp for a prolonged period. The difficulties and the dangers of wartime travel never seemed to have bothered Sarah Hill. She took her young son, George, and embarked on the long and difficult journey from St. Louis to Nashville. She wrote about the problem that faced her: "How to reach Nashville was the question, for I did not hesitate a moment about going, but Nashville was a base of military preparation for a big campaign, and it was a difficult matter for a mere woman with a child to get through the lines." There were in fact severe restrictions on travel by civilians on trains and steamboats, and military rules prohibited the presence of women at the front lines or in army camps. But Sarah Hill was not a "mere woman." She was endowed with an indomitable will and possessed a great deal of stamina and courage. Somehow, she obtained the needed pass to travel from St. Louis to Louisville, and with the help of Colonel John M. Palmer, an early supporter and friend of Lincoln, she found a seat on the train going from Louisville to Nashville. She had no pass but when the guards demanded to see her pass, Colonel Palmer told them that she was in his party.

By a lucky coincidence, General Ulysses S. Grant also boarded the train in Louisville and sat next to Mrs. Hill in the compartment obtained for her by

Colonel Palmer. Mrs. Hill and Grant had a delightful conversation. She notes in her memoirs that the officers of his staff looked much more imposing than did Lieutenant General Grant who "wore a plain blue coat with old tarnished shoulder straps designating his rank." While chatting with the famous general, Mrs. Hill must have prayed that he would help her in her dire predicament because she had no pass and no ticket. She knew that the conductor would have undoubtedly put her and her son off the train at the next stop if she failed to produce the necessary papers. Luckily, when the conductor approached, General Grant quickly interceded saying: "This is Mrs. Major Hill. You will please pass her. Her escort, who is on the train following this, has her ticket and pass." Thus rescued, Mrs. Hill talked at length with the General about their mutual friends in St. Louis.

In the course of the conversation Sarah Hill remarked that there was a lot of talk in the country about nominating Grant, already then a war hero, for the Presidency on the Republican ticket. The election was to take place in November 1864, and it was generally assumed, at times even by Lincoln himself, that he would not be nominated because the leaders of the Republican Party were convinced that the President was unpopular and did not have enough support to be elected. Radical Republicans were unhappy with Lincoln's moderate approach to the issue of slavery and to Reconstruction of the

South, and many people of the North were weary of the war and wanted a new leader in the White House. The Democratic party, which promised to end the war, was sure that its candidate would be elected President. Facing this dilemma, some Republican leaders, as Mrs. Hill told Grant, wanted to nominate him for the Presidency. When she asked Grant whether he would rather be a full general as was proposed in a bill then pending in Congress or be President, General Grant thought for a while and then said: "I do not think I would make a good President. I prefer the Generalship. That is for life and my family would be provided for. There are too many things to consider in the Presidency, anyway, I am going to stay with the war until it is ended. I think no farther than that now."

Assuming that Mrs. Hill's recollection is accurate, and we have no reason to think otherwise, Grant's statement is remarkable on several counts. With his usual modesty and ability for self-analysis Grant astutely prophesied that he did not have the qualifications to be an effective President. His concern for his family's financial security rings true. Grant was a man of modest means all of his life because his many financial ventures usually ended in disaster. In spite of the fact that during his two terms as President corruption was rampant and his friends enriched themselves by legal and illegal means, Ulysses S. Grant had no money when he left the Presidency and his family was not provided for.

When he was told that he had cancer of the throat, he decided to write his autobiography in order to provide some financial security for his family. His publisher was Mark Twain, and the autobiography, a remarkably good book in which Grant took the credit he deserved for his accomplishments as a general, but expressed his disappointment in his record as President, was a financial success.

The credibility of Mrs. Hill's conversation with Grant, which took place sometime around January 15, 1864, is confirmed in a letter written on January 21, 1864, by Grant to J.N. Morris, a friend who lived in Quincy, Illinois. In that letter Grant wrote: "I am not a politician, never was and hope never to be, and could not write a political letter. My only desire is to serve the country in its present trials. . . . I infinitely prefer my present position to that of any civil office within the gift of the people."

Mrs. Hill's encounter with General Nathaniel Bedford Forrest, the famous Confederate cavalry general, came in Trenton, Tennessee. This meeting gives the reader an important insight into the man who at the end of the war founded the Ku Klux Klan in Pulaski, Tennessee. Sarah Hill's journal helps explain the tactics of fear, terror and brutality which were the mark of the tactics used by the K.K.K. Bedford Forrest, a handsome, dashing and daring general, perfected these tactics in the Civil War, and after the defeat of the Confederacy, decided to use them against the blacks to prevent the freed slaves from using their new found right to vote.

The image of Forrest as represented by his portraits is that of an aristocratic Southern general who cut a magnificent figure of a cavalry officer. In fact, Nathaniel Bedford Forrest was a poorly educated son of a blacksmith, who was a laborer and a slave trader. Using his innate abilities for leadership and business he became a rich planter and an alderman in Memphis. When the war began, Forrest equipped, at his own expense, a cavalry regiment and fought with courage and distinction at Fort Donelson and at Shiloh. Following his promotion to Brigadier General, he caught a large Union force by surprise at Murfreesboro, Tennessee and took 1,200 Union soldiers prisoners and captured half a million dollars worth of guns, ammunition and war materials. His lightning raids became a legend and a scourge to the Union troops in Tennessee.

Mrs. Hill heard of General Forrest in Trenton, Tennessee, where she came after a harrowing journey to nurse her ill husband back to health. The doctors had given up hope for E.M.'s recovery. But Mrs. Hill did not. She took her husband from the hospital to a private home and slowly helped him recover. After Major Hill returned to his regiment, Mrs. Hill stayed in Trenton with E.M.'s brother, Elihu, who lived there. Suddenly rumors began to spread that Bedford Forrest was planning a raid on Trenton to capture ammunition depots and destroy the railroad. There was no Union force in Trenton sufficient to repel the raid and its occupation was a foregone conclusion. The inhabitants of Trenton, Mrs. Hill relates, were terrified because of Forrest's reputation for cruelty and ruthlessness. "Great excitement," she writes, "and anxiety prevailed." When the Confederate troops entered the town, "Forrest's cavalry charged madly down the streets yelling and firing promiscuously, shooting up the town." Forrest had about 1,200 men and after the capture of the small Union garrison, the Confederate troops "spread out over the town committing many depredations. They charged up and down the streets firing wildly into houses among unoffending women and children." The Confederates burned some homes of known Unionists and looted stores belonging to them. The aim was clearly to warn the citizens not to give support to the Union. Forrest, as he was to do later with his K.K.K. raids, used intimidation and fear to achieve his aims. Sarah Hill perceptibly notes "the attack of Forrest with his large force on this unprotected little town was a good deal like a big bully beating a little boy."

A few days after the capture of Trenton, General Forrest summoned Mrs. Hill to appear in his headquarters. Sarah Hill was not easily frightened, even by Bedford Forrest, and she refused to come. But the officer who delivered the message warned her that she would be taken by force. She describes Forrest as a "fine looking man, tall and lean, but muscular, with a face that showed he was accustomed to rule. The eyes looked hard and cold, and the mouth looked cruel." General Forrest after confirming that Sarah Hill was a wife of a Union officer on active duty ordered her to take an oath that she would not aid the Union. Without hesitation Mrs. Hill refused. Forrest relented but ordered her to remain under house arrest, warning that if she left the house, she would be taken prisoner. Mrs. Hill said to him: "We know your tender mercies to prisoners, but you are not making war on women and children, you have to make your retreats so rapidly. They would only be obstacles to you on the run, and you will leave this town more rapidly than you entered it when you learn the Union army is coming." Forrest's face, Mrs. Hill writes, looked "black and hard." He dismissed her repeating that she would be under house arrest. Whether Mrs. Hill was, indeed, as fearless as she reports is impossible to ascertain, but the incident, even if partly fictional, provides an interesting picture of the image that Bedford Forrest gave to the people of the North.

Historians ought to find Mrs. Hill's account of her wartime meeting with Andrew Johnson of great interest. Johnson, as is well known, stumbled and fell as he walked up the stairs to be inaugurated Vice President of the United States. He was elected to this office in 1864, as Lincoln's running mate. It was obvious to those present that the Vice President elect was drunk, and that his aides had to carry him to an office in the Capitol. Textbook writers and biographers have for years explained that Johnson was a non-drinker, and that since he suffered from a bout of influenza, he took a tumbler of whisky to steady himself. This one drink made him drunk because he was virtually a teetotaler.

Mrs. Hill has a different story to tell about Johnson. She relates that she was present in the summer of 1864, at the reception in Johnson City, Tennessee which was attended by Andrew Johnson, who was at that time the military governor of Tennessee. When Johnson tried to give his speech, he mumbled incoherently and was obviously drunk. On the train which brought the guests back from Johnson City to Nashville, Sarah Hill saw him and remarked: "Johnson was drunk, he was stupid." Sarah Hill's account would suggest that Johnson was no stranger to heavy drinking long before the 1864 Inauguration. Whether Mrs. Hill was influenced in her negative portrait of Johnson by his unpopularity at the time of the writing of her memoirs must be left to the judgment of the readers.

Mrs. Hill saw John Wilkes Booth when he played "Shylock" and "Taming of the Shrew" in a theatre in Nashville. She described him as a "very handsome dark man" and a very good actor. She thought that "he was under the influence of liquor" because he "frolicked" so much on the stage. Her impression was that "he was of wild undisciplined nature and inclined to dissipation." She reported that it was widely rumored that his leading lady was his mistress. Sarah Hill did not seem to be scandalized by this spicy rumor.

In her descriptions of Sherman's march to the sea, the burning of Atlanta and of other Southern cities, Mrs. Hill reveals her ambivalent emotions about the events she is describing. On one hand, she seems to justify the ruthlessness displayed by Sherman's army and quotes his famous statement that "war is hell" in partial justification of the sufferings inflicted on the population of the Confederate States. Mrs. Hill notes with pride that her husband was part of Sherman's victorious troops. But, it is also clear that Mrs. Hill, who even earlier in the war was impressed by the grandeur of the homes of the planters and the graciousness and charm of the "Southern way of life," was dismayed to see and hear of the havoc wreaked on the heart of the Confederacy by Union troops. It must be remembered that Mrs. Hill wrote her memoirs many years after the Civil War, and that her attitude at the time she set her reminiscences onto paper, reflected the changed conditions in the nation. There was a reconciliation between the North and the South, a successful effort to "bind the nation's wounds," and a growing distrust and dislike of the Negroes in both North and South. When she wrote her book, the Jim Crow laws were already in force in the South, and the people of the North did not seem to be very much perturbed by them.

Characteristically, even the passage of time has

not dimmed Mrs. Hill's recollection of the emaciated and sorrowfully neglected Northern soldiers whom she saw returning from Confederate prisons. She vowed, when she saw the evidence of the inhuman treatment of these prisoners, never to forgive the South for this crime. In this aspect, Mrs. Hill also reflected the temper of the times on which she wrote her memoirs. All Republican candidates for high offices still continued to conduct what was called "bloody shirt campaigns" which stressed the terrible sacrifices made by the North in the Civil War and the cruel treatment of Union prisoners in Confederate prison camps.

We will conclude this introduction by summarizing briefly what these memoirs tell us about the authoress. Sarah Hill was a remarkably loving and devoted wife. No hardships, not even fear of enemy fire, was enough to deter her when she decided to see her husband when he was ill or wounded. As we noted on one occasion, she went to see E.M. with her very ill son even after the doctor told her that her child might die on the way. Her duty to her husband came first even before the survival of her son. It was her good fortune that both husband and son survived.

Sarah Hill was a strong minded woman. Sometimes her strong personality created difficulties for her husband. On a prolonged visit to her husband's army camp in Kingston Springs, Tennessee other officers and soldiers complained that they were under a "petticoat rule." Major Hill had to publicly rebuke his wife and ask her to forgo expressing her opinions on war matters. Shortly thereafter, a rumor of an impending raid by General Forrest, brought about an order for all women to leave the camp. Mrs. Hill reluctantly went home to St. Louis, however, she later found the rumor to be a false alarm.

We must not remain with the impression that all was hardships and gloom for Mrs. Hill in her travels and her stays in various army camps. On the contrary, her descriptions of her life in army camps near Nashville and Waverly in Tennessee are filled with accounts of rides through beautiful countrysides, parties and dances. Sarah Hill was vivacious and fun-loving. She innocently flirted with the officers and liked to, and often did, dance all night. At one great ball, she writes "we danced till sunrise the next morning forgetful of war or rumors of war." After so-called "inspection tours" of the engineering works around Waverly, Mrs. Hill reports that most of the nights were spent "frolicking and dancing." We, of course, know that horror and carnage and frolicking and dancing were intermingled in all wars throughout history.

Sarah Hill must have had a phenomenal memory because her memoirs are remarkably accurate and her ability to reconstruct conversations is very impressive. It is a pleasure to meet Mrs. Hill through these reminiscences.

EDITOR'S ACKNOWLEDGMENTS

THE EDITOR wishes to acknowledge the help he received in the pleasant task of editing this manuscript from the staff of the Joseph Regenstein Library of the University of Chicago, the Newberry Library, the Chicago Historical Society and the Illinois Historical Society.

Special appreciation is due to the well informed reference librarians of the Missouri Historical Society in St. Louis for their generous and competent assistance in clearing up some obscure historical and geographical points in the manuscript. A number of the illustrations in the book were supplied from the Civil War collections of the Missouri Historical Society. We gratefully acknowledge the assistance given us by Mrs. Judith Ciampoli, Curator of Pictorial History.

The family of the late Mrs. E.M. Hill was quite helpful in supplying much needed information along with valuable family illustrations and documents. We wish to express our thanks to the grandsons of Mrs. Hill—Mr. Thomas Chandler of Osterville, Massachusetts and Mr. Marvin Chandler of Carmel, California.

DR. MARK M. KRUG

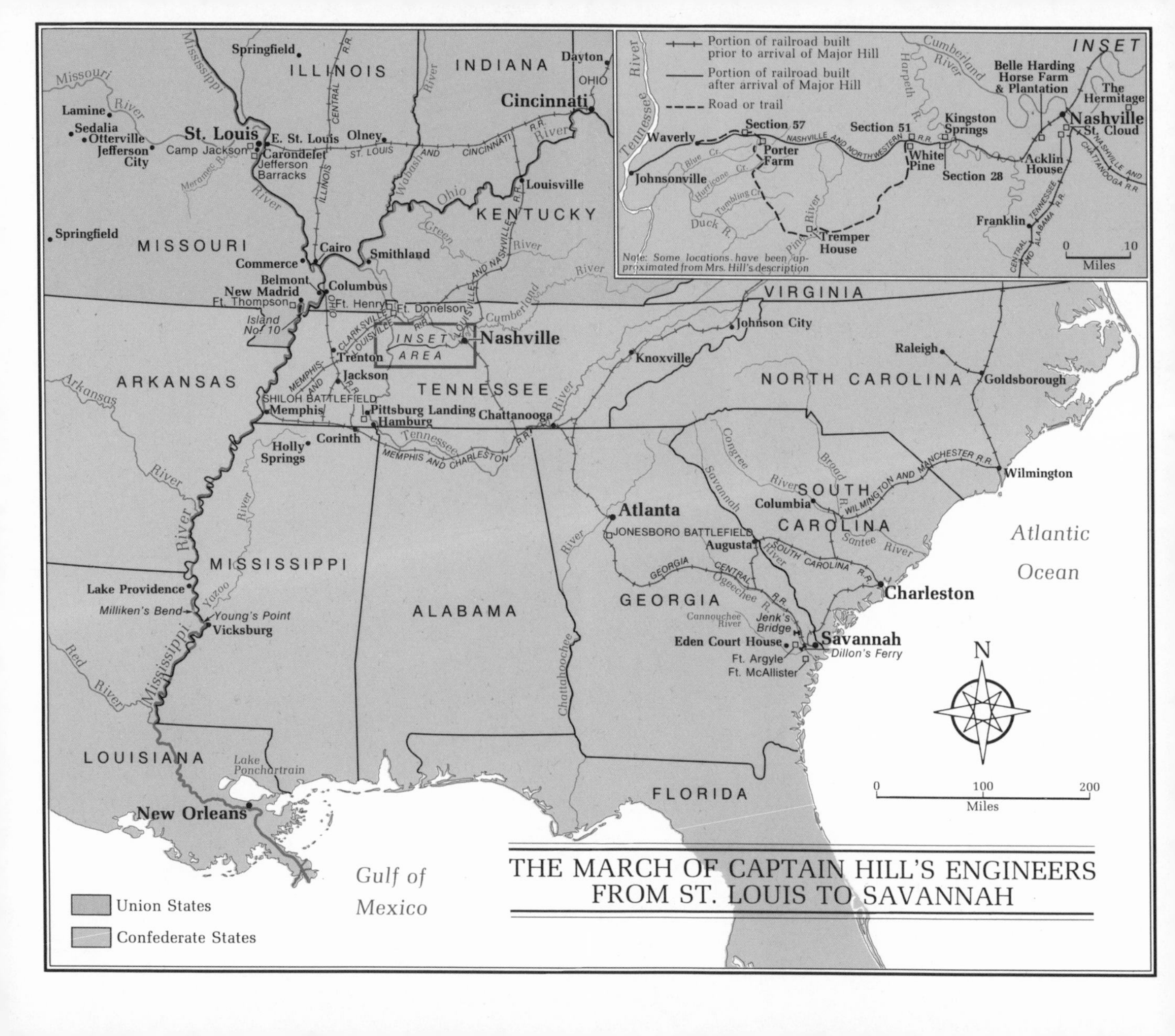
INSET
Portion of railroad built prior to arrival of Major Hill
Portion of railroad built after arrival of Major Hill
Road or trail
Tennessee River
Cumberland River
Harpeth R.
Belle Harding Horse Farm & Plantation
The Hermitage
Nashville
St. Cloud
Waverly
Section 57
Section 51
Kingston Springs
Porter Farm
White Pine
Section 28
Acklin House
Johnsonville
Blue Cr.
Hurricane Cr.
Tumbling Cr.
Duck R.
Piney River
Tremper House
Franklin
NASHVILLE AND NORTHWESTERN R.R.
NASHVILLE AND CHATTANOOGA R.R.
CENTRAL TENNESSEE AND ALABAMA R.R.
Note: Some locations have been approximated from Mrs. Hill's description
0
10
Miles
ILLINOIS
INDIANA
OHIO
KENTUCKY
MISSOURI
ARKANSAS
TENNESSEE
VIRGINIA
NORTH CAROLINA
SOUTH CAROLINA
GEORGIA
ALABAMA
MISSISSIPPI
LOUISIANA
FLORIDA
Springfield
Dayton
Cincinnati
Missouri River
Lamine
Sedalia
Otterville
Jefferson City
St. Louis
E. St. Louis
Olney
Camp Jackson
Carondelet
Jefferson Barracks
Meramec R.
ILLINOIS CENTRAL R.R.
OHIO AND MISSISSIPPI R.R.
Wabash River
Ohio River
Louisville
LOUISVILLE AND NASHVILLE R.R.
Green River
Springfield
Cairo
Smithland
Commerce
Belmont
Columbus
New Madrid
Ft. Thompson
Island No. 10
Ft. Henry
Ft. Donelson
Cumberland River
CLARKSVILLE AND LOUISVILLE R.R.
INSET AREA
Nashville
Johnson City
Knoxville
Raleigh
Goldsborough
Trenton
Jackson
MEMPHIS AND OHIO R.R.
SHILOH BATTLEFIELD
Memphis
Pittsburg Landing
Hamburg
Chattanooga
Corinth
Holly Springs
Tennessee River
MEMPHIS AND CHARLESTON R.R.
Arkansas River
WILMINGTON AND MANCHESTER R.R.
Wilmington
Congree River
Broad R.
Savannah River
Columbia
Atlanta
JONESBORO BATTLEFIELD
Augusta
Santee River
SOUTH CAROLINA R.R.
GEORGIA CENTRAL R.R.
Ogeechee R.
Cannouchee River
Jenk's Bridge
Charleston
Eden Court House
Savannah
Dillon's Ferry
Ft. Argyle
Ft. McAllister
Atlantic Ocean
Chattahoochee River
Lake Providence
Milliken's Bend
Young's Point
Vicksburg
Yazoo River
Mississippi River
Red River
Lake Ponchartrain
New Orleans
Gulf of Mexico
N
0
100
200
Miles
Union States
Confederate States

THE MARCH OF CAPTAIN HILL'S ENGINEERS FROM ST. LOUIS TO SAVANNAH

Mrs. Hill's Journal – Civil War Reminiscences

Her Story

MY CHILDREN have desired that I should narrate some of my personal recollections of the Civil War. I will try to do it as best I can, relating some of the incidents that have remained most firmly impressed in my memory, and which after more than half a century has elapsed, are just as vivid and clear as when they occurred. Of the time when a nation went through a baptism of fire and blood, and her dearest and best were offered as a sacrifice on the altar of their country.

In writing of my husband he will be mentioned as E.M. That was his familiar appellation in our family.

It seems difficult to realize that over half a century has elapsed since that memorable day in April when the gun was fired on Fort Sumter which boomed across the world and announced the beginning of one of the fiercest and bloodiest wars in the annals of history. When people of one nation, one faith and one family were pitted against each other in deadly combat, and which meant the destruction or salvation of a government, "of the people, by the people and for the people."

A little explanation about our family matters is

necessary to begin. We were living in St. Louis at that time, not far from the old Fair Ground, in a little cottage which was our own home. We had our baby boy and E.M. was connected with my father in a large construction and building business which was quite successful. Life looked very fair and bright to us, for we were young, healthy and strong and were prospering.

After the election of Lincoln in November of 1860, the cauldron of rebellion in the South was seething and many believed that he would never be inaugurated. Father and E.M. had both voted for Bell and Everett, as being the more conservative candidates, thinking Lincoln and his platform too radical.[1] They were Republicans, though living in a slave state.

One evening in April, E.M. came home looking very pale and as though he had received a great shock. He dropped into a chair and appeared so unlike himself I was alarmed and begged to know what the trouble was.

"I fear it is war," he said, "for South Carolina has fired on the flag and it cannot go unnoticed. The

[1] Mrs. Hill's father and her husband Eben Marvin voted for John Bell of the Constitutional Union Party which opposed the threatened secession of the Southern states and the disruption of the Union. Bell's party also demanded the strict enforcement of the Constitution and of the existing laws which protected the institution of slavery. Bell lost Missouri to Stephen Douglas, the head of the Unionist Democratic Party by a few hundred votes. Edward Everett the famed Massachusetts lawyer and orator was Bell's running mate.

South has been preparing for this many months, and this is the pretext for war, while the North is not ready and never has believed this thing would come."[2]

There was no dinner partaken by us that night for we realized what the consequences might be, and living in a border state, which was even then trying to secede, the conflict would probably be fierce and sanguinary.[3]

[2]South Carolina attacked the U.S. Fort Sumter on April 21, 1861. The greatly outnumbered and isolated garrison, commanded by Major Robert Anderson, surrendered to the Confederate troops. The firing on Fort Sumter was, of course, not the cause of the Civil War just as the murder of Archduke Ferdinand in Sarajevo in 1914, was not the cause of World War I.

It can be argued that the causes of the Civil War can be traced as far back as 1800 when the first conflict between the North and the South over slavery began. Repeated efforts to find an acceptable compromise failed.

Allan Nevins in his splendid work on the Civil War wrote: "looking backward, we can now see that a conflict between North and South had been certain when Lincoln was inaugurated. Nothing the government might legitimately have done could have averted it. The seven states of the 'cotton kingdom' were determined to erect a separate republic; the United States was determined to maintain the Union. At some point battle was certain. It would have taken place at Pickens, if not at Sumter; in Texas, if not at Pickens; or on the banks of the Mississippi, if not in Texas."

[3]Missouri was a border state between the Union and the states which seceded from the United States of America during the period December, 1860, and March, 1861.

Missouri was a slave state but its population was, as the 1860 Presidential election has proven, overwhelmingly for the preservation of the Union.

Events which are matters of history occurred rapidly after that and need not be gone into in this narrative. State after state in the South seceded and Missouri tried to,[4] but St. Louis, which had a large German population that remained steadfastly loyal to the Union, kept it from so doing.[5] Four regiments of German citizens were enrolled as militia for the protection of the city. They were called the Home Guards and were commanded by Carl

[4]Mrs. Hill's statement that Missouri tried to secede from the Union is only partly true. The slave owners, who had about 100,000 slaves in Missouri, and those Missourians who came to the state from the South generally favored the position taken by the Confederate States of America. They were led by Governor Claiborne Jackson. However, when in February 1861, Governor Jackson called a special state convention, not one secessionist delegate was elected. By a vote of 89 to 1 the convention resolved that Missouri had no cause to leave the Union.

[5]About a third of the population of St. Louis consisted of German immigrants who came to Missouri in the 1840's and 1850's. They left Europe after the collapse of the democratic revolution in the Austro-Hungarian Empire and in the various German states.

Since many of them fought against these despotic regimes in the "Spring of Nations" revolutions of 1848 and 1849, they were strongly opposed to slavery and considered the Southern states oppressive and autocratic.

When in 1860, the Democratic party split on the issue of secession and slavery, the German immigrants switched their allegiance to the newly founded Republican Party headed by Abraham Lincoln, William Seward, Salmon P. Chase and others. In the 1860 election, Lincoln carried St. Louis primarily because of the solid German votes that he received.

Carl Schurz,
famous leader of St. Louis German-Americans,
journalist and Civil War general.

Franz Sigel,
Commanding General of the German Home Guards,
Major General, Union Army.

Illustrations courtesy Missouri Historical Society

Schurz[6] and Franz Sigel.[7] These men were armed and drilled and ready for any emergency that might arise where they would be needed, but more especially for the protection of the United States arsenal at Carondelet.[8]

Whenever they appeared on the streets they were subject to abuse and vituperation from the secession element in St. Louis, but they would march on in their phlegmatic, stolid fashion and pass unnoticed

[6]Carl Schurz was born in Cologne, Germany. He came to the United States at the age of 31, in 1852, after the failure of the liberal revolutions of 1848 and 1849. Like other German-American immigrants of those years, Schurz was opposed to slavery and to secession. He joined the Republican party and supported Lincoln in the 1860 campaign.

Schurz served in the Union army and rose to the rank of general. After the war, Schurz was a journalist and an editor of several newspapers. In 1868, he was elected to the U.S. Senate from Missouri. In 1879, he became Secretary of the Interior in the Cabinet of President Rutherford B. Hayes.

[7]Franz Sigel was an artillery officer in Baden, Germany during the 1848–49 revolutions. After immigrating to America, Sigel became the leader of the German-Americans in St. Louis.

Early in 1861, Sigel organized the Home Guards which kept St. Louis in the Union. He helped Captain Lyon to capture the United States Arsenal and Camp Jackson. In recognition of these efforts Sigel was appointed Colonel of the Third Infantry of Missouri Volunteers and then was raised to the rank of Major General. He fought with distinction in many Civil War battles and campaigns.

[8]Carondelet was at that time a riverfront townlet on the outskirts of St. Louis. The town was in the Southern section of St. Louis and its population was largely German-Americans. The U.S. Arsenal was located nearby.

the taunts and epithets flung at them by the crowds along the sidewalks.[9]

In May the State Guards under Gen. Frost[10] went into camp at Lindell's Grove not far from the heart of the city. It was called Camp Jackson, after Gov. Claiborne Jackson.[11] Ostensibly it was for drill and the yearly meeting of the State militia—a usually gala occasion. This time it was known to the military authorities that the militia was concentrating for an attack on the Arsenal and Jefferson Barracks—to capture the stores, ammunition and men—then they would hold St. Louis and Missouri could join the Confederacy.

Col. Lyon, who was in command at the Arsenal, prepared for action.[12] A demand was made on Gen. Frost to disperse the State Guards and retire from

[9]The German Home Guards patrolled the streets of St. Louis so pro-Confederate forces could not take over the city.

[10]General D.M. Frost, a native of New York, commanded the Missouri state militia. His headquarters were at Camp Jackson located on the west edge of St. Louis.

[11]Camp Jackson—a camp of state militia. In May 1861, Camp Jackson had a garrison of only 700 troops. Mrs. Hill has in her memoirs confused the chronology of events. The United States Arsenal was captured by Captain Lyon and his troops, mostly Germans, in April 1861. The attack on Camp Jackson took place on May 10th of the same year.

[12]Nathaniel Lyon was born in Ashford, Connecticut. Lyon graduated from West Point, fought in the Mexican war and served on the Kansas border when Missouri slave owners attempted to turn "Bloody Kansas" into a slave state. From that time he hated slavery and the South. With the help of Frank Blair, Jr., Captain Lyon received the command of the U.S. Arsenal.

Jefferson Barracks
located just south of St. Louis and Carondelet
about 1861.
Courtesy Missouri Historical Society

St. Louis Arsenal about 1866.
Courtesy Missouri Historical Society

Camp, which was refused.[13] Calling out the loyal Home Guards, Col. Lyon marched them out to Camp Jackson and surrounded it before the State Guards were aware of what was being done. There was some show of resistance and it promised to be a terrible slaughter; as it was there were several volleys of musketry exchanged. Men, women and children were killed. The camp was captured and the men disarmed and marched to the Arsenal as prisoners instead of conquerors.

Winston Churchill in "The Crisis" has related this incident in a graphic and truthful manner, and the effect it had in retaining Missouri in the Union.

That afternoon, quietly sewing in my home, the musket fire was distinctly heard, and was attributed to practice and drill at the camp. Many people went out to visit with the men and see the drills. It was almost entirely the secession element, and was made the occasion of much defiance to the Union.

I could hear shouts and cries in the distance and became aware of something unusual occurring. Soon a neighbor, Mrs. Kempin, an Englishwoman and a secession sympathizer, rushed in wildly excited, crying, "The Black Dutch! The Black Dutch are

[13]General Frost, the commander of the Missouri State Militia, offered to surrender the camp peacefully. Captain Lyon was ready to accept the offer, but a mob of pro-slavery rowdies hurled insults and stones on the Union soldiers. When a pistol shot was fired from the crowd, the soldiers returned the fire and twenty-eight people were killed and many more wounded.

killing them all. They are shooting women and children in cold blood, and they have taken those brave men and are marching them to the Arsenal as prisoners." She was almost incoherent with fright.

While deploring the shooting and killing which was begun by Gen. Frost's men, yet there was a feeling of satisfaction that at last the government was taking some action to protect its property and the city from becoming a prey to the Confederacy.[14]

When E.M. came home that night he was very grave and quiet. He said the wildest rumors were afloat, that martial law had been declared. All the Home Guards had been called out; volunteers had been requested to guard and protect the city from attack by the rebels. A terrible state of uncertainty existed; private feuds cropped out and no man's life was safe. He cautioned me to stay closely at home, to keep quiet and have little to say on current matters. It was known that he and father were Union men and the Southern element was very bitter against them.

The following day E.M. had a narrow escape. Mother was sending me a small basket of home cooking by him, which she usually did on baking day. After leaving the streetcar, there was quite a distance to walk before reaching our house, part of the way across a deserted brick yard. E.M. was

[14]There is no evidence to support the statement that General Frost's men "began the shooting and killing." The first shot was fired by someone in the crowd which assembled to protest the camp's capture.

General Nathaniel Lyon,
Commander of the Arsenal at St. Louis.
Courtesy Missouri Historical Society

hastening across this when a couple of men stepped out from behind a brick kiln and attacked him, saying, "Now, you bloody Union man, we are going to clean you out and all others like you." E.M. did not stand on the order of his going, but sprinted away from there lively, the two men in pursuit. Finally they fired on him two or three times and he thought he was hit. He soon reached a street where there were houses and they did not follow. He reached home white and breathless, and when we unpacked the basket we found where a bullet had gone through it and through a package of cookies inside.

That was bringing matters close to home and I implored him not to take any more short cuts to the streetcars but keep to the streets, though many men were shot down causelessly on the streets.

Another incident occurred that increased the tension to almost breaking point. One of the German regiments was being marched to the Arsenal to relieve the one on duty. When passing the Centenary Methodist Church on Fifth Street, the steps of which were crowded with hostile people flinging vile epithets at them, someone in the crowd fired a revolver at the marching men, wounding one. It was like a match to tinder. The Germans fired a volley into the crowd before the colonel had time to give an order. Several were killed and wounded. The Germans were enraged and threatened to clean out the city of the rebel element.

It was incidents like this that kept the opposing

parties inflamed and vindictive, and St. Louis was in sore straits during those dark days. A reign of terror now ensued; martial law was declared. Frank Blair, the organizer and leader of the Home Guards was given command of them.[15] Captain Lyon was rapidly promoted and put in command of the city. Wild rumors were afloat that the Germans, incensed by the attacks made on them, were going to take reprisal for the insults heaped on them and were about to attack secessionists and loot the city. A panic was the result of these reports and hundreds of southern families fled from the city, taking with them their slaves and what valuables they could most easily carry. Many of them boarded the steamboats and went South to join the Confederacy and never returned.

Schools were dismissed and the children sent to their homes and warned to keep off the streets, for minor disturbances were occurring in all directions. Business was demoralized. Society, churches and

[15]Mrs. Hill is referring to Frank Blair, Jr., a prominent Missouri politician, strong Union man and a Lincoln supporter. Frank Blair Jr., was the son of Francis P. Blair, a leading political figure in Baltimore and a brother of Montgomery Blair, a Postmaster General in Lincoln's Cabinet.

Frank Blair, Jr., served as Colonel of the First Infantry of Missouri Volunteers and supported Captain Lyon's capture of the U.S. Arsenal and of Camp Jackson. After a brief service in the House of Representatives, Blair returned to the Union Army and served as a Major General under Sherman in Mississippi and Georgia. Later Blair was a United States Senator from Missouri.

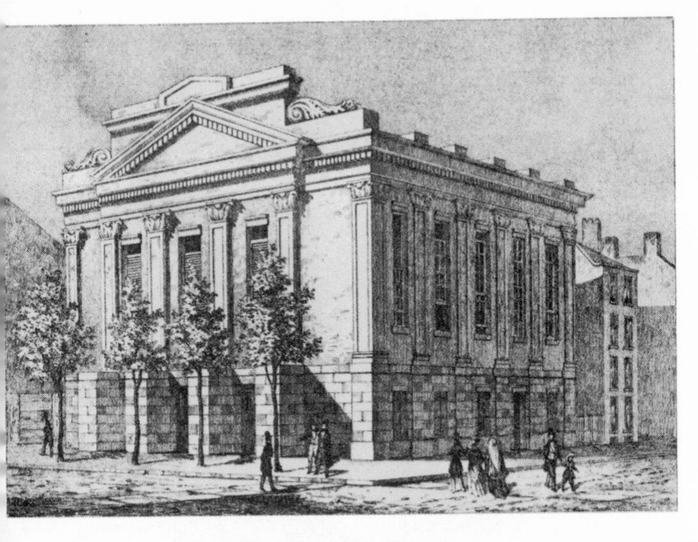

Centenary Church and Parsonage,
Pine and 5th St., St. Louis.
Courtesy Missouri Historical Society

families were disrupted, and people who had been life-long friends now ranged themselves on opposite sides and became enemies. Even the children were partisans. My little sister had a playmate and companion. They had always played happily together, but now Alice, who was a "rebel," insisted that little sister, who was "Union," should be a "rebel" in their plays. At last Phebe revolted and turned on Alice with the declaration that she was not going to play with Alice Babcock any more, for she would not be a "turncoat," and she did not.

The disruption and separation permeated all classes and a feeling of suspicion and uncertainty hung heavy as a pall. In my father's business, building and construction work ceased. One entire block of six three-story brick storerooms on Broadway, which he was building for Judge Bates,[16] who was Attorney General in Lincoln's cabinet, were not completed till after the close of the war. Both my father and E.M. were Union men from the first, and it was particularly hazardous for my father to remain loyal to the Union. He was a member of the Eighth Street M. E. Church, and was active and prominent in the Church work. This church was a hotbed of secession and many acts of treason were planned and carried out by its members. When

[16]Edward Bates was an outstanding St. Louis lawyer and judge. Bates was a Henry Clay Whig and a foe of slavery. In 1880, Bates was a contender for the Republican presidential nomination. After Lincoln's victory, Bates served as Attorney General in Lincoln's Cabinet.

they found out that father remained firm in his loyalty to the Union, it was the parting of the ways, and his brethren and friends dropped away from him and ostracized him and his family. His business was broken up, most of his workmen enlisting either for the North or South, many of them going into the Southern army and joining Gen. Sterling Price, who was organizing a division for the Confederate service in the hope of yet taking Missouri into the ranks of secession.[17]

Oh, it was all so dreadful, and you wondered if God reigned! Hell surely was let loose during those dark days. Lincoln's call for 75,000 men for three months service had come, but it was soon seen how inadequate they were to stem the tide of rebellion, and that a long and terrible war was imminent, till one side or the other was exhausted.

E.M. grew very restless and felt that his country needed the help of her loyal sons, and was anxious to offer his services. Womanlike, I clung to him and felt I could not give him up at that time. Father could not go for he had a large and expensive family completely dependent on him, and he had to gather together the tangled skeins of his business and try to save something from the ruin. It was in a deplorable condition.

[17]Before the Civil War, Price was a member of Congress, served as a Colonel in the Mexican War and was elected Governor of Missouri. General Price had sympathy for the Union, but went over to the Confederacy after the capture of Camp Jackson by Union troops under Captain Lyon.

Sterling Price,
General commanding Confederate forces in Missouri.
Courtesy Missouri Historical Society

In June a little daughter was born to us. She only lived a few hours. Then the conviction came home to E.M. that his first duty was to his country. Father said go and he would care for E.M.'s wife and boy, and with a sinking heart I bade my dearest to give himself to his country. Now thousands of women, both in the North and South were in like case.

Then came the Battle of Bull Run with the terrible defeat and rout of the Union forces and the knowledge of how unprepared the North was for war. It swept the last lingering doubt away and there was no holding back of loyal, true men after that. Never to be forgotten is the feeling as we looked long into each other's eyes, after reading the fearful news, and realized what it meant for us. No word passed between us, but we knew the sacrifice had to be made, and it was for me to be brave and make it as easy as possible for my husband.

The next day E.M. went to see Col. Frank Blair and offered his services. He sent him to Col. Bissell,[18] late colonel of the Tenth Missouri Cavalry, who had been given authority by Gen. Frémont to raise a regiment to be known as the Engineer Regiment of the West, and to be recruited not only in Missouri but from the adjacent states. He advised E.M. to go across the river and recruit in Illinois. It

[18]William H. Bissell was elected Governor of Illinois in 1856 with the support of Abraham Lincoln. Appointed Colonel in the Union Army, Bissell commanded the unit of the Corps of Engineers in which Eben Hill served.

was to be a regiment of mechanics and artisans for pioneer and engineer work. Substantial inducements were offered in the way of extra pay and freedom from guard duty.

The next day he bade me good by and started for Illinois to recruit a company of men for the new regiment, and my baby boy and I were alone in our little home. I tried to carry a brave front and be heroic and patriotic, but when the dinner hour came and his place and chair were set at the table and the thought would obtrude that perhaps never again would he occupy it, my heart would sink and instead of eating I would sit and cry while little George would say, "Don't Mama. Don't Mama. Papa come back."

One day Father came in unexpectedly and found me in this plight. He gathered me and the baby up, put us into the buggy, locked the door, leaving the dinner table set, and carried us home, and would allow me to go back only to pack my things and close the house. My dear Father, how good and thoughtful he was.

Frequent letters came from E.M. He was being quite successful in recruiting the class of men desired for the new regiment. Among other things, a very rigid physical examination was required, so that only strong healthy men were accepted.

The first week in August he reported to Col. Bissell with sixty-six men and was ordered into camp at Lafayette Park where the regiment was being

General Frank P. Blair, Jr.,
Major General, Union Army,
United States Senator from Missouri.

Courtesy Missouri Historical Society

mustered for organization and drill. A quotation from the history of the regiment will be apt here:

"Company D was recruited partly in St. Louis but mostly from Illinois. When it came to the organization of the company there was some clashing of interests. E.M. Hill representing sixty-six men and Griffith with twelve men each claimed the Captaincy. The twelve men recruited by Griffith refused to be mustered unless their leader was made Captain, and without them an organization could not be effected. The sixty-six men stoutly protested against so unjust a claim, and with a good degree of reason and justice, claimed that he who represented so large a majority should be entitled to the honor of the command."

It was in this state of affairs that Col. Bissell interfered with the statement that the parties could have one hour to compromise the matter, at the expiration of which time, if the different squads were not consolidated, he would take the matter in hand himself and distribute them among the other companies. Finding Griffith unyielding, E.M. quieted the clamor of his men by quietly admitting the claim of his opponent and the company was organized on August 15, 1861, with Griffith Captain, E.M. First Lieutenant. Col. Bissell, however, refused to tolerate the injustice of Capt. Griffith, and that officer was summarily dismissed without even receiving a commission. Soon after, Charles R. Thompson brought into the company a squad of recruits, filling it up to the maximum, and on October 31, Company D was mustered into the service for three years or longer, with E.M. as Captain and Charles Thompson as First Lieutenant. During all this clash and confusion of interests, it was a time of anxiety and trouble to E.M. He was actuated by the purest and most patriotic motives, and the self-seeking and manifest injustice of others annoyed and repelled him. He was ready to yield a personal advantage for the good of the many, and he did not want to see the men whom he had enlisted, scattered around through the various companies of the regiment.

During the time these events were taking place there was little opportunity for communication. In those days the wonders of the telephone were unknown. The government service monopolized the telegraph lines, and it was difficult to get a private dispatch over the wires, as we discovered later, to our sorrow.

E.M., from the day he had started to recruit his company, up to the time of which I am writing had only been able to make us one brief visit of a few hours to procure necessary clothing. Mail facilities were extremely uncertain, and an occasional penciled note sent by a messenger, when one could be found, was all the word I received from him in several weeks. Visiting by relatives to the men in camp was not permitted, and only by special permission was a woman allowed to see her husband, father or son. E.M. tried to get leave for me to come out and see him, but the colonel thought it might establish a precedent that would occasion him much difficulty. He said that if an order came from Gen. Blair, allowing a visitor, it would be obeyed and not occasion inconvenience to him. Acting on this hint, my Father went to Gen. Blair, who was a personal friend and neighbor, and procured the order without any trouble. This he took to Col. Bissell and they arranged that the following Sunday, Father should bring the little son and me and leave us with E.M. while he went on to Gravois where he had an appointment to preach in the afternoon, and he would call for me on his return, so giving us two or three hours to visit with each other.

It was a hot windy Sunday in September, and a drive of six or eight miles to the Park. We took a large basket of cooked provisions and a bundle of clothing for our soldiers. When we reached the camp we found it a busy place. To unaccustomed eyes it looked like a busy ant hill with each ant doing something unrelated to what the others were doing. Beautiful Lafayette Park, with its brilliant flower beds and stretches of green sward, looking like emerald velvet, was turned into a great military camp. Regiments from adjacent states were sent here for organization and drill. Later they went to Benton Barracks for muster and equipment.

On the grassy lawns that policemen had so watchfully guarded, now camp fires were burning and men were cooking the evening meal. Tents were erected and laid out in streets. It was hot, dry and dusty, and clouds of dust blew and added to the general discomfort.

We found him for whom we were looking, on the farther side of the park, where the men for the Engineer Regiment were received and put into camp. E.M. was a very busy man and was out with his company drilling. Father left me and went on to his appointment, and I watched the various activities with interested eyes. It was a motley crowd, and after watching them drill and how unused they were to military training, I was not surprised at the defeat and panic of our men at Bull Run. They were so raw and unprepared and had looked on the war as a summer holiday affair, in which thought most of the North had participated, till they were wakened by the terrible battle and bloodshed.

Col. Bissell had gained some semblance of order in his camp. New men were coming in every day. The large squads, as in E.M.'s case, were made the nucleus of companies to which the small squads were attached. There were all sorts and conditions of men and they were dressed in all sorts and conditions of clothes. E.M. in his gray summer suit, drilling with his men using sticks for guns and all dressed differently, did not give a soldierly effect, but the good material was there and it took but a few weeks for them to present a very different appearance and later to show the good stuff that was in them.

After E.M. was at liberty, he took me around to

see the camp and to meet his friends, some of whom I came to know and prize in the following years. Many of the men were trying to cook their suppers over the camp fires, but they made awkward work of it. Probably but few of them had ever cooked a meal for themselves, and in their clothing they also showed a lack of feminine ability. They were fast discarding what was not necessary to their comfort and convenience, while learning to take care of themselves.

We prepared a little feast from the well filled basket in E.M.'s tent which he occupied with Lieut. Thompson and E.M. invited his brother officers in to share it with them. It was really pathetic to see how those young fellows appreciated and enjoyed the well cooked food and delicacies. Father soon came and that was the time for good by. It was well that none of us could know or realize under what circumstances we should see each other again.

Father was much occupied during these busy days with new contracts. He had secured several from the government for barracks and buildings. The old Fair Grounds had been made a vast barracks, called Benton Barracks. Here the Western Army was mobilized, armed, equipped and sent out to active service.[19] Gen. Sterling Price was gathering an army of Confederates in the western part of the

[19]By the "Western Army" Mrs. Hill means "The Department of the West" of the Union Army which was at that time under the command of General Frémont.

state with the avowed intention of attacking St. Louis, and Federal troops were being hurried forward to prevent his advance.

On the following Sunday, Father drove out to the Park hoping he might get a word with E.M., for we had received no message from him that week. When he reached the camp, he found a strange regiment occupying it and was told that the Engineers had been ordered to Benton Barracks and had broken camp there, several days before. Father returned from a fruitless quest, and the next day went out to the Barracks. Great confusion and activity was apparent there and he could get no tidings of the Engineers. Scant courtesy was shown a mere civilian. However, he persevered in his search. No one seemed to know anything about them, but finally he found the right trail and reached the proper source for information and learned that the regiment had been ordered to Lamine to build fortifications and earthworks, in expectation of Gen. Price's advance. They were sent before being mustered or equipped and were armed with spades and shovels.

Father returned home a sad and disappointed man, for he now realized more than ever what the war would mean to him and his loved ones. He greatly missed E.M. in the business, especially now, when there was promise of increased activity from the new contracts. My only brother was a lad of seventeen, and had just finished his high school course. He was wild to enlist, but Father restrained him, saying, "Not yet, not yet, my son. Later you can go if it is necessary." And he kept him busy in the office with the books and office work.

A few days after, several letters and messages reached us from E.M. He had written and tried to telegraph us, but they had all been delayed in the transmission. It was now incumbent on me to have courage and fortitude and make it as easy as possible for the parents who shared my trouble and so tenderly cared for E.M.'s wife and child. There was much we could all do in a small way to help the cause. Father was intensely loyal, and gave largely of his means individually. On Sunday he would go out to the Barracks to visit and talk to the men, and when permitted, hold a religious service if only a little prayer meeting. He always took a large basket of cooked food and dainties which Mother and her daughters prepared, and which he passed around to the privates. He was always welcomed and even the officers in command were courteous to him. His was a religion that he took into all the affairs of his life and he lived it every day, always asking the blessing of God on his acts.

Our home was on Morgan Street and many of the new regiments marched down that street on their way to boat or railroad station to embark for the front or seat of war. Most of our neighbors were rebel sympathizers and unfriendly, and kept their houses closed when the Union columns marched past. But we always gathered at the front gate with

Camp Benton at St. Louis.

Courtesy Missouri Historical Society

flags and handkerchiefs waving and cheering the boys and wishing them Godspeed. It was small welcome or encouragement they received from the residents in that part of the city. Mother would prepare large pails of lemonade and many a hot, thirsty boy thanked us for the cool refreshing drink. Later, when it became cold, we had hot coffee for them, and they would call out "God bless the Union ladies," and we would wave and cheer them.

Brave boys were they, and after all these years my old throat contracts and eyes fill, as memory recalls those boys, for the majority of them were boys less than thirty years old, boys fresh from the plow and the simple homely life of the farm, clear-eyed, tanned and stalwart, boys from their colleges and schools, who closed their books, and earnest and enthusiastic, had given themselves to the service of their country. They were so brave and gallant in the vigor and strength of their young manhood, full of youthful hope and ambition. They were soon going to "whip the rebels." They looked so gay and fine in their new uniforms, with their knapsacks strapped on their backs and the shining muskets glinting in the sun. Tears which I could not repress would stream down my face as I watched them and realized that many would never return, for I had given my best and dearest and my heart went out to the boys and to the women who were left behind and had to "labor and wait." But we gave the marching men a word and smile of friendly cheer as they passed by and for which they always seemed pleased and grateful, and we served them the "cup of cold water" in His name.

The Sixth Iowa, to which E.M.'s brother E— belonged, went past one day. E— stepped out of the ranks for a minute to bid us good by. He had been greatly attracted to my younger sister, Gina, a very brilliant and clever girl. None of us took his attentions to her seriously, but this day, after bidding us good by, he turned to her and looked deep into her eyes, drawing off a ring which he wore and that had been made from a gold nugget he had dug in California. They held each other with their eyes, the ring was drawn off his finger, she raised her hand and he placed it on her finger, never letting his eyes drop from hers. Then he turned, and without a word from either, rejoined his regiment which was still passing, and that was their engagement. We all saw it but could say nothing. Gina went to her room and we saw no more of her that day. Father was not present but when told of the incident was greatly disturbed. Gina was so young, and he did not want her influenced in that way. It certainly was a singular affair, but E— was in earnest and hoped she would be.

One day in the latter part of September 1861, Father went out to Benton Barracks on business. As usual he carried many delicacies for the boys in camp and was warmly welcomed. Returning to the city, he was caught in a severe storm and came home drenched to the skin. A severe cold resulted, his vitality was greatly lowered through mental troubles and worry, and he did not rally as he usually did from physical ills. He became worse, the family doctor was called, who pronounced it not serious and administered the usual remedies, which were severe and drastic, and did not improve his condition. Other physicians were called in. The cold had settled in his bowels and he suffered intensely with inflammation, which later became hemorrhage of the bowels. No relief was obtained, and in two weeks my dear Father passed away.

We now know in the light of modern science that it was acute appendicitis that killed him, and today an operation that would save a life could be performed, but even the disease was unknown then, and a valuable life was sacrificed at a time when it was most needed. My Father was in the prime of life, being only fifty-three, a hale, vigorous, clean blooded man who was rarely ailing. His last illness was a violent attack from the first. His death was a dreadful calamity to his family, who were so dependent on him, and just at this time when financial and industrial affairs were in such a state of chaos.

I lost my best and dearest friend in my father. Being the eldest child, we had been very congenial and from a little girl I had been his companion, and his was the greatest influence in my life. I will hasten over this time, for even after all these years, I cannot dwell on it. When he went, the family was like a ship at sea without a rudder, at the mercy of the waves.

When we knew there was no hope of his recovery, we telegraphed for E.M. and wrote to him every day imploring him to come home. Father so desired to see him. He was conscious that the end was approaching and he wanted to place the care of his family and business in E.M.'s hand. Our frantic appeals brought no response and every night Father would listen for the whistle of the train that came in from Jefferson City, and wait for E.M.'s coming. We went to headquarters and tried to get a pass to go out to Lamine for him, but without avail, and Father died without seeing him again.

The night after the funeral, about midnight, a ring came to the bell and when we opened the door, there stood E.M. He had received telegrams and letters the night before, which were held up and delayed in transmission. He had spent the night in getting an order permitting him a short leave of absence, and the next day started for St. Louis. When told that Father was gone, the shock was almost too much for him. He staggered and would have fallen, if we had not caught him. That was a sad household and we all mourned for the dear one who left us so bereft, and there was no sleep for any of us that night.

E.M. could only spend three days with us, and did what he could in that short time to arrange business matters for Mother. These things are mentioned to show how uncertain everything concerning civil affairs was. War and military requirements were absolute, and we and our griefs were as nothing compared to the weightier concerns. E.M. returned to Lamine and we attempted to readjust our lives to the changed conditions. It seemed as though a great pall had descended on us and we were being smothered under the weight of grief and trouble.

The Engineers at this time were at Lamine and Otterville engaged in building forts and earthworks, repairing roads and bridges, drilling and preparing for the varied labors that were a part of the requirements of an Engineer Regiment. The officers were formed into a school with regular lessons assigned them, which had to be studied and recited at night to the colonel when they reported to him. It was a severe test for many of them. Their regular daily duties had to be performed and this night school was the extra work. For many weeks in the early part of that winter E.M. had only two hours sleep in the twenty-four, but he never missed a lesson and received high marks in his studies, though resolution and endurance were needed to fulfill the heavy demands made on them both physically and mentally. Yet the severe disciplines laid the foundation for the future efficiency and skill which gave the Engineers their high standing and fine reputation in the Western Army. It made them equal to any emergency. It was a survival of the fittest, for the weaklings dropped out.

The winter came early that year and the Western Army was ill prepared for it. Cold and rainy weather prevailed. In the camps in Missouri, notably around Sedalia and Otterville, there was much sickness. Severe colds and pneumonia and an epidemic of measles broke out in the Engineer camps. Many of the men were very ill and several died. Sanitary conditions were bad and the men had not become inured to the hardships and exposure of army life. The outlook for the Union was dark and gloomy that first winter of the war. The Confederates, better prepared in every way, were gaining the advantage. The Union forces were repelled at all points. The Mississippi River was closed to navigation below Cairo. Gen. Price was gathering a large army in western Missouri and preparing for a movement on St. Louis, intending to blockade the river at that point and invade Illinois.

Sickness and death were playing sad havoc with our men lying in camp, neither properly clothed or fed by the Government. Gen. Frémont was in command of the Department of the West. He had been a girlish idol of mine from reading of his achievements as a Pathfinder, but my illusions vanished, for he was "weighed in the balance and found wanting." The "pomp and panoply of war" appealed more to him and his staff than the dire needs of his men in the field. E.M. wrote pitiful stories of the suffering of his men, not yet hardened to the exigency of camp life and the difficulty there was in

J. C. Frémont,
Commanding General, Department of the West.
Courtesy Missouri Historical Society

cutting through the "red tape" to procure necessary supplies. He only voiced or wrote the indignation and dissatisfaction felt by many men to whom the welfare of the army was of more importance than military rank or precedence. Gen. Frémont[20] had outlived his usefulness as a military man and was soon superseded by one who was more practical and far seeing.[21]

Right at this time a quiet, little man from Illinois was coming into notice as a man who could do things. No fancy uniforms for various occasions were necessary for him. He had received a commission of colonel from the Governor of Illinois and

[20] John Charles Frémont was a famous traveler who in 1842 explored the route to the West from Missouri to Oregon along the Columbia River. He was married to Jessie Benton, the beautiful daughter of the powerful Senator from Missouri, Thomas Hart Benton.

At the start of the Civil War, Frémont was given the commission of Major General, and was appointed to command the Department of the West with headquarters in St. Louis. His ambitions and his lack of administrative abilities caused a great enmity between Frémont and the prominent Missouri politician, Frank Blair, Jr.

Frémont lost his command in September, 1861 when he refused Lincoln's request to rescind a proclamation which he issued in August, 1861 ordering the confiscation of property and slaves of Missouri citizens who were fighting for the Confederacy. Subsequently, Frémont proved unsuccessful in his commands and eventually left the army.

In 1864, Frémont was a candidate for President on a splinter Radical Republican ticket, but he withdrew his candidacy.

[21] Frémont was succeeded by General David Hunter.

been assigned to a regiment of infantry. He was a West Point man and had served in the regular army. There was nothing remarkable about him except that he was a financial failure. He went about among his men with his trousers tucked in his boots, an ill fitting old blouse coat, a slouch hat and an everlasting cigar in his mouth—not a very promising appearance for one who became a renowned general, yet that was Ulysses S. Grant, who gained one of the first Union advantages at the battle of Belmont.[22]

During these sad days there was no time or place for private griefs. Loyal women in St. Louis had their hearts and hands full ministering to the many needs which were constantly arising. Every loyal household became a soldiers' aid society, and in our family we worked more especially for E.M. and his company. I went to see Mr. Pierson of the Ubsdell and Pierson Dry Goods store, the largest and most important store of that kind in the city in those days. He had known my father very well and we had always shopped at his store.

I asked him for a donation and he generously responded when told what was wanted, and that afternoon sent us a number of bolts of bed ticking,

[22]General Ulysses S. Grant, acting under the command of General Frémont, in a bold move, crossed the Mississippi and attacked a small Confederate garrison at Belmont, Missouri. He lost 600 men in the action and military historians are divided whether the battle of Belmont was a Union or a Confederate victory.

flannel, calico, cotton batting and yarn. We immediately set to work and made the sewing machine hum night and day. Mother, my aunt and we four older girls worked unceasingly and soon had a large box filled and ready to send to our soldier boys at Lamine. We made bed ticks which could be filled with hay or straw, could be easily emptied and refilled and took up but little room on a march. We made and tied comforters thick and warm. They were for the sick men, and we made at E.M.'s suggestion, a number of sleeping caps or helmets of flannel which were eagerly sought and greatly appreciated that cold winter. And we made quantities of flannel shirts and kept the knitting needles clicking, fashioning socks and mittens. How the boys rejoiced over the contents of that box, the forerunner of several during the winter.

Soon after father's death, mother found she could not keep up so large an establishment, and we moved downtown into a smaller house. My brother went to work for a large iron and steel company. Mr. Crozier, the proprietor, was a close friend of the family and took my brother with him, and my sister Gina got a number of music pupils, while E.M. shared his resources with the family. Aunt found a position. The younger girls went to school and Mother kept the house and cared for my little boy.

The women's Soldiers' Aid Society had been organized and I offered my services which were gladly accepted and I was a busy woman those dark days of the winter of '61 and '62. A large vacant block of stores on Fifth and Chestnut streets was taken by the government for a hospital, and the store rooms on the ground floor were used as Headquarters of the Medical Corps. The three upper stories were used for the hospital. Later the Sanitary Commission occupied some of the empty lower rooms, and our Soldiers' Aid had two rooms on Chestnut Street. Afterward we became Auxiliary to the Sanitary Commission, but we started before that was organized.

At first there was little system or order in our work, each and every woman doing what she could, our main object being to help the sick soldiers, and we found plenty of work. Of course we were all giving our time and labor to the cause. The doctors and surgeons availed themselves of our help, and every day we women gathered at the rooms and scraped lint, tore and rolled bandages, knitted socks. We solicited donations of delicacies for the sick. Many boxes were packed and sent to the soldiers in the field hospitals. We were called on to assist the surgeons in their operations and to nurse the patients. There were no regular nurses then and volunteer nurses were scarce. There was much confusion and lack of system in the hospital work, I might almost say ignorance at first. To illustrate, Mother spent much time making soups, broths and dainties, for she had had much experience in cooking for the sick. My sister and I would visit the hospital three or four times a week, always carrying a well-filled basket of broth and delicacies. These we would distribute ourselves among the patients who had come under our notice. We were not forbidden and there was no protest from any one against it. Many other women did the same thing. The boys watched eagerly for our coming and I will say that we were careful to feed only the convalescents. My sister often accompanied me and we were known as "the two women in black." Beside that personal work, I was placed on the hospital visiting committee of which Mrs. Cozzens was the chairwoman. Her daughter, Phebe, was also on the same committee and I grew to know them very well. They were a fine family, the father being chief of some civic department. There were three daughters, all beautiful girls. Phebe was the most brilliant and intellectual, with great executive ability, she was a valuable aid to her mother. In after years she became distinguished as a lawyer and lecturer. At this time she was engaged to a young officer in the army, and was to be married in the Spring, but they had a lovers' quarrel. He was on detached service in St. Louis at the time, but after the quarrel he rejoined his regiment and was killed at Fort Donelson. Being of an intense temperament, she was completely prostrated, for she truly loved him and his death greatly changed her.

But to return to our hospital work, we were frequently called on for nurses, for there was great lack of help in that line. Many days and nights of that winter I spent beside the beds of the sick, wounded and dying, assisting the surgeons in their gruesome work. They said I had good nerves and was not afraid of the sight of blood. The use of anesthetics was little known, and the doctors often called for me. They said I was quiet and efficient and obeyed orders and understood quickly.

After the battle of Springfield where the brave Gen. Lyon was killed and where Frémont's bodyguard made a brilliant charge, a number of the wounded were brought to our hospital.[23] Several of our Committee were up all night after they arrived, helping the doctors attend to their needs. One young fellow I well remember, a splendid specimen of young manhood, had a badly shattered right arm, which the attending surgeons declared must be amputated at once. He protested and fought most vigorously against it, and would not consent to the operation. He said he was not going through life with one arm, that he was going to fight the rebels till they killed him, and if he could not use his sabre he could still shoot. He was so insistent and determined that finally the surgeons yielded and set

[23] Lyon was killed during the Battle of Wilson's Creek not the battle of Springfield. The reference to Frémont's bodyguards refers to the cavalry regiment made up of Hungarian immigrants, all veterans of the 1848 revolutions in Europe. This regiment acted as Frémont's personal bodyguard. In the battle of Springfield, these Hungarians led by Colonel Charles Zagonyi routed some of the Confederate forces.

Death of General Lyon during the Battle of Wilson's Creek.

Courtesy Missouri Historical Society

to work to save the limb. He refused to take a sedative and lay there white and grim while the doctors probed and extracted splinters and pieces of bone from the shattered elbow. They were over an hour before they finally dressed and bandaged the wound. Twice he fainted and the cold sweat poured off his pale face, but he never made a moan. It was a wonderful exhibition of courage, and the poor fellow deserved to save his arm. I attended the doctors in this case, held the basins and towels and did what was demanded of me without faltering, but after it was all over and I reached home the reaction took place and the tired nerves made themselves felt. We women who were called on to go through such scenes, lived on our nerve in those days.

The next day when I went to the hospital, I found the young man greatly exhausted after the night's ordeal, but hopeful of recovery. He had a wonderful physique and was a clean blooded boy. At his request I comforted him by writing to his mother and sweetheart in Northern Illinois. He subsequently recovered and returned to the army, but was unable to be a cavalry man, for his arm was stiff from the elbow, the joint there being partially gone. This is one of the many experiences we were called upon to pass through in our efforts to assist as best we could. We helped to dress wounds, washed and bathed the sick, closed the eyes of the dying, attending to the last sad rites at the deathbeds of many, wrote letters and read aloud to the convalescents, and never forgot a cheery presence and encouraging word or smile for our boys to whom the reality of war was so sadly being demonstrated.

Christmas time was a dark and gloomy period, not only in our own family, whose loss of the dear Father had been so recent, but the whole nation was plunged in grief and mourning. The Divine message, "Peace on earth, good will to man" had little meaning, for the horrors of war were ever before us. There were no festive gatherings or merry making. We as a family devoted all our efforts and what means we could spare, toward the cheer of our boys in E.M.'s Company D. The younger girls made "Betties," or housewives, for each man in the company. They were small cases that could be rolled up and carried in the pocket, containing thread, needles, pins and buttons, and were a great convenience and very popular with the men, who now had to sew on their own buttons and mend their torn garments.

We older ones made more of the desired sleeping caps and knitted socks and mittens, so that each man in the company was supplied. For a week we cooked and baked and finally packed and sent to the Engineers at Lamine two large boxes, one containing articles for wearing and the other enough Christmas cooking to give all the boys of Company D a taste of the goodies. In the latter box there was a roast turkey, boiled ham, baked chickens, boiled

The famous Hungarian regiment of General Frémont's bodyguards. Headquartered at St. Louis, Missouri. (from Harper's Weekly, September 21, 1861)

Courtesy Missouri Historical Society

tongues, plum pudding, mince and apple pies, four or five loaves of cake, and a quantity of doughnuts and cookies and ginger bread. The boxes reached the camp in season and in good condition and the contents were distributed among the boys on Christmas morning and were a great success, assuring the boys they were not forgotten. Of course, there were a number of individual gifts received among them, but we tried to include the whole of Company D in our offering, and we were more than repaid for the pleasure afforded to them on that day.

Most of my Christmas day was spent beside a poor man dying of typhoid fever. He had been brought in from one of the camps in Missouri. There was little hope for him from the first. He was from Iowa, had a good farm there, and a wife and three little girls, and was so anxious to get well for their sakes. I had nursed him most of the time since he was received in the hospital, and he clung to me for hope and courage, but this day he realized his condition and it was so pitiful to hear him call for his wife and babies. The end came toward evening after a hard day, and for his wife's sake, I did for her loved one what she would have liked done, for I did not know how soon I might be in a similar place.

Many entertainments were planned and given by the loyal women of St. Louis for the benefit of the Soldiers' Aid Society during the winter of '61 and '62. One of the most notable was a series of tableaux. One evening they were all classic. Another evening they represented celebrated scenes and incidents in history. They were given in Mercantile Library Hall, and some of the most prominent women and girls, socially, took part in them. It was quite an original form of entertainment in that day, and was very successful. We added many dollars to our treasury.

Phebe Cozzens was a leading spirit in this enterprise, and was in several of the pictures where a rich dark beauty was required. Miss Post, the daughter of Dr. Post, a noted Presbyterian clergyman, also took a prominent part. She was very beautiful, tall and statuesque, with a perfect Grecian profile, and was lovely as a Greek goddess or the Goddess of Liberty. Of course many scenes were given appealing to the loyalty and patriotism of the spectators, and they had to be given over and over again. We women had worked hard preparing for the entertainment and were much gratified with our success.

We also arranged with Dr. Berkeley, the Rector of St. George's Episcopal Church (it was then on Locust near Sixth Street), to give a series of readings. That also was an innovation. He was a fine elocutionist, with a rich deep voice and perfect delivery. His church was always filled on Sunday by many who went to hear him read the service, which he did in a dramatic but very reverent manner, bringing home the beauty and the meaning of the service as I have never heard it before or since.

He gave three readings at the Mercantile Library

Mercantile Library Hall, St. Louis.

Courtesy Missouri Historical Society

Hall, the largest room in St. Louis for gatherings. I had heard Adelina Patti and Madame Colson, also Brignoli sing there. It was used for all large affairs. Dr. Berkeley's readings were even a greater success than the tableaux had been. The reading of the "Charge of the Light Brigade" was wonderful, and electrified his audience, while his rendering of patriotic selections set the people wild, and he was cheered and recalled many times. His services were a free gift, and the Hall was also given to us for that time, so that we netted a large sum, which was much needed in our work. We were gratified with our success, but decided on no more entertainments for that winter. It distracted our attention from the more needed work required of us in the nursing and care of the sick and wounded soldiers that came under our attention, but it was a change, especially for the young people, from the cloud of gloom and sadness which enveloped the country and the city during that dreadful first winter of the war.

In January, 1862, we received word of the severe illness of E.M.'s brother E—, who through exposure and severity of the weather had been stricken with pneumonia. He was with his regiment, the Sixth Iowa, on duty in Missouri. For a while his life was despaired of. As soon as possible he was sent to St. Louis, and we found him in the hospital, but so enfeebled and his lungs in such bad condition that he was discharged from the service. We took him home and he soon partially recovered, but he never became a well man. One Sunday night in February, my sister went to church and returned after the service with Rev. Frank Morris and Mr. Collins, an old and tried friend of the family. A very sad wedding took place in the little parlor. We were all in deep mourning and the bridegroom looked like a wraith. We had all protested, and the family were all opposed to the marriage from the first, and Father especially. Sister wanted the right and privilege of nursing and caring for him, and he was anxious to make her his wife on any condition, so regardless of entreaties or remonstrances, they persisted in being married. Poor Mother could do nothing but acquiesce, but she was heart broken. My sister was a remarkably bright girl in many ways and was the cleverest one in the family. A girl of fine mind and intellect, she had a promising future, being the possessor of a beautiful voice which was being trained and cultivated. Strakosch heard her sing and offered to take her to Europe for study and to sing for him, but Mother would not consent, so she had pursued her studies under the best teachers in St. Louis. We all felt that it was a great sacrifice to make, for E— had but little means, his health was uncertain and his disposition peculiar.

In a few weeks he recovered sufficiently to travel, and took my sister with him. They went down to Columbus, Kentucky, which was a distributing point for the army just then, and opened a little shop for the repairing of watches. He was a watchmaker and jeweler by trade. The doctor had told him he must live in the South. He followed the army as it conquered its way South.

When the Engineer Regiment was recruited, extra pay had been promised them, as the Engineers were a higher arm of the service and their work was more arduous and required skill and mechanical ability, and by the promise of extra pay, a better class of artisans and mechanics had enlisted in that Regiment. As the winter progressed and they had been kept constantly at work by a strenuous and active colonel, building bridges, roads, fortifications, and repairing railroads, they had endured great privations and hardships. Still there was no talk of the extra pay. Dissatisfaction and murmurings began to manifest among the men. There was much red tape to be untangled. Finally, the colonel sent E.M. to St. Louis with a requisition for the money, giving him the power of attorney to collect it, and he reached St. Louis the latter part of February. We had not seen each other since the previous October and it was a happy meeting. E.M. spent several days endeavoring to cut the red tape which bound up military matters so tightly. He was determined not to return without the money, for it had been promised to the men in good faith. They had been in the service six months and thought it time the promise should at least be partially fulfilled, and the feeling of discontent was seriously injuring the discipline of the regiment.

At last E.M. was able to make an appointment with Gen. Cullom, Chief of Engineers, to see him, and went to the Planters House one afternoon at three o'clock, and was shown to Gen. Cullom's room.[24] To tell the truth there was very little belief in the Engineers Regiment, as Engineers, among the chiefs and their staffs stationed in St. Louis, and E.M. realized he had a difficult task before him to demonstrate and convince the officials the Engineers were what they professed to be. Gen. Cullom was his last hope and it was necessary to have his endorsement before he could get the money. The general was pleasant but non-committal and questioned E.M. about the regiment and the work they had been doing the past winter. He quizzed him pretty close on many details, but they talked as man to man. Supper time arrived and the general invited him to supper and afterward they returned to his room, and talked till midnight.

The regimental business was dropped before supper and after that, they discussed military matters and engineering problems and it was midnight before they realized how long they had been talking. The general thanked my captain for a very pleasant evening and made an appointment with him for the next day. This is the way the general put it, "Well,

[24]General George Washington Cullom was Chief of Staff and Chief Engineer on the staff of General H. W. Halleck. General Cullom supervised construction and engineering on the western rivers and was active in the siege of Corinth, Mississippi.

Captain, I have enjoyed this talk with you and thank you for a pleasant evening. By the way, about this regimental matter, you come to my office to-morrow afternoon at three o'clock and we will see what can be done." I waited up for E.M. for I was consumed with anxiety and my heart was in my mouth when he came. He began to tell me of the interview, and as he related the conversation, it dawned on him that he had been subjected to a searching examination and quiz on engineering matters, and Gen. Cullom had been drawing him out, but so skillfully E.M. had never suspected it. How glad we were that E.M. had given so much study to the science. Though he had been a successful civil and mechanical engineer before the war, yet there was a vast subject to learn in Military Engineering, and Gen. Cullom was one of the most noted engineers in the regular army. We did not know what this quiz might portend, but hoped for success.

When E.M. reached the general's office the next afternoon, he found a different man from the genial host and gentleman of the night before. He was an officer on duty with many cares and responsibilities. He received E.M. and handed him a letter to be delivered to Col. Bissell, then gave him an order duly signed and endorsed on the disbursing officer for five thousand dollars, and directed where to get it cashed. That was all. E.M. thanked him and immediately made his way to the place designated.

There he had to wait a couple of hours till his turn was reached. But finally he received the five thousand dollars in crisp bank notes, and realized his mission was a success. When he reached home, my heart was throbbing in my throat and I gazed at him with an intenseness and excitement difficult to conceal, but his face was impassive and non-committal and I knew he did not want to be questioned before the family. However, he remarked that he expected to return to Lamine the next day. When we gained the privacy of our room, I begged to know if he had succeeded and he drew out the package of bank notes and showed me.

He wanted the matter kept as quiet as possible, for he felt the responsibility of his position. That night after the household had retired, we counted the money and found it correct and he started for Lamine before six o'clock the next morning. There was much satisfaction over the success of his mission. Among the men, the money was at once divided among them, and allayed the feeling of unrest and suspicion that had been growing for some time. The letter to Col. Bissell from Gen. Cullom, and which E.M. was the bearer of, commended the colonel for his method of drilling and teaching his officers, and also said if Captain H— was a specimen of his student officers, they could make a regiment worthy of being engineers. He spoke of the exhaustive examination he had given the captain, and how well he had passed, and E.M. was gratified that he had been successful in the test and, therefore, had accomplished his mission.

Before many weeks were passed, orders were received making them regular engineers, with the increase of pay and the advance in rank, and there was no more dissatisfaction with their rank and pay.

Soon after this came the news of the fall of Fort Henry and the battle of Fort Donelson, in which the Union Army was victorious.[25] It was almost the first success of our army, and was a hard fought and desperate battle, and the little gray man with his bull dog grip had compelled victory after three days hard fighting. How anxious we all were, and when the word came that our flag floated over both forts, the city went wild with excitement and rejoicing. Men and women went up and down the streets waving flags and singing, glad of the opportunity to at last have something to rejoice over. But soon the steamboats came with their loads of maimed and wounded and we had the dread side of war.

That success greatly heartened and encouraged the North, and military men as well as the people began to realize that we had a general on our side who knew his business as well as Gen. Lee, but Gen. Grant had bitter enemies who tried to traduce and injure him. But he went quietly on his way,

[25]Fort Henry and Fort Donelson surrendered to General Grant in February, 1862. The capture of Fort Donelson was a great victory for the Union because it opened a route for the capture of Nashville and the invasion of the South.

doing his duty and serving his country with loyalty and faithfulness.

The Western army and navy were now being massed for an expedition down the Mississippi River to open it for navigation. Columbus, Kentucky and New Madrid were the points first aimed for and then Island No. 10 with its formidable forts and batteries had to be captured before boats could pass it.[26] The Engineer Regiment was ordered down the river to the vicinity of New Madrid. They came in from Lamine and went right to the boats that were to take them down the river. E.M. could only spend a couple of hours with us, and as the expedition promised to be a summer campaign, it was very uncertain when we should see each other again.

He was very anxious that the baby and I should go to his people for the summer. They had written to him wanting us to come and believed the summer spent in the quiet of the Northern Vermont home would prove beneficial to us both, especially after the strenuous winter just passed. Affairs at home had so arranged themselves that I could leave Mother in comparative ease, and it seemed a good opportunity to pay the promised visit. When the time came for us to part my heart was broken, and it made it hard for him, but this time I seemed to have

[26]Island No. 10, named by the Army Corps of Engineers, was strongly fortified by the Confederate forces who were in a position to control navigation on the Mississippi. The island was taken by a flank movement by the Union troops under the command of General Pope.

Charge of General Smith's division
during the capture of Fort Donelson, Tennessee.
Courtesy Missouri Historical Society

The gunboat attack on the water batteries at Fort Donelson.
(from Harper's Weekly, March 15, 1862)
Courtesy Missouri Historical Society

Positions of Taylor's and McAllister's batteries during the Battle at Fort Donelson.
(from Harper's Weekly, March 15, 1862)

Courtesy Missouri Historical Society

lost the power of repression and self-control, and sobbed my heart out in his arms. The good bys had to be said and it was as bitter for him as for me.

The next day I went to the hospital and devoted myself to the poor wounded fellows from Donelson, and strove to forget my own griefs in the sorrows and miseries of the poor boys who were giving their all to their country. Mother took care of my baby and I gave my time both night and day to the sick and wounded soldiers. In that way I could forget my own troubles.

While the regiment was in Missouri they had been in no battle or engagement. Gen. Sterling Price was threatening a movement on St. Louis and the Engineers were busy building fortifications and throwing up earthworks, and the winter's work was really a school of instruction in Military Engineering. The very able officers and men took advantage of the opportunity which afterward gave this regiment such a noted and enviable position in the Western Army, while the severe winter passed in camp had inured them to the severities and hardships of active camp life and fitted them for future activities. Many were the stories told of their experiences in Missouri among the hostile planters and farmers. Some of these stories are related in the history of the regiment.

As the men were nearly all Republicans, they did not look with much favor on slavery, and when the slaves in the vicinity of the camp would run away and come to our men, there would be no special effort made in persuading them to return to their owners, and they would come in search of their slaves foaming with wrath. Several drastic orders were given by the Department Commander in St. Louis, forbidding the harboring of slaves by members of the army, and insisting on the return to their masters.

One Negro who attached himself to E.M.'s mess as cook and general servant, had been returned to his master, an old farmer, several times, but insisted on still running away. Finally E.M. bought him off the old man for a trifling sum and a bill of sale was made out, and E.M. owned a slave. But only for a short time, for the poor fellow, who was a devoted servant to the men who had saved him from death at the hands of his master, succumbed to disease in the trying campaign around New Madrid.

E.M. and his lieutenants were involved in several of these so called "contraband" affairs, however the colonel, who was charged with seeing that the orders were enforced, was in sympathy with the feeling of the regiment on the slavery question. He overlooked many violations of the order, which soon became obsolete, for the slavery question was a vital one, much as the government ignored it at this time. But all this is history.

On the 4th of March, 1862, the Engineers started down the river to join Gen. Pope, under whose command they were, during the ensuing campaign for the reopening of the Mississippi River.[27] They were disembarked at the little town of Commerce, and marched the rest of the distance to New Madrid in three and a half days. It was their first extended march, and first night bivouac. The weather was very severe and the men greatly suffered. At night, wrapping themselves in their blankets, they laid down on the hard frozen ground to sleep. The warmth from their bodies would melt the frost under them and many in the morning found themselves frozen to the ground.

The regiment went into camp in the rear of New Madrid, on the eighth of March.[28] The fight at New Madrid was the first time E.M. was under fire and it was an exciting experience to him. He had been ordered with his men to move a quantity of gun powder which was exposed to the enemy's fire, to an earthwork magazine just finished by the men to receive it. The enemy had opened a galling fire and the engineers were right in the path of it, but the powder had to be moved and his men were watching E.M., so he and Charlie Thompson, his lieutenant, went at it and assisted the men. They were all frightened blue and did want to get away from there, but that powder had to be moved and E.M.

[27]Major General John Pope was later appointed Commanding General of the Army of Virginia.

[28]The capture of New Madrid, Missouri and Island No. 10 were important events in the River War for the domination of the Tennessee and Cumberland river system, and for the use of the Mississippi as an invasion route to the South.

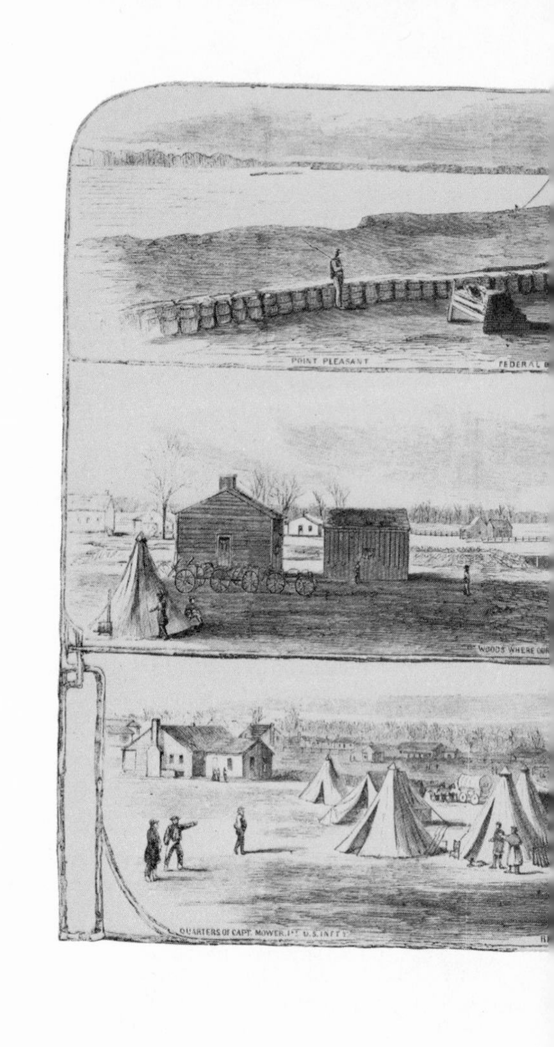

POINT PLEASANT
FEDERAL B
WOODS WHERE OUR
QUARTERS OF CAPT. MOWER, 1ST U.S. INF'TY

Views at New Madrid and Point Pleasant, Missouri.
(*from Harper's Weekly, April 12, 1862*)
Courtesy Missouri Historical Society

knew that to keep his men in line, he must remain in line himself. Once when he raised his arm to point and direct the moving of a keg of powder, a cannon ball passed under his arm and the swift motion of the ball so close to him whirled him round, dazed for a moment. That same ball killed a man of an Ohio regiment who was some distance behind E.M. and cut off the legs of another man. Our boys laid themselves flat and hugged the ground close, but they stored the powder in a safe place. Soon after, the colonel came and ordered them to a less dangerous point and they certainly obeyed that order with alacrity. It was not a funny experience at the time, but years after, E.M. and Charlie and others of the officers would laugh over it and at each other at the blue funk they were in, when the shot and shell began to fall around them and they dared not run or even flatten themselves to the ground as they so much wanted. In talking of it afterward E.M. said he was so terrified that he was sick, but the only coherent thought he had was to get that powder in a safe place before it was exploded by the fire from the enemy. When he looked at Charlie Thompson the young fellow's face was blue, and Charlie said E.M. was blue too, and his eyes like coals of fire. He watched for E.M. to hunt a safe spot so he could go too, but E.M. kept on like a man hypnotized, and he had to stay, too.

The next night New Madrid was evacuated and the following day, our troops occupied the rebel camp. The Confederates had left in a hurry, for even their camp fires were burning, and much of their clothing and camp equipage was left. E.M. picked up a prayer book lying on the table in the tent of the general commanding, and sent it to me as a souvenir of his first battle.

The next point to capture was Island No. 10, which being strongly fortified, blockaded the river completely, and to make an attack on it meant the loss of many lives. No boats could pass through the narrow channels without danger of capture or destruction. Our men had marched around back in the country through swamps and morasses, wading many times up to their waists through the water. They came out to the river, south of the Island, but could do little without the aid of guns to fortify. Commodore Foote, who was in command of the river fleet, would not permit his transports to run past the rebel batteries, knowing it was certain destruction for them, and Gen. Pope was imploring for support and that the attempt be made.

At this day it looks tame in the writing, but I well remember how fierce the anxiety and excitement were about attempting to pass Island No. 10. Finally in the fertile brain of Col. Bissell an idea was born which appeared feasible and practical if allowed to be carried out. After reconnoitering the surrounding country and its conditions, he believed it could be done. I will quote from his own story of the New Madrid Canal.

"I was determined Gen. Pope should have his boats if I had to take them across the country. In the morning standing upon the levee, while the guide was bailing out the canoe, I saw an opening in the woods back of the over-flowed field, and the thought came over me that this was the way to take the transports through. This was an old wagon road extending half a mile back into the woods. There it terminated. The guide said it was two miles from there to the nearest bayou. I took out my memorandum book and asked him to make a map of the route of this bayou, from the nearest point to where we then were, to New Madrid. This he did showing a straight line through the timber of two miles. This we carefully explored and I said to myself, "The Engineer Regiment has talent enough to take a fleet of boats through those woods." The result proves that the old organization could be depended upon for anything. Upon reaching terra firma I went to Gen. Pope's headquarters at once and reported the refusal of Commodore Foote to help us with the transports. Gen. Pope was indignant, and expressed himself with great vehemence and warmth. In other words he was "hot under the collar." The general and his staff had just finished their supper and as I was eating mine, someone suggested something about a "canal." The general laughed about any "canal" when the whole country was under water ten feet deep. I then took out my memorandum book, and showing the sketch to the general, told him the whole thing was provided for and that our regiment would put him across the river in fourteen days. He at once called me into another room, where the whole plan was explained. I knew that he had graduated at the head of his class at West Point, and was distinguished in the engineer service, and when he said the plan was a good one (if the regiment could carry it out), he showed his faith in it by giving me unlimited orders on everybody under his command, for everything that might be asked for."

PUBLISHED BY CURRIER & IVES.

Entered according to act of Congress in the year 1862 by Currier & Ives, in the C

BOMBARDMENT OF ISLAND "NU

By the Gunboat and Mortar fleet,

The Bombardment commenced on Saturday afternoon, March 15th. 1862, a
of war, fell into the hands of the gallant forces, unde

…ict Court of the United States. for the Southern District of New York. 152 NASSAU ST NEW YORK.

EN" IN THE MISSISSIPPI RIVER.

…mmand of Flag Officer A.H. Foote.

… until midnight of April 7th, when the whole Island with all its vast munitions … e Foote.— "A Nations thanks are due them".

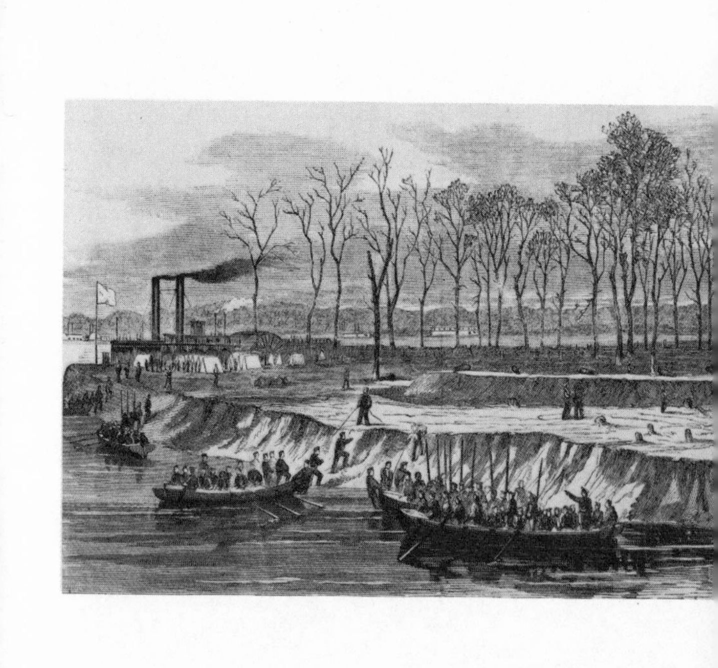

Island No. 10 after the Surrender.
(*from Harper's Weekly, May 3, 1862*)
Courtesy Missouri Historical Society

That was the beginning of the canal which was made around Island No. 10. It was completed in the time specified and was one of the greatest achievements of the war. Transports and gunboats passed through this canal and one of the strongest and most impregnable points held by the Confederates was rendered untenable, and they surrendered. Large numbers of prisoners were taken, and vast quantities of ammunition. This is all a part of history and need not be dwelt on here, only in so far as the Engineer Regiment was concerned. The country rang with the brilliant and successful manoeuvre and it gave the regiment a status and reputation it well deserved and which was maintained throughout the war.

There were but few letters from my captain during these strenuous days. Every officer and man were putting forth their best efforts to make a success of the undertaking. They were more than men. They were heroes. No thought of hunger or fatigue or want of rest found lodgment in their minds. Each man did the work of three and though many of them worked night and day in water waist high, there were none sick from the exposure, and I know my soldier was giving the best in him, and they achieved deserved success, though there were some who tried to steal their laurels.

I quote from Gen. Pope's report:

"Col. Bissell having reported that a route could be formed for a channel sufficient for small steamers, I immediately directed him to commence the canal with his whole regiment, and to call for any assistance for men or material necessary for the work. It was my purpose to make the canal deep enough for gunboats, but this it was not found practicable to do within a reasonable period. The work done by Col. Bissell and his Engineers was beyond measure difficult. The canal is twelve miles long, six through very heavy timber was made fifty feet wide by sawing off trees four and five feet under water. Of Col. Bissell and his Engineer Regiment I can hardly say too much. Untiring and determined, no labor was too much for their energy. They have commenced and completed a work which will be memorable in the history of the war."

Then he goes on and gives a list of names, particularly deserving of credit, and on the roll of honor among the others was my captain's name. How proud and gratified I was. That newspaper in which I read the report has been preserved and cherished all these years till, alas, it is only shreds and pieces!

The regiment was now divided up, companies being detailed for detached duty. E.M. was charged with making the improvements at Fort Thompson, and to make it impregnable from attack by water. About the middle of April, soon after the battle of Shiloh, the Western Army embarked and went up the Mississippi River to the Ohio, then up the Ohio to the Tennessee, where they disembarked and prepared to take part in the siege of Corinth.[29] The

[29]The siege and the battle of Corinth, a strategically located city in northeastern Mississippi, took place on October 3 and 4, 1862. General Grant's forces were victorious.

Engineer Regiment was with Gen. Pope's command, and took part in all the operations around Corinth.

The battle of Pittsburg Landing or Shiloh, was fought April 6 and 7, 1862.[30] It was a fierce and bloody battle, but the Confederates retreated to Corinth, Mississippi, and the Union forces held the ground they had fought over. The loss of life was appalling and the blood of brave men was poured out like water. So fierce was the musket fire that many trees were stripped entirely of leaves and small branches. The field hospitals were entirely inadequate to deal with the wounded, and transports were sent from St. Louis as soon as word reached us of the battle, fitted up with cots and all necessary supplies known to medical science in that day. Doctors and surgeons were called on and a call for volunteer nurses was sent out. In our Soldiers' Aid Society the organization and system was much improved and Mr. Yeatman was already at work with his great Sanitary Commission. Our Society was called on to furnish as many nurses as possible. Mrs. Cozzens was made chairman of the committee and she selected those who had more or less experience in the hospital work during the past winter

[30]Pittsburg Landing in southwestern Tennessee was a gathering place for the forces commanded by General Grant in preparation for the battle of Shiloh. The battle of Shiloh, April 6 and 7, 1862, was one of the bloodiest battles of the Civil War. Over 80,000 Union and Confederate soldiers participated in the battle which ended in a Union victory.

from among the volunteers of the Aid Society. She was really to be the head nurse and we were to work under her orders. I was one of the chosen and felt it a great honor for I was the youngest woman on the Committee. But my zeal probably made up for my lack of experience, though the past winter's experience had been of great service to me in the caring for the sick and wounded. Mother said for me to go and she would care for my baby boy. I knew he was safe with her.

One misty cold morning in April our little fleet of transports started down the river on our sad and gruesome errand. There were a dozen women on our boat, under the direction of Mrs. Cozzens. We had been co-workers for many months and were earnest and thorough in our work. We all wore black dresses with large white aprons while on duty, and that was most of the time. While on the way down, the long saloon was fitted up with two rows of cots the whole length, and they were made ready with clean fresh bedding, to receive our poor boys. We were very busy all the way assisting the surgeons in their preparations and realized the serious ordeal that was before us.

We women all had a hope that we might be able to visit the battlefield and see where one of the great battles of the war was fought. We did not know how long we might remain at the Landing, but had no doubt there would be an opportunity to go ashore and make an expedition to Shiloh. When

U. S. hospital ship Red Rover *on the Mississippi River.*

Courtesy Missouri Historical Society

at last we reached Pittsburg Landing late in the afternoon, a scene of indescribable confusion and horror met our gaze. Horses, mules, men, cannon, commissary stores, and ammunition seemed piled together, and lying and sitting around on the wet and muddy ground, were maimed and wounded soldiers, suffering and dying for lack of attention. It was a dreadful and horrible sight. Many of the poor fellows had been unable to get their wounds dressed since the battle. The hospital tents were overflowing, and the doctors were working night and day.

As soon as the boat was tied up to the Landing, they began bringing the wounded on board. All night they kept coming and all night doctors and nurses worked over the wounded and dying. Many limbs had to be amputated, and the saloon where the operations took place looked like a butcher's shamble. By morning our boat had all the wounded it could carry, and we were ordered to St. Louis as rapidly as we could get there, and by nine o'clock we were steaming back up the river and that is all we saw of the battlefield of Shiloh.

After the Engineers reached Hamburg, E.M. was detailed to report at St. Louis on official business, really to make a requisition for the tools to be used in building the fortifications around Corinth, which was to be the next point of attack. He came unexpectedly, but we were rejoiced and happy to see him, even for the short time he was there. My captain showed the effect of the hard campaign around New Madrid and Island No. 10. He was lean and toughened and looked years older, but said he was well though tired. He was greatly concerned about the baby and me, and insisted that we start East at once. It was an arduous winter and the Shiloh experience had been a heavy drain physically and mentally. So many poignant things had happened.

The baby, too, looked thin and pale. He was a delicate little fellow, and I had neglected him more than I meant to for other duties. Mother had been most kind in the care of him, but she had many burdens and a large family dependent on her. E.M.'s brother living in Dayton had written inviting us to visit him and his family on my way to Vermont. E.M. thought it would be a good time to go and insisted on my going, as the complete change would benefit both the baby and me. I was loath to give up my work with the soldiers or to leave Mother, but felt their judgment was better than mine, for I certainly was very tired and overwrought and needed a change.

After E.M. returned to his regiment, we began to make ready for my journey, which in those days was quite an undertaking for a woman and child to make alone, and it was with great reluctance I retired from my work in the Soldiers' Aid Society, in which I had been so deeply interested. With my aunt, sister, brother and myself and baby gone it would greatly lessen the labor and care of my mother, who would still have her four little girls to provide for.

One bright April day I bade adieu to St. Louis, not knowing under what circumstances I should see it again. The next morning I was met in Dayton by my brother-in-law, and taken to his pretty cottage where a warm welcome greeted me from his wife and baby girl.

The clean quiet town with its attractive homes surrounded by beautiful gardens and lawns, the broad tree lined streets, the bright spring sunshine, and shrubs and flowers blooming, making the air fragrant and the yards brilliant with color, were revivifying to the tired and faded senses after the gloom and grime and mud filled streets of St. Louis during the past winter. Then there were the peaceful and well ordered lives of the people going about their usual avocations, apparently without thought or concern regarding the war. Seldom was a soldier in uniform seen. It was a startling change from the rush and feverish excitement of the past year, and took some time to become accustomed to so great a change. Gradually the tension that had kept the nerves all taut was relaxed, and we enjoyed what seemed a paradise to us, and both soon showed improvement. M— and F— were most kind and insisted on our remaining there till we were in a more normal condition. Their friends were delightful and we soon became at home. Those quiet months and the great kindness shown E.M.'s wife and boy, who were strangers to them, are recalled with great pleasure. The weeks slipped by and each day in this lovely spring time was a joy and delight, and the little boy grew rosy and plump.

E.M. wrote frequently from the front at Corinth. The Engineers were being worked to the utmost by the higher powers. They had proved how resourceful and efficient they were, and many demands were made on them. The companies were scattered no two in the same place, but all where skill and technical ability were needed, and they proved themselves every time. At last E.M. wrote to me and his brother, saying he was not at all well, and the doctor advised his getting a sick leave for thirty days to go home and get well before the summer campaign began. M— immediately wrote for him to come to Dayton, where we would nurse and care for him, and certainly no nicer place could be desired for a sick man. How thankful and grateful I was that he could be there. He came very soon, looking so pale and gaunt, almost a wreck from loss of rest and overwork, as well as exposure and hardships of the New Madrid campaign. We put him under the care of the best doctor in the city, and I had my own soldier to nurse till he was restored to health.

After two weeks of electrical treatment, which was then in its infancy, and salt water baths, and the perfect quiet and rest, great improvement was manifested. He soon became convalescent, and was able to share in the little outings and picnics which were given for him. The weather was ideal, the friends congenial, and many delightful affairs were enjoyed those bright summer days, only one of which threatened to end disastrously. We had started on a boating trip down the Miami River. We were to float down the river about ten miles, picnic in the woods on the bank and return by moonlight. There were three boats filled with a gay and jolly crowd, all young married people, with our children, three of them. The day was very warm, but it was a charming ride and everyone was at their best. We had partaken of our dinner and were preparing to embark when someone remarked they heard thunder, and on investigating we found that there was a storm almost on us. Being in the woods, we had not noticed the clouds approaching. There was no shelter in sight, but on reconnoitering found there was a farm house across some fields about half a mile away. There was nothing but to go there, and we began the tramp over the rough plowed fields. The storm broke in all its fury before we were half way. The wind almost swept us off our feet and quite took our breath. The lightning was sharp and fierce and the thunder one continuous roar, while the rain came down in sheets. We were soon drenched to the skin, and it was a wet bedraggled crowd that finally reached the hospitable shelter of the farm house. We women were badly frightened too, for the storm seemed to increase and we were twelve miles from home. However, we discovered there was a railroad station about a mile off, but no train into Dayton that stopped there till seven o'clock. It was still raining hard when the farmer drove the women and children over to the station. The men had to walk through the mud and water. We left all our picnic equipment with the farmer and his wife till we could send for them. We were a sorry looking lot of people that reached Dayton after our festive start of the morning.

We found the storm still raging there, the streets flooded with water and it was with difficulty that we could procure vehicles to take us home, glad and thankful to reach its shelter safely, especially after we had learned of the damage done and lives lost. It was a thrilling experience, but fortunately none of us suffered from the drenching and exposure.

Capt. William Keeling, Quartermaster of Gen. Sherman's Army, a cousin and foster brother of E.M. and M—, came and spent several days with us. The boys had not seen each other for a number of years and it was a happy reunion. How they did enjoy recalling their boyhood days on the old farm in Northern Vermont. As I was soon going there, they proposed filling a trunk with things that would be useful to Father H— and the sister who lived at home, but the articles at that time would be in the nature of luxuries. There were several pounds of parched coffee which cost them a dollar a pound, tea at three dollars a pound, twenty-five pounds of sugar at twenty-five cents a pound, tobacco for Father H—, a piece, or bolt, of cotton cloth at fifty cents a yard, dresses for the aunt and sister at fabulous prices. The trunk full of simple necessary articles represented a large amount of money, but how enthusiastic those boys were and with what pleasure they would keep buying something the folks at home would like, and tuck it into the trunk. It certainly was a wonder box. My sister-in-law, who had visited them and knew the family, suggested more discrimination in some of the gifts. The boys had a fervor of generosity and it was well to allow them to indulge in it, but afterward, when I saw how the gifts were received, I wished they had sent the money. It would have been more serviceable and acceptable, but they did not know that.

The month of furlough soon slipped away and my captain, restored to health and strength and looking fit, was ready to return to duty. We had put war and its horrors away from us and after he had recovered, they had been days of quiet unalloyed pleasure to him. The time came all too soon when we must part again, but how much we had enjoyed this brief respite in the cozy home of his brother, and the unfailing kindness and hospitality they had shown us. We left the same day—E.M. saw Georgie and me off for the East, then took the next train for the South, and our idyll was a thing of the past.

The summer of 1862 my little boy and I spent with E.M.'s Father and family, who lived in the quaint little village of Highgate, in the extreme northern part of the state of Vermont. Father Hill had sold the farm and old homestead on which his family had been born and reared, and on which his father before him had lived and reared his family, and which was part of the original grant made to the Marvin family by George the Third of England. E.M.'s grandmother was a Marvin and the old farm was a part of her dower. Father H— was now living in a very comfortable and pretty home in the village. As his sons grew to manhood, they left the sterile acres which afforded them but a meagre living, and as so many young men of New England did at that time, went West to open up a newer and more fertile country.

Just now the four Hill sons were in the Union Army, serving their country. They were worthy descendants of patriots, for Father H— had been a soldier in the War of 1812, and Grandfather H— had been a soldier in the War of the Revolution, from the state of Connecticut, where the Hill family had originally settled when they emigrated from England in the latter part of the 17th century. So really, they were a family of soldiers and devoted to their country.

But to return, we spent a very quiet summer. A pall of sadness had settled over the entire country. In the smaller Eastern states, all the young and able-bodied men were in the army. Every family had contributed its quota. The Army of the Potomac was suffering defeat. The bloody battles of Malvern Hill, Gaines Mills, Chancellorsville and Fredericksburg were fought and no advantage gained, and it was now realized that the war would be a long and bloody one, till one or the other side was exhausted and physically spent.[31]

The summer was a very sad and gloomy one. Scarcely a day passed but the tidings would reach the quiet little village of the killing or wounding of some of its sons, and funeral sermons and orations were more frequent than any other oratory.

Father H— was greatly attached to his little grandson, and in their waking hours they were seldom apart. With good old Betty, the family horse, and buggy, we took many delightful drives over the hills and through the valleys in which my soldier had passed his childhood and boyhood till he reached his majority, and which he had loved to talk about till I felt familiar with all his boyish haunts. We drove over the farm, gathered plums from the plum thicket, went through the old house which had originally been a spacious log house, but had been so transformed and built over, you

[31]The Battle of Malvern Hill, which was fought on July 1, 1862, was a qualified Union victory.

The battle of Fredericksburg in December, 1862, was one of the worst defeats suffered by the Union Army. Under the inept command of General Ambrose E. Burnside, the Union forces lost about 13,000 men.

The battle of Chancellorsville fought in April and May, 1863 was another terrible defeat of the Union armies commanded by General Joseph Hooker.

would never suspect its original character, but the logs were still there and added to its substantiality.

We went to the sugar woods and saw the camp and all paraphernalia for gathering the sap and making maple sugar, which E.M. said was the most plentiful thing they had in their childhood. We went to the little red school house and saw girls and boys at school, just like those who went there when E.M. was a boy, and he drove by the comfortable farm house where E.M.'s first sweetheart lived. She was now married and the mother of four children. I afterward met her and we laughed over her experience. She said, "He was a mighty good boy, and a master hand at making love." I told her I could well believe that, and we laughed some more.

We attended services at the old stone church, gray and ivy covered, surrounded by its graveyard in the old New England fashion, and where Father Hill had been church warden for fifty long years. Father H— seemed pleased with my evident interest in the early life of my soldier. He was certainly a dear and delightful old man, and my sojourn among them that summer is one of my pleasantest memories.

In the meantime, it had been a summer of much danger and trying labor to E.M. with small visible result. After the capture of Island No. 10, and the opening of the Mississippi to Memphis for navigation, the regiment which had become famous through the canal they had built, so as to go around the Island instead of past it, was scattered at many and various tasks. Arriving at Hamburg, Tennessee, it was discovered that the Corps of Gen. Pope and Gen. Buell were separated by a deep creek, and would, in case of attack, be unable to communicate with each other.[32] Companies D and F were detailed under Capt. Hill to build a bridge which was commenced about dark and finished about daylight the next morning, after an all-night's work.

Many were the activities of the Engineers during that hot and trying summer. They were in the siege and battle of Corinth. It was here that E.M. had a horse shot under him. The horse, a magnificent bay animal, with saddle and accouterments complete, was a gift from Gen. Pope to E.M. as a slight appreciation of his faithful services, and he was highly prized, both for the giver's sake as well as the horse's. This day, E.M. and other engineers were with Gen. Pope on a reconnoitering expedition over the fortifications the engineers were engaged upon, when the enemy got their range and opened fire on them. A cannon ball struck the horse, almost severing his head and he was instantly killed, but E.M. said he (the horse) remained standing several moments before falling. E.M. hastily alighted and they all got away from there in double quick time,

[32]General Don Carlos Buell, a West Point graduate, served in a Kentucky command post during the campaign against Confederate General Braxton Bragg. Buell's inept leadership caused his dismissal in 1863.

for they were pouring a hot fire into them, but he did mourn the loss of his beautiful horse.

During this summer details of the regiment were in several battles around Corinth and a number of the men were killed, wounded, and taken prisoners. Such terrible stories were reaching us of the horrible brutalities committed on our men in Southern prisons that I wrote E.M. I would rather he was killed in the discharge of his duty than to be taken prisoner and sent to one of those hell holes. I had such a horror of them it did not seem as though I could bear to have my soldier meet such a fate.

In July E.M., assisted by Lieut. Parker, with a detail of sixty-five men was ordered on a wrecking expedition on the Mississippi River among the boats, barges and floating batteries sunk or destroyed by the Rebels in their surrender of Island No. 10 and New Madrid. One immense battery had been cut loose hoping it would float down the river, past the Federal forces and be saved by them for future use, but it stuck on a small sand island submerged during high water, and there it remained. The falling river had left it high and dry and half buried in the sand. This battery was a formidable affair and the men were engaged nearly three weeks in dismantling it, not an easy task with the burning heat of July sun pouring down on them on a barren sand bar, with myriads of mosquitoes holding high carnival and adding to their discomfort. On Island No. 10, where the camp was, it was only a degree better and there was much sickness and suffering amongst the men.

Mrs. Parker had come to visit her husband, Lieut. Parker, and proved herself an angel of mercy. She established herself as Dr. Knower's head nurse and was indefatigable in her care and attention to the sick men and was so cheerful, bright and sympathetic, she kept up their failing courage. E.M. wrote they would hardly know what to have done without her. She was so ready and resourceful, and with so much common sense, for really the conditions were dreadful. They remained there till the last sunken steamboat was raised, the last cannons, guns and ammunition were loaded on steamboats and sent to Memphis, and then returned to Jackson, Tennessee, where the regiment was now stationed.

Many of the men had to go into the hospital, for the heat, malaria, mosquitoes and continuous hard labor had also done its work, and many of them were sick men who returned to Headquarters. E.M. sent me one relic from Island No. 10, a silver plated butter knife from the cabin of a sunken steamer which he was examining at the bottom of the river, in diving dress. We used it for many years.

While at No. 10, a steamboat, the *Crescent City*, was turned over to E.M. to move the wreckage, guns, ammunition, and stores captured with the Island. Often, the boat made trips to Memphis and Cairo with its cargoes. On one occasion, when they were at the latter town, Col. Palmer, commanding

YAZOO

View of steamers sunk by Confederate forces between Island No. 10 and New Madrid, Missouri. (from Harper's Weekly, May 3, 1862).

Courtesy Missouri Historical Society

an Illinois regiment, came on board and gave E.M. orders to take a detail of his regiment to some point down the river. The colonel had quite a sense of his own importance and was very domineering. E.M. refused to obey the order, saying that he only took orders from ranking officers. That made the old fellow furious, that a captain of Engineers should address an Infantry colonel in that manner. He sputtered and swore and threatened to put E.M. under arrest. E.M. quietly drew his orders from his pocket and showed them to the colonel. They were issued by Gen. Pope, commanding the Department directly to E.M. and outranked the colonel. "Now," said E.M. "you get off this boat and get off quick. I command here." The colonel swore some more, but E.M. had the satisfaction of seeing him beaten. He was a brave old fellow, but tyrannical and bullying. He was afterward Gen. Palmer, and many years after the war became a candidate on the Democratic ticket for President or Vice-President.[33]

After they had completed their work on Island No. 10, the detail returned to Jackson, the Post Headquarters. E.M. was frequently sent on business or orders to the river. On one of these occasions he was able to render a service to Mrs. Grant. She had

[33]Colonel, later General, John M. Palmer was an Illinois politician and a supporter and friend of Lincoln. He served in the Union army, first as a colonel, then as a major general. He fought in the battle of Chickamauga and in the siege of Atlanta. Later, Palmer was Governor of Illinois and a United States Senator.

come down from Cairo under the escort of one of the general's aides, but he had to return to Cairo and he asked E.M. to escort her as far as Jackson, where the general was to meet her. E.M. willingly acceded and took charge of her. She was a pleasant, motherly woman with a large fund of good common sense. There was no train going out that day but a troop train for the front, consisting of freight cars, not even a caboose on it. She was not at all well, and anxious to reach her husband so decided to go on that. E.M. helped her into a freight car filled with soldiers inside and outside, got her baggage on board so she could have a seat on her trunk, and off they started. E.M. tried to make it as comfortable as possible, and the soldiers were quiet and respectful. She chatted with E.M., for they had mutual friends in St. Louis, and many topics of interest to converse about. After awhile, she told E.M. she would have to ask his help to get her off the car when they again stopped, that she was suffering greatly with an attack of diarrhoea and would have to get off, as there were no accommodations on the train. E.M. could see she was in great distress, but she was so sensible about the limitations and seemed to place confidence in him. As soon as the train stopped he got off and lifted her down, took her over to a fence near by, and turned his back on her, shielding her as well as he could from the gaze of the soldiers who swarmed on the train. The men who were in and on the car in which she rode, to their honor looked intently on the other side of the road. E.M. lifted her back into the car and she thanked him very much for his kindness and was very friendly with him the rest of the way. When they reached Jackson, the general was there to meet her and they went South that evening. A short time afterward E.M. received a very cordial and friendly note from her, thanking him for his kindness and his delicate consideration toward her, in what was a very trying experience. Afterward, Gen. Grant spoke of the incident to me the day I traveled with him from Louisville to Nashville.

As the summer passed, E.M.'s letters became less buoyant and cheerful and there was a note of depression in them that was unusual, for while he was not an enthusiastic temperament, he was always hopeful and well balanced. He wished so often that I was nearer, it seemed so far away in Northern Vermont. I felt he was not well and I was anxious to go West. Father Hill and the family were most kind and wanted me to spend the winter with them, but when I read E.M.'s letters to them they did not urge me. The sister in Montreal came home and she helped me with Georgie's clothes and my own sewing. After a pleasant summer spent in that beautiful scenic country and with E.M.'s people, my little boy and I started back for the West. We spent a week in New York with a childhood and girlhood friend and then went to Dayton, Ohio, reaching there early in November. From there we were going to St. Louis. Upon reaching Dayton, Georgie developed a severe cold taken on the journey and was feverish. I called in a doctor and he thought it only a cold, but the child grew worse and the third day he pronounced it scarlet fever. I was greatly troubled, for my sister-in-law's little girl and two little boys next door had been playing with the child and were exposed to it. He was a very sick child and my heart was heavy. On Friday I received a telegram from Elihu, at Trenton, Tennessee, saying, "Come at once. E.M. very ill in hospital here. Wants you." I wired back that I could not come for George was sick with scarlet fever and could not be moved. Saturday afternoon another dispatch came, saying, "If you want to see E.M. alive, come at once." I could not leave my baby and sent for the doctor to know if I dared move him. He said not. It might be his death. I told him there was no other way, I would just have to take him. He said I should do it at my own risk, and I replied I would have to take the risk. I do not think we either of us thought of the risk of contagion for there was not as much attention paid to those matters at that time. It was Saturday night, and no trains ran on Sunday. If I started then, I would have to lay over in Cincinnati till Monday so there would be nothing gained. On Sunday another telegram came saying that he was sinking and there was little hope, and to come at once. I looked at my baby, who was delirious and a very sick child and I became nearly frantic with the hopelessness of it all. Such a dreadful day and night. It was especially bad for us, the women with our dread and fears, for my brother-in-law was away with his regiment and little Julia was already sick with the dread disease, but we had good and kind friends to help us. At five A.M. on Monday morning on the first train out of Dayton, I started for Trenton.

The doctor had given me necessary directions and medicines. We rolled the little boy in blankets and I carried him. He knew little of what was going on. We reached Cincinnati and had to wait there three hours for a train going West. Finally, about noon, we started and went in a desultory fashion, stopping at every little way station. There was no sleeping car and the coaches were dirty old ramshackle affairs. It developed that this train was to pick up soldiers along the way returning from furloughs, who had been called back to their regiments in the field, and was to land them at Cairo, Illinois.

There was a big forward movement being organized at Memphis and Jackson, Tennessee, and new regiments were being hurried to the field and men absent on furloughs were being called in and the railroad and transportation service was much demoralized and congested. When we left Cincinnati there were few passengers in the car and I made the baby comfortable on the seat in front of me, turning the back over so that it made a double seat. He seemed to be in a comatose condition and was very quiet. The conductor asked if he was sick, but I did not tell him the nature of the illness. He was a gruff, surly fellow and told me I could not occupy that seat. I offered to pay him for it but he would not consent to that, but said when the car filled up I would have to move the child.

Every mile passed brought me nearer to E.M. and I felt the way to reach him would be managed. At every station a crowd of half drunken men and loud women would get on the train and as night came on the car filled up with a noisy ribald lot of men and women who seemed to have left decency and respectability far behind them. One man squeezed into the seat beside me with an oath that I would have to move that "young un" from there.

Soon another crowd got on about midnight, worse than any of the others, for they were drunk and abusive and the women were even worse. The conductor was afraid of them and feared trouble. The car was crowded, all the seats taken and he told me I should have to move the boy. Still, I offered to pay double price for the seat but he refused. Just then a great burly fellow, half drunk, brutally sat down on my boy's feet and legs saying the seat was his and he was going to have it. I was desperate. "Very well," I said, "Take the seat, but you will be responsible for the death of a child who is sick with scarlet fever," and I turned back the blanket and showed them the swollen and scarlet face of the unconscious little sufferer. That startled and sobered them. They grunted and got up, and some of the women shrieked, "Put her out. Put her off the train." The conductor said, "Look here. You have no business on this train with that child. You will have to get off at the next station." The fight was on and I was ready for it with the only weapon I had, "bluff." I said to the conductor, "This child is very ill with scarlet fever. We are called to his father who is dying at Trenton, Tennessee, and we are going there, and if you dare put us off, you will not hold your position a week, for I shall report this matter to Gen. Pope and Gen. Grant who are personal friends of my husband. Moreover, I have been taking the numbers and regiments of these men and I shall report their behavior to their commanding officers, some of whom I am well acquainted with." That ended the matter. I was undisturbed the rest of the night. No one wanted to sit with me, and I had the two seats to myself.

Some of the women would growl and insist on my being put off, but the men left me entirely alone. That dreadful, dreadful night! For a while toward morning I feared my baby would leave me. I was oblivious to the drunken rowdyism going on around me. The loud women and their vulgarities, the ribald songs and coarse low jokes. It seemed more like a dream of hell. I did not seem to have any consciousness of myself or my surroundings. I watched my baby and my heart went out to my husband. I prayed, how I prayed, that terrible night, that my dear ones would live. I did not pray for myself or ask the Good Father for anything for myself, only that my husband and child might live. In the gray dawn of a cold winter morning we reached Cairo. There we had to take a steamboat for Columbus, Kentucky, and there a train for Trenton, Tennessee. Everyone was for himself, and no one offered to help me, so I put the little boy over my shoulder, wrapped in his blanket, took my bag and made my way to the boat, two blocks distant through the mud and mire and reached the boat just as they were about to pull in the gang-plank. Two minutes more and I should have had to remain in Cairo till the next day. The boat was crowded, but I managed to find a seat and hold my baby in my lap. I wanted a cup of coffee and finally got a Negro to get me one. We reached Columbus about noon and I took the train for Trenton. My boy seemed only just alive. I have but a hazy recollection of that ride to Trenton. I was in a dazed condition. For two nights I had not slept and had scarcely eaten, and the anxiety and suspense had benumbed my faculties. The only thought was to reach E.M. with his boy before they both died.

At Trenton, Elihu met us at the train. I could not speak when I saw him. I could only look at him.[34] He took the boy from me and slung him over his shoulder and said in his gruff manner, "Don't look at me like that. E.M. is alive. Now no fainting, and

[34]Elihu Hill, a brother of E. M. Hill, lived in Trenton, Tennessee.

you had better get that look off your face before you see him. Come on. I will carry the lad." It was like a douche of cold water in the face, and he only spoke that way to cover up his own feeling. I followed him without speaking for some distance till we reached the building used for a hospital. "Now," he said, "E.M. is conscious and expecting you. It is what has kept him alive. Hold on to yourself and you may be able to pull him through."

We went into a large room full of cots, and there in one opposite the door lay my soldier. Even when he lay in his casket forty-two years after, and I took my last look at his dear face, did he look so death-like as he did that day when I first saw him. So thin and white, and his eyes so glassy and sunken, surely the shadow of death was over him, and my first thought was "only just in time," but the look of ineffable relief and gladness came into his dear face when he saw me. He could only whisper my name as I took his hands and kissed him. "Now," I said, "you are going to get well." "Yes," he whispered, "Don't leave me."

The shock to see him in this condition was a terrible one, but I was so thankful and relieved to find him alive. I held on to myself, for this was no time to think of self. There was work for me to do. Elihu put George in bed beside his father. He had not known that his boy was ill, and even then we did not tell him the nature of his illness. I saw the doctor, who said there was a slight chance for E.M., but he was greatly prostrated and it would take long and careful nursing to bring him around and he must be kept very quiet. I asked him if he could be moved and he feared it was not possible yet. But I was willing to take the risk, and we decided that Elihu should find a room in some quiet, remote house, and the ambulance could take my sick boys there. Elihu had a place in view which he thought would be what we wanted and started off at once to secure it if possible.

I then questioned the doctor about E.M. and found that the exposure and hard work of the summer on the river had done its work, culminating in congestive chills and dysentery. He had two of the chills and another would be fatal. He was so prostrated and weakened that there was little rallying power left and to add to his suffering, he had been blistered with Spanish fly plasters and in his delirium, rolling and tossing, the plasters had been spread all over his stomach and bowels till he was a raw sore from his neck to the lower part of his abdomen, and that had become infected and was covered with sores. When the doctor turned down the bedclothes and showed me his condition, I was horrified. He had become very ill at Jackson and rapidly became worse, till they had no hope for his recovery. They sent him to the hospital at Trenton, because his brother was living there, and Elihu had immediately telegraphed for me.

Elihu soon returned with the news that he had

secured a comfortable room with an elderly couple with no one else in the family and where we would have good attention. He had made the necessary arrangements and they were preparing the room for us and would be ready to receive us when we came. The doctor remonstrated, but I think he was rather glad to shift the responsibility. He, however, helped to move my soldier and went with us to the house. When we got there, E.M. fainted as we moved him from the ambulance, and George was still unconscious. For some time we feared that E.M. would not revive, but slowly he came back to life. We put the boy in bed beside his father and at last I had my two boys where I could take care of them and fight death from them. I thought only of life for them and felt they would get well, and set myself to work to do my part.

When I could look around, I found we had a large comfortable room in what was called a two pen log house. There was a great open fireplace, a rag carpet on the floor, a good bed and a couch in the room and everything was spotlessly clean. There was an open hallway through the center of the house, and the old couple lived in the rooms on the other side of the hall. They were quiet, kindly people and were glad to have us there as a protection. Across the yard was the kitchen and servants' quarters. They kept a Negro cook and her husband, who was a general utility man, and also a housegirl who was deputed to wait on me. The house was situated near the river bottom on the outskirts of the town, remote from the noise and confusion of the barracks and the more thickly populated part. It certainly proved a haven of quiet and peace in the ensuing days when the life of my two hung in the balance.

The days that followed seemed like a dream. I lived only for my sick ones. For two weeks no one was permitted in the room except the doctor. All that was done I did. The servants were not even allowed to enter but left wood and water and necessaries at the door. During this time I never went to bed, but got what sleep I could with my head on the pillow beside my husband, and my hand clasped in his. He seemed fearful of my leaving him, and his nerves were so shattered he clung to me like a little child. Little son was in a very feeble and weak condition. Now the fever had left him and perfect quiet and freedom from any excitement had to be maintained for them both.

The terrible blisters were healing and I kept them cleanly dressed with the few antiseptic remedies that were known at that time, and when they began to heal I knew the work of recuperation was taking place. Our good cook made nourishing broths and soups and we had good pure milk and fresh eggs, and they both soon began to build up, but the convalescence was slow and tedious and as strength gradually returned, E.M. began to chafe at the weakness and confinement. He wanted to be back in the thick of things. Gen. Grant was making a big move down through Mississippi and the Engineers had gone to Holly Springs. Just at this time a number of the new regiments recently enlisted and organized were being hurried to the front. Every day trains loaded with soldiers would go through the town shouting and cheering. E.M. was always eager to learn about them and I would make inquiries so as to tell him.

One day we heard the cheering and noise and I asked someone who was passing what regiment that was. He replied, "—th Ohio." When I told E.M., he turned his face to the wall and burst into tears. He wept and sobbed like a broken-hearted child and his grief was uncontrollable. I was appalled, for I had never seen him lose self control so utterly, and I feared the consequence. I begged him to tell me what the matter was. All he could say was, "It was my regiment." I feared he was delirious and tried to quiet him. The paroxysm finally passed and he was able to tell me his trouble. When the regiments were being organized, he had applied to the governor of Ohio for the command of one of them. E.M. was ambitious and promotions in the engineer service were slow and uncertain and he saw his opportunity to command one of the new regiments. Col. Bissell, Gen. Pope and Gen. Grant had given him fine letters to the governor recommending him as competent and efficient in every way and a brave and loyal soldier. He sent them with his application and had been notified to report at Columbus and take command of the —th Ohio.

Though he was sick even then, he made his preparations to start for Ohio the next day but was stricken that night and knew nothing more about it till told of the —th Ohio going to the front. He had not discussed the subject with his brother officers except the colonel and perhaps one or two others. Every one had their own interests to look after and they all expected him to die, and took no further interest in the matter. He had not written to me about it and was keeping it for a surprise, expecting to meet us in Dayton when we reached there. It was a bitter disappointment and he took it very hard, but I tried to show him the cheerful side, that it was one of the fortunes of war and if he had gone into the Infantry service, he would probably have been killed in battle. "Better that, than to die of disease," he remarked.

As strength returned, he viewed the disappointment in a more philosophic spirit and was reconciled to return to duty with his old comrades and make the best of things. His good constitution and clean living were the great factors in his restoration to health and how happy I was to see him daily gaining strength. The little boy too was well over the fever and was now able to play out of doors. It was a brief interlude of great happiness and peace and thankfulness.

While here I had my first experience with an

earthquake. It was a warm morning in December, quite unusual weather for that season. I had gone to the kitchen across the yard for some warm water and as I turned to pick up the bowl, a singular noise as of rocks tumbling on the roof sounded and then in an instant the water began to slop over the side of the bowl and the floor to sway under my feet like the deck of a ship at sea and it seemed as though the earth was falling from under me and I became nauseated. The servants rushed out into the yard, crying, "Earthquake!" and I followed. When I looked up, every one was doing the same. Another tremor followed and the houses swayed like drunken men, chimneys toppled down, but that was about the worst damage. In some houses there were great cracks. Our house stood the shake well. Only dishes and loose articles were damaged. When I reached our room I found the clock and mantel ornaments had fallen down and E.M. said the old house creaked like a rusty hinge on a door. He was not alarmed for he had a previous experience at New Madrid and once at Charleston, S.C., before the war. All that day I had a feeling of terror and fear that solid old mother Earth should prove herself so uncertain was a new sensation that one did not enjoy.

After a two months' illness my soldier was able to rejoin his regiment at Holly Springs.[35] He was fully

[35]In December 1862, the Confederate General Nathaniel Bedford Forrest struck at General Grant's supply base at Holly Springs and captured 15,000 Union troops.

recovered and fit. It was a day or two before Christmas when he left us, and he decided it was better for me to remain where I was for the present. Our little boy was very frail and delicate and here he could be out of doors most of the days, which was better than being shut up in a city house in St. Louis. The people with whom we were staying were very kind and did much for our comfort, and while the town was occupied by Federal troops it was perfectly safe for us. Then too, my sister was not at all well and we should be near each other. So I bade my soldier good by and he returned to his comrades and duty with renewed health and vigor. We did not celebrate Christmas that year. No one felt like rejoicing, for "Peace on earth, Good will to man," was not in evidence. There was nothing but battle and murder and bloodshed going on. The troops that had been quartered at Trenton were gradually withdrawn and sent South to join Gen. Grant in his movement to the rear of Vicksburg, the next great objective point for the Western Federal Army.

By the New Year there was only a garrison left in charge of the large quantity of stores which had been gathered here for the army. There were also many wagons and mules corraled here, and a number of sick in the hospital which was in the Female Seminary, a large building on a hill overlooking the town. Soon after, rumors began coming in that Gen. Forrest and his men were on a raid and were making their way to Jackson and Trenton to capture stores and destroy the railroad.[36] The commanding officer sent for more men to protect the government property, but everything was being hurried to the front and his requests were disregarded. Scouts began coming in with the word that Forrest had a large body of cavalry and had started on a raid, but it was uncertain where he would strike or when. There was great excitement and anxiety in the town, but my baby and I in our quiet retreat heard little of it, till Elihu came and advised our going to the hotel where he and my sister lived and remaining there with them till the danger was past. He was a civilian in business and would probably not be troubled. I did not see the wisdom of such a move and had no fear, but he had promised E.M. to look after me and had a responsibility in the matter. He could do that better if we were all together than if I was half a mile from the hotel. Then too the old couple with whom I was staying would be safer without a Yankee officer's wife in the house, so we went to the hotel though I didn't want to.

Pickets were stationed on the causeway through the river bottom which led to the bridge and a

[36]Nathaniel Bedford Forrest was a Confederate cavalry general. His lightning raids on Union supply depots were widely feared by Union troops. He was ruthless and treated prisoners with cruelty. Forrest, a son of a blacksmith, was a wealthy planter and slave trader.

After the Civil War, Forrest founded the Ku Klux Klan in Pulaski, Tennessee.

guard placed there. Scouts were sent out and the men in garrison began building a barricade of cotton bales around the station and railroad buildings. Most of the sick were sent to Jackson. There was still a large force there and that town was less likely to be attacked. Great excitement and anxiety prevailed. We hardly knew what to expect. One morning we noticed from our windows much activities in the corrals. The teamsters were hurriedly harnessing mules to the wagons and driving off toward the warehouses. Then Elihu came in with his arms full of boxes and parcels and informed us that Forrest was coming and would reach the town in less than an hour. He had brought his most valuable articles from his shop and wanted us to conceal them for him. He had much gold and silver coin which the citizens had paid him for goods, besides a quantity of currency. My sister padded the front of her dress with money till she had quite a buxom bust, and we took the watches and jewelry and fastened them to the inside of our hoop skirts onto the tapes which formed the skirts. We had a good deal of fun while doing it, and when we finished we were walking watch and jewelry shops and so loaded down with the weight of our wares, we could hardly walk. There was not much fear of our being searched unless someone aroused suspicion toward us. In the general excitement Elihu had passed in and out unnoticed, and he had now returned to his shop and would remain there as long as possible to protect his property. He cautioned us not to leave our room on any account, and no matter what happened to remain quietly where we were unless the hotel was fired. We were not to worry about him. His safety lay in quietly attending to his business and mingling unconcernedly with the citizens.

Soon we noticed increased activity on the streets, men running to and fro, shouts of "They're coming! They're at the bridge." Distant shots were heard and presently soldiers ran by, making their way to the fortified barricade at the station. They were the pickets being driven in. In the corrals the teamsters were wildly and frantically driving their wagons and teams into the woods. Presently the sounds of yells reached us coming nearer, the shrill "Ki yi" of the rebel yell reached our ears, and Forrest's Cavalry charged madly down the street yelling and firing promiscuously, shooting up the town. They charged the barricade, but were met with a hot fire from the little garrison, which emptied several saddles. They turned and charged on the corrals and soon overtook the teams that tried to escape, wounding the men and capturing the teams. A gallant defense was made and bullets flew thick. The zip zip of the guns and the ping of the bullets could be heard and many shots struck the hotel. Some went through our windows and we realized we were in the midst of a battle, even if it were only a skirmish. While they again charged the station and were repulsed, we suddenly heard the boom of a cannon and again another boom and we knew the end was near. They had a couple of their guns in position on the hill by the hospital and were firing at the station, where the few Federals were making their stand. Soon the buildings and cotton bales were on fire and there was nothing to do but surrender. The little band had made a gallant fight, but was overpowered by numbers. Forrest had about 1,200 men with him in this raid. Two or three were killed and several wounded. After the capture of the garrison, they spread out over the town committing many depredations. Their first object was, of course, the tearing up and destruction of the railroad, and loading the wagons with stores and sending them away. What they could not transport they set fire to and burned. Then they turned their attention to the citizens who had harbored or sheltered any Federal soldiers during their occupation of the town, or who were known to have Union proclivities. It was here their brutal savagery was shown. They charged up and down the streets, firing wildly into houses among unoffending women and children. They went into the homes of citizens who were suspected or known to favor the Union cause, broke up pianos with axes and made bonfires of them and the furniture. Many houses were burned to the ground and their occupants turned out homeless in the winter weather. Stores were looted. There seemed to be no discipline or restraint. They were turned loose in that little town and in a few hours had destroyed more property belonging to their own people than had been done by the Federal thousands that had occupied the place for months.

During these terrible hours my sister and I remained in our room, witnessing the fearful scenes enacted before us. We, like others, were in danger of our lives, for bullets flew thick around us and several panes of glass in the window were shattered. We watched the capture of the wagons and saw several of the men shot down and left lying on the ground. From the front window we saw the charge to the little fort and were in the midst of the firing. We were keyed up to the highest pitch and I do not think we were really conscious of what we did. Ever afterward, in recalling what was to us a thrilling experience, the funny side of it would appeal to us and we would laugh till we almost had hysterics. Even to this day I laugh when I think how funny we two women must have been. When the firing was the thickest and bullets were flying fast, my sister stood at the window, a perfect embodiment of fury and cursed the Rebels and the Southern Confederacy. Yes, cursed like a trooper. I never heard her use a profane expression either before or after that experience. She was a woman of innate refinement, very choice in her use of language, and free from all slang and loose expressions, while I was more careless in that respect. In a dazed sort of way, I wondered where she had got all those "cuss words."

There she stood, a little woman, her black eyes blazing, with murder in her heart, pouring out the vilest vituperations on the passing Rebels and wishing she could kill them all. I was sitting on a chair in the middle of the room, with my skirts, and they were voluminous, drawn tight around my little boy in a futile effort at protection, and I was praying at the top of my voice. What I said I do not know, but I was determined God should hear above the din of battle and so I shouted my prayers and sister shouted her curses and we had each changed character. It certainly was very very funny, but we were really so terrified we were not conscious of what we were doing.

The fury and confusion gradually quieted down. Forrest established his headquarters in a private residence not far from the hotel. After dark Elihu came to the hotel. We had been very anxious about him. He had remained in his shop all day, very quiet and non-committal but he was always that. The raiders had been in several times and helped themselves to what they wanted. They had taken all the revolvers and ammunition that were in sight and helped themselves to some of the watches and trinkets and told him to send his bill to "Uncle Sam." He would pay it. He did not remonstrate with them or object, for it would arouse their suspicion and would have done no good. Fortunately, there was little liquor in the town, and there was not much drunkenness. Elihu procured some food for us, as we had eaten nothing since the morning and were feeling exhausted and spent after the day's thrilling experiences. He returned to his store to guard his property as well as he could, and we remained in our room. We each had a revolver and knew how to use it if occasion demanded it, but we did not go to bed or take our clothes off. We carried too much of value concealed about our persons. We slept but little and it was a fearful night for many others in the town as well as ourselves, though the hotel was left unmolested. In the morning my sister was unable to go to breakfast, but my child had to be fed, and I went to the dining-room with him. We had just been seated next to the proprietor at the head of the long table, when three young Confederate officers came in and took seats opposite us at the table. They appeared rather nice boys with considerable swagger, and clattered to their seats with much laughter and loud talking. After they were seated and commenced their breakfast, Georgie, who had been observing them very closely, piped up in his shrill little voice, "Mama, are those men Rebels?" There was a moment of tense silence, then I replied, "Yes, dear, but we will not talk about that now."

"Well, they won't get my Papa will they?"

I told him no, his papa was safe and they could not get him, he must eat his breakfast now. One of the young fellows laughed and remarked I need not be so sure about that. I looked at him and said,

"You will be the first to retreat." I added that the attack of Forrest with his large force on this unprotected little town was a good deal like a big bully beating a little boy. Why hadn't he gone to Jackson, the base of supplies and where he would meet a force equal to his own?

The boys sat up and stared at me and turned very red. The landlord began talking fast about his loyalty to the Confederacy and engaged the boys in conversation, while I quietly finished my breakfast. I just had to say that to them, and when I had got it out of my system I felt better, but they did eye me closely and I expected a hereafter. It came that morning when I was notified to report to Gen. Forrest at once. I refused at first to obey it, but the officer who served the notice said if I did not accompany him I would be placed under arrest and taken there by force if necessary. I decided that for my brother's and sister's sakes it was better for me to go quietly and not involve them in any trouble. I could take care of myself. So we proceeded to Forrest's headquarters and found a motley crowd gathered there—many of his own men, some Federal prisoners, suspected citizens, and I was the only woman, with my little boy. I had insisted on Elihu's keeping out of the matter and not showing in it in any way, for I was fully able to care for myself and knew they would not harm me. Gen. Forrest was a fine looking man, tall and lean, but muscular, with a face that showed he was accustomed to rule. The eyes looked hard and cold, and the mouth looked cruel. Perhaps it looked that way to me for I had heard much of the cruelty of the man. Evidently the young officers had reported my unwise speech of the morning. He looked very sternly at me and asked my name and asked where my husband was. I told him on active service with Gen. Grant. He asked if my husband was a Yankee officer and what I was doing here. I told him who my husband was and that he had recently rejoined his regiment from a sick leave which had been the reason for my being here, to nurse him. He was very short and gruff, but I was not afraid and was extremely angry to be questioned so closely. He wanted me to take an oath of some sort about aiding or succoring the enemy, meaning the Union men, which I utterly refused to do, remarking that they were my people and that he and his men were the enemy. He frowned and said I was to consider myself under arrest and could not leave the hotel except under guard, and if I gave any trouble I should be treated as other prisoners were. I was furious and I could not resist the impulse to reply, "Yes," I said, "We know your *tender mercies* to prisoners, but you are not making war on women and children, you have to make your retreats so rapidly. They would only be obstacles to you on the run, and you will leave this town more rapidly than you entered it when you learn the Union army is coming." I thought for a moment he would strike me, his face was so black and hard, but I felt better for bearding him. He turned to an officer and said, "See that she does not leave the hotel on any pretext whatever." I was a prisoner sure enough and was escorted back to the hotel by an armed guard who remained there. I did not return to my room but wandered around in the building from the parlor to the kitchen and on to the verandahs. I was an object of curiosity, but I was not afraid and I wanted to keep away from my brother and sister so as not to mix them in it. Elihu remained in his store and G— who was not well, kept to the seclusion of her room and I stayed in the parlor most of the time, reading and sewing and entertaining my little boy. We appeared at the table regularly at mealtime, though many of the Confederate officers took their meals there. Some of them were quite nice and friendly and I had pleasant talks with them and I found that many regretted the war and bloodshed as much as the North did, but the sum total with them was in the statement "We had to go with our State." We bantered back and forth about the deeds of prowess of either army, and they were very good natured and I accepted the situation and made light of it, so thankful and happy every hour in the day that my soldier was safely out of it. The third day rumors were reaching us that a brigade of the Federal army from Jackson was marching to relieve the town and would be here the next day to attack Forrest.

The next morning much excitement was manifest

on the streets and there was great running to and fro. We soon learned that Forrest and his troopers had left early in the morning and the Federals would be there by noon. The rear guard of the raiders was then filing past the hotel. The women of the house had gathered in the hall and at the front door to see them pass. They were a motley crowd for they had confiscated most of the family carriages and buggies, also the horses of the citizens, and they were occupied by the wounded Rebels. The prisoners with ropes around their necks like halters and their hands tied behind them were hitched to the back of the vehicles, just like cattle, but received less consideration. One poor fellow, who had managed to slip away unperceived, took refuge with the women in the hallway. A trooper on horseback rode up to the steps and called out asking if there were any "Yanks" in there. A woman shrilled back there was one hiding and to come and get him. The poor fellow cowered down, but his time had come, for the bully rode his horse up the steps and right into the hall among us women and ordered him out. The soldier refused, when he was struck over the head with the butt of the other's revolver, and dazed and beaten, he was driven out to the street. I expected to see him shot and do not know why he was not. There was little compassion shown to sickness or suffering among captured men. My heart burned within me, but what could one woman do, and she in a way a prisoner too, so the poor boy had to meet his fate. The cavalcade stopped in front of the hotel and a sick soldier haltered and tied to the back of a buggy driven by a slouching Rebel, looked up at us women and exclaimed, "For God's sake, ladies, give me a drink of water." No one responded, but I could not refuse that cry for help and rushed to the back of the hall and got a cup of water from the bucket that stood there and carried it out to the fainting man and held it to his lips. The man in the buggy said, "Here, give me that." "No," I replied, "the blue before the butternut with me." He reached over to take the cup when I grasped his wrist and held it fast. "Not this time you don't," I said. I was so furious and keyed up there was the strength of ten men in me and I could have dragged him out of that buggy easily. Just then an officer rode up and ordered him to move on and started the horse, but my sick soldier had drunk his cup of cold water. The last of the raiders left hurriedly and in a very different manner when compared with how they had entered the place. They left destruction and ruin everywhere. The town had been looted and devastated more in the three or four days of Forrest's occupation than in the months that the Union forces had been stationed there. For a few hours a great stillness and quiet seemed to pervade the place. Then in the distance we heard the shrill notes of the fife and the roll of the drums, playing "When Johnnie Comes Marching Home," and soon the boys in blue with the stars and stripes waving came marching down the street. I never was so glad to see anything in my life as that flag, and felt that our troubles were over for that time.

The commanding officer of the Union forces established Post Headquarters in a private house across the street from the hotel. A day or two afterward I witnessed a funny scene which I will set down to illustrate the bitterness of feeling existing toward the Northern soldiers by women who ordinarily were ladies of refinement, gentleness and good breeding. It always seemed strange to me that their hatred and vindictiveness should take the form it sometimes did and betray them into acts of positive coarseness and vulgarity. The flag was suspended on a rope across the street and hung directly over the sidewalk, so that pedestrians passed under it. I have seen women turn out and walk through the muddy streets to go around it rather than to walk under it. This day a young aide came out of headquarters hurriedly, and reached the street just as a young woman was passing. From her appearance and dress she was evidently a lady. She stepped in front of the officer and as he saluted, she deliberately spit in his face. Quick as a flash he grasped her arm, with one hand, drew his handkerchief with the other, wiped his face and then rubbed her face good with the handkerchief. It was all done in a moment. She shrieked, "You dirty Yankee! You are no gentleman." "Well, you are no lady," he answered, "so we are equals," and went on his way, while she just foamed with wrath. It was very funny.[37]

There was a great outcry about a Federal officer assaulting the daughter of a prominent citizen, and many demanding his court martial. Nothing came of it, however, for it was proved that she was the aggressor. The commanding colonel issued an order, however, that anyone insulting officers in discharge of their duties would be summarily dealt with, and also an order forbidding people from going around or insulting the flag. That quieted matters and the place soon became orderly.

I returned to my quiet haven with the old couple, took my soldier's picture out of hiding and settled down to await orders from him. It had been a strenuous time in many ways and I was glad of the quiet and liberty with my friendly host and hostess.

Gen. Grant's campaign through Mississippi to Holly Springs was a failure for many reasons, with which I was familiar at the time and which are matters of history, but need not be gone into here. E.M. was with his regiment at Holly Springs and when Grant's army evacuated the place and returned Northward, the Engineers went to Jackson again.

[37]The incident cited here by Mrs. Hill was not an isolated one. In many Southern cities occupied by Union troops, Southern ladies would publicly insult Union officers.

In New Orleans these humiliations of his officers caused General Ben Butler, the Union Commander of the city, to issue an order that any Southern woman insulting an officer or the United States flag was to be arrested as a prostitute.

Soon after reaching there, he came to Trenton for a couple of days. While in Holly Springs, he had heard of Forrest's raid and the capture of the town and was very worried till he heard from me later for he could not surmise what might happen to us. He told me the Engineers were ordered to Memphis, that the campaign to get in the rear of Vicksburg had been abandoned owing to the difficulty in keeping the line of communication open. The next forward movement in force would be by way of the river where they were now beginning to rendezvous. He counseled my remaining here for the present, till they were settled in camp at Memphis. The Engineers had much to do, for the Federals were going to abandon along the line of this railroad and concentrate around Vicksburg. The road would be destroyed as much as possible, and before that he would send for me to join him at Memphis for a short time before they started down the river. He also advised his brother to leave because he would be away from Federal help, but Elihu decided to remain there. We were so glad to see my soldier again. He looked so well and strong and was in better health than he had been for a year. He had become inured to the hardships of the life.

The latter part of January, 1863, a message reached me from E.M. directing me to join the Engineer company under Lieut. Hooker, which would pass through Trenton on a certain day. This would be the last train over the road, for it was being destroyed behind them. I was to accompany Lieut. Hooker to Jackson and then to Memphis where the headquarters of the regiment now were and where the Engineers were concentrating from different points before proceeding down the river to participate in the siege of Vicksburg. I bade goodby to my kind friends who had sheltered us and been good to us. We met Lieut. Hooker, as directed, on the last train that went over that road for several months, stayed all night at Jackson and proceeded to Memphis the next day. It was a thrilling ride in several ways. The train was a special one, going through on official business for the government. It consisted of two dilapidated passenger cars without any toilet conveniences and a baggage car. There were no passengers except the military officials for whom the train had been provided and I was the only woman with my little child on board, for I was the last officer's wife to leave the abandoned district.

Lieut. Hooker was most kind in his care of us and tried to make it as comfortable as possible. The journey was fraught with much danger, for the country was infested with guerrillas, and a strong guard had to be placed along the road to prevent their tearing up the track. One place we were passing through some dense thickets, when someone in the car cried out, "Down, down, quick," and Lieut. Hooker shoved me and the boy down between the seats and told us to lie flat, and he suited the action to the words. We had hardly done so when a volley of musketry was discharged outside and the bullets came crashing through the windows and the side of the car. Fortunately their aim was too high, and no one was hurt. One of the guards on the train had spied a figure in the thicket ahead and had given the alarm. The men on the train were so accustomed to adventures of that kind, they treated it with complete indifference, but to me it was a serious matter and I was nervous.

At every station there were rumors of attacks or expected attacks. We stopped at one town and were advised to move on quickly. Several sick men were put on the train and the garrison was preparing for an attack from a body of Rebel cavalry that had been reported marching on the town. The engineer put on steam and got away from there in short order. When we had gone about two miles, off in the distance we saw a body of horsemen galloping toward the town we had just left. They were too far away to do us any harm, but that rickety train surely did speed away from that neighborhood, and with the rough uneven track, we were threatened of being left beside the road. The old coach swayed from side to side, but we soon put a safe distance between us and the hostile band. We afterward learned that they attacked the town and were repulsed, but not before they had torn up the railroads and done much damage. Ten minutes later we would have been caught in the skirmish. It was a narrow escape.

We reached Memphis safely in the evening after a very hard journey in many ways. E.M. met me there and I gave a great sigh of relief when I saw him. Lieut. Hooker turned his charges over and was relieved of responsibility and I know he was glad, though he had been most kind and considerate. E.M. took us right out to the camp which was about two miles from the city. It was a dark cold night and my first experience of camp life. His tent was a large round one, called a Sibley tent. On one side boards were laid on cleats which raised it about two inches off the ground. A good thick covering of clean straw or hay was laid on this and then blankets tucked over the straw and that was the bed. The other furnishings were a couple of folding camp chairs and a camp chest which served for a table and trunk. In one side was a folding camp table with tin wash basin and bucket of water. It was all novel to me and I was rather pleased over sharing my soldier's real camp life, although he said this was quite luxurious. His cook was a fine young man named John Meek, a private in his company. He cooked over an open fire in dutch ovens and he made the best biscuit and corn bread and coffee I ever tasted. We had real camp fare and ate off tin plates and drank from tin cups, without table cloth or napkins. When it came bedtime we blew out our candles and crawled in between the blankets. During the night a severe storm came up, and when we wakened in the morning we were covered with two inches of snow that had drifted in over us. E.M. wanted I should go into the city to a hotel, but I preferred to remain in camp, for I knew that was where he wanted me to be, near him, for they were preparing for a long and arduous campaign and it would be many months before we should see each other again. When I decided to remain with him it pleased him.

The cold and the storm continued and we, George and I, had to remain in the tent. We had a little camp stove set up and were able to keep warm. I occupied myself putting my soldier's clothes in order and mending and darning for others, and we thoroughly enjoyed the good meals John Meek prepared for us. He was such a happy good-natured fellow, a real mother's boy, and no matter how great the difficulties he encountered in his cooking, he was always cheerful.

E.M. had little time to spend with us for all was hurry and bustle loading stores and equipment on the *Crescent City*. I had been in camp with E.M. about ten days when the regiment was ordered to embark. E.M. found a boat going to St. Louis and secured passage on it for me and the boy. I bade good by to my many friends in the regiment and my soldier took us on board the boat and put us in the charge of a friend of his who was going to St. Louis on business, Capt. McMurry of the 1st Missouri Artillery, and another good by had to be said, for how long neither of us knew. It might be forever. The Engineers were embarking, and they left that night for down the river. I had taken a severe cold while in camp which had settled in my throat, and it was months before I could speak above a whisper.

The trip up the river to Cairo was devoid of interest. Sad and depressed, and not at all well, everything took on a melancholy aspect. It was cold and stormy and the boat made slow progress on account of the cakes of floating ice. There were few passengers, only one that was attractive; a lovely little lady in deep mourning. She was the wife of a Confederate officer in Hood's army and had been with her husband for some time in the Red River country. She had been passed through the lines and was going to St. Louis to be with her mother, who lived there, and we discovered that our mothers lived only a few doors apart so that we became quite friendly. We were about the same age and had been through many similar experiences. Capt. McMurry proved himself a fine escort and was amusing and entertaining, a good deal of a wag and full of fun.

When we reached Cairo we could go no further by boat on account of the ice, so we took a train for St. Louis. When we reached Olney, or Olin, a junction point with the St. Louis and Cincinnati R.R. we had to change cars there. It was dark and we were dumped out on the platform of a little station shack, apparently on the prairie far from a habitation. The captain could find no one to make inquiries and we were hungry and wanted supper. He was starting on an investigating trip when we saw someone coming with a lantern and waited. A long lank individual approached. "Be you passengers on that train?" he drawled. We said we were and inquired when the train for St. Louis would arrive. "Wal," he said, "There is no train for St. Louis till tomorrow morning. I beant looking for passengers from Cairo to-night. They mostly come on the morning train. I guess maybe you uns ull have to stay at my hotel to-night." We thought so too, so we followed him across the frozen prairie to his house which was some distance from the station. The town, at that time, had been recently started and there were only half a dozen houses in the place and this man had recently erected a two story building for the "traveling public." We were soon in the light and warmth of this welcome shelter. There was an office room smelling of new pine lumber, for the wood work was unpainted, a counter or desk on one side of the room and a register very new, lay on the desk. We were invited to sign our names, but deputed the captain to do it for us. I noticed when the proprietor looked at it, he seemed to perk up and at once showed us into the parlor on the other side of the hall, and lighted the fire in the big wood stove. He remarked he would do all he could to make us comfortable and that supper would be ready in a little while. We noticed how deferential he and his wife were and how very attentive to our wants. We spoke of it to the captain but he laughed and said it was alright. Mrs. Brooks and I decided to occupy the same room and I had a couch put in for my little boy to sleep on. They nearly fell over themselves in their attentions, but as we were the only guests we thought nothing of it.

The next morning it was so cold we asked to have our breakfast served in the parlor where a good fire was burning. While we were at breakfast the man came in and said the train was coming. "But," he said, "you'll have plenty of time to finish your breakfast and get to the depot. It won't be here for half an hour." He told us to look and we looked from the window and as straight as a crow flies the iron rails stretched for miles and miles over the flat level prairie. The distance seemed illimitable and far away, no bigger than a pin's head, was a little black speck and that was the train. In fact, it was forty minutes from the time we first saw it, before it reached the station. The old fellow insisted on showing us every attention. The captain settled our bill and the wife came in from the kitchen wiping her hands on her apron, to bid us good by and to tell us how honored she was by our staying at their house. We stared at her, but I noticed the captain grinning and knew there was a joke somewhere. After we were on the train and started, he began to laugh and exclaimed, "The old fellow stuck us, by Jove. He made you ladies pay for your title." Then we wanted to know the reason of it all, for two plain little women in black hardly expected to be treated as distinguished guests. He began to laugh and said just for a joke he had registered our names as Mrs. Major General Hill, U.S.A. and Mrs. General Brooks, C.S.A. and did not tell us for fear of our giving him away. Especially so since they had exerted themselves to do us especial honor. But the joke was turned on him when he came to pay the bill and found we had to pay for the privilege of being general's wives. We had much fun and sport over the experience and thought the joke was on us.

We reached East St. Louis in the afternoon and had much trouble in crossing the river. It was almost closed with ice and it was a difficult matter to keep a passage open for ferry boats to cross, the only way for passengers from the East and South to reach St. Louis. Instead of ten minutes, we were two hours in crossing, but at last home was reached. I bade my pleasant traveling companions good by, and was glad to be home with Mother once more after the varied experiences of the past months.

Many changes had taken place during the year that had elapsed since I went East. Mother had moved into a large house and was a very busy woman providing for her family. It was almost impossible to make collections on old debts and Father's estate was in a very tangled condition, so there was a real necessity for Mother to provide for her children, and it was a very active life she now led. I soon resumed work with the Soldiers' Aid Society.

Here, too, there were many changes. The Sanitary Commission had been organized by Mr. Yeatman, an eminent and patriotic citizen of St. Louis, the object of which was more efficient and sanitary service to the sick and wounded soldiers in the field hospitals, and to assist regimental doctors and surgeons with medical supplies and proper foods for the sick and convalescent. This was before the days of canned tabloid food and it was a difficult matter to get perishable foods to the sick soldiers in the field before spoiling. This also was before the day of manufactured ice, when ice was a luxury instead of a necessity. The Soldiers' Aid was now an auxiliary of the Sanitary Commission. Their activities were as great as formerly, but were supervised by the Commission. We were still busy scraping lint, rolling bandages, hemming towels, making comfortables and sick-bed clothing, soliciting dainties and food for the sick, packing boxes for the hospitals in the field and many other industries that came up from time to time.

In the city hospitals also a great change had taken place. Chaos had been reduced to order and system. The large block of buildings on the corner of Fifth and Olive Streets had been taken for a general hospital. The Sanitary Commission occupied several of the store rooms on Fifth Street and the Soldiers' Aid Society, one store room on Olive Street. No longer were women allowed to visit the hospital at all hours, ladling out hot soup and beverages to the patients and feeding them rich dainties in a promiscuous fashion. The contributions were gladly received, but now the hospital steward received them and they were taken to the kitchens and fed to the patients by the nurses under the direction of the doctors. No longer were well-meaning women allowed to take charge of the sick and nurse them in a desultory, haphazard fashion, though with the most patriotic intention and the greatest sympathy and tenderness for the suffering men. Now there was a large corps of volunteer nurses who could devote their entire time to the service. They were thoroughly organized and worked under the orders of physicians and surgeons. On certain days and at certain hours our committees were allowed to visit the patients, take flowers for the sick, books for the convalescents, and write letters and messages for them. Everything was better organized and systematized and it made for better care of the sick and wounded and enabled us to accomplish so much more than in the old way.

In June a very beautiful affair was given in aid of the Sanitary Commission. It was called a Sylvan Fete and was really a feast of flowers. The Lindell Hotel on Washington Avenue was just completed. It was the largest and most pretentious hotel west of the Mississippi, and was considered a very handsome edifice and occupied the whole block. We were allowed to use the ground floor for our fete and we were weeks preparing for it. Four large rooms were decorated to represent the four seasons and the girls in charge of them were costumed in harmony with the decorations. There was a queen of flowers and in the evenings a series of tableaux and fancy dances were given, emblematic of the seasons, in the large hall or office of the building. We made bushels of paper flowers for the decoration. The fete lasted three days and wagon loads of fresh flowers were sent in every morning for distribution and to sell. Phebe Cozzens, who afterward became famous as a woman lawyer and eloquent speaker was the queen of flowers. She was a very beautiful girl of the brunette type, a remarkably clever and bright girl, with great executive ability, and she marshalled and led her flower maidens through the mazes of the processions and dances with great vivacity and ability. The whole affair was a brilliant success and netted the Sanitary Commission a very large sum of money, many thousands of dollars.

In the Spring, a change occurred in my mother's affairs. The U.S. government had established a large shipyard for the building of the iron-sheathed gunboats for service on the rivers. The yards were established south of Carondelet, not far from Jefferson Barracks, and it was some distance from the town. The officials and head men were having great difficulty in finding places to live, within a reasonable distance of the works. Some old and influential friends of my father came to Mother and asked her

The gunboat New Era, *just built at St. Louis, Missouri.*
(*from Harper's Weekly, October 12, 1861*)

Courtesy Missouri Historical Society

to take charge and manage a house where these men could have a congenial home and be together. There was a large house on the bluff overlooking the works and the river, about five minutes walk from the yards. It was a stately old mansion of former days, surrounded by orchards and beautiful grounds. It was now vacant and the place was falling into disrepair. The owner and the family were living in the South, but the twenty room house was an ideal one for the purpose contemplated.

Some of the friends who were interesting Mother in the project had large contracts with the government for iron and steel and materials for the building of the gunboats, and they had thought it a fine opportunity for Mother, as well as making living conditions more pleasant for the working officials in whom they were interested. They promised to put the interior of the house in living repair and to keep the house full of paying guests, Mother to furnish the house and help and to have all the proceeds. If Mother needed help to start, they would loan her the money. We hesitated and thought the matter over. I wrote E.M. on the subject. He thought Mother had the ability to manage such an establishment and said we would finance her, so she would not have to borrow money outside or pay interest.

Mother decided to accept the proposition and moved down to the place in March. She had much furniture of her own, and bought comfortable furnishings for the many bedrooms. She retained two rooms and a parlor on the ground floor for herself and family. When the house opened, twenty-seven men engaged board and rooms, and many more wanted to come, but the house was filled.

Now began busy days for the family. The greatest difficulty which we encountered was in procuring and keeping help. It was so far from the city and town they would not stay, but Mother and the two older girls and myself were healthy and strong and we were not afraid to work. In one of the Negro cabins on the place lived the Negro caretaker and his wife, old slaves of the family. He took care of the garden and the cow, and his wife did the laundry work and scrubbing at the "big house." It was a delightful place in many ways, and our little ones, Mother's two little girls and my little boy, spent most of their days out of doors in the old orchard and grew so rosy and strong and were no care. Indeed, we were all very happy and busy and glad to be out of the city, and Mother was prospering and she enjoyed catering for the gentlemen who were her guests.

In the meantime the Engineers were kept quite busy in the operations about Vicksburg. They are matters of history and fully detailed in the History of the Regiment. I shall only speak of matters in which E.M. and his men were interested. That was a wonderful campaign fraught with constant danger and much suffering. The Engineers reached Young's Point opposite Vicksburg during the latter part of February.[38] They found the town an impregnable fortress, a series of high bluffs overlooking the river and all strongly fortified, guarding the passage of the river. Across from these bluffs the country was low and flat, a rich and fertile land, with immense cotton and sugar plantations protected from the overflow of the river by high levees. Several attempts had been made to run past the batteries by gunboats and transports, but they had usually ended disastrously. One attempt only had been successful, I believe.

Arriving at Young's Point the regiment was at

[38]The siege and the capture of Vicksburg on July 4, 1863 by the Union troops commanded by General Grant were a decisive victory for the Union and signalled the defeat of the Confederacy.

President Lincoln, elated by the victory, issued a proclamation to set aside "a day for national thanksgiving, praise and prayer."

An excerpt from a letter dispatched by Lincoln to Grant on July 13th may help to explain Mrs. Hill's description of the role played by the Corps of Engineers in the siege of Vicksburg.

Lincoln wrote: "When you first reached the vicinity of Vicksburg, I thought you should do what you finally did—march the troops across the neck, run the batteries with the transports and thus go below, and I never had any faith, except general hope that you knew better than I, that the Yazoo Pass expedition and the like could succeed. When you got below and took Port Gibson, Grand Gulf and vicinity I thought you should go down the river and join General Banks and when you turned northward, east on the Big Black, I feared it was a mistake. I now wish to make the personal acknowledgment that you were right and I was wrong."

once employed cutting a road through timber from army headquarters to the canal in course of construction across the point. The work occupied two days, during one of which it rained in torrents. The men, however, worked the whole time and while constructing one bridge, were compelled to stand to their waists in water. There was not sufficient ground outside the levee to admit of a camp. The men had to remain on board the boats. Having completed this work, the regiment was ordered to Lake Providence, Louisiana, under command of Col. Bissell. After arriving there, companies D and G, commanded by E.M., were immediately ordered to Baxter's Bayou about eight miles away and proceeded there on foot the same day, making camp near the mouth of the Bayou on a flat piece of ground. These two companies were subjected to the most trying ordeal the succeeding two days, by rain which fell in torrents and covered the ground on which the camp stood to the depth of several inches, leaving no place on which one could stand dry footed. The whole locality was under cultivation and the ground being saturated with water was a perfect bog. There was no possible means of stepping without sinking knee deep in the soft loam. A serious attempt was made to construct a passage for the river fleet around Vicksburg as had been done around Island No. 10, and the Engineers were set to work cutting the levees, cleaning out bayous, opening navigation through Baxter's Bayou, and finally the steamboat, *Sam Young*, which was occupied by the Engineers, made a trip through the opening in the levee, passed over the falls into Macon Bayou, and through other streams and bayous into the Mississippi River, proving that what a dozen regiments had failed to do, this regiment had successfully accomplished alone in a few days. But owing to the distance to be traversed through the enemy's country, before again reaching the Mississippi River, and the great hazard attending the navigation of the bayous and small rivers, the trial was never made.

In all the operations around Vicksburg during the siege, the Engineers took an active part, erecting and building batteries, mounting heavy guns and mortars, cutting levees, doing mining and sapping work in the enemy's fortifications in the rear of Vicksburg. They excavated the levees across the river opposite the enemy's batteries and built masked batteries for guns. The work had to be done at night and in silence, for during the day the enemy's fire would have been trained on them. As it was, they lost several men in the dangerous work.

After the guns were in position, a perfect rain of shot and shell was kept up on the devoted city both night and day. The gunboat fleet above the town and the fleet below the town in conjunction with the land batteries kept up a terrific and incessant bombardment, while Grant with his army like a huge serpent coiled around the rear of the town was drawing the coil still tighter. After severe fighting, the Federals held the railroad, the only means of communication the Confederates had. At last, Grant and Sherman had the enemy penned up in the town and quietly waited to starve them out. There were many sorties, and the Federals made several assaults, but it was found that the place was almost as impregnable to assault in the rear as it was in front. During this time the Engineers in the nature of their work, and the rapid movements they were called on to make, suffered many hardships, not the least being their meagre fare. They were confined almost entirely to bacon and hard tack, and even that was eaten raw at times, when there was neither time nor place to cook it. The boxes of food and dainties that were sent from the Sanitary Commission were for the sick and wounded. Such was the congested and uncertain state of transportation, it was difficult to get personal packages through to the men. If we had the Sanitary Commission frank on them, they went to the hospital. However, Mother and I tried to get some boxes to E.M. for he said they were suffering for fresh vegetables. There was nowhere to forage in that country.

We packed and sent a box every week, usually in care of one of the surgeons of the regiment. Sometimes the box went through and reached E.M., but often it did not. We consoled ourselves with the thought that it was welcomed by whomever received. The great difficulty was in sending fruit and vegetables that would keep on the long trip and in the hot weather. It was before the days of canned food, and there was little use in sending cooked food. We tried sending a boiled ham once, but it was not very satisfactory, so we confined ourselves to potatoes, onions, cabbage, apples and lemons and smoked meats, and whatever dainties we could find in sealed bottles and packages. We always put in two or three loaves of cake for the boys, which they loved, fruit, pound and spice cakes being the best to send. E.M., of course, always shared with his comrades and he wrote we would surely feel repaid to see the delight with which the receipt of one of those boxes was hailed and how much they were enjoyed. Still it was such a small thing to do when we were aching to do so much more. I rarely sat down to a meal in those days but what I thought of our boys with their hard tack and salt pork and their days and nights spent in swamps and water, exposed to all manner of dangers and without the proper food to support and nourish them.

Gen. Grant drew his coils still closer around the doomed city. Still the hail of grape and canister was kept up, and Pemberton and his army and the citizens were shut up as in a cage.[39] Tales of distress and want began to creep out, of great suffering and death, of people digging caves to hide from the terrible bombardment, and finally the end came on July 4, 1863, when Gen. Pemberton surrendered to

[39] John Clifford Pemberton was a Confederate general commanding the forces at Vicksburg.

Gen. Grant and the Federal army marched in and took possession with the stars and stripes flying, drums beating and soldiers shouting themselves hoarse. It was a great and wonderful day. The Confederates had been starved into surrender.

Gen. Grant was most generous and humane in his treatment of his prisoners, and there were many thousands of them. They were paroled, and he ordered that rations be issued to them for a time. Many of them were in starving condition. Most of the horses and mules had been killed for food, and cow peas were ground for flour. The cows had been killed and there was neither butter or milk, and even water was scarce, for the city's supply was cut off and their dependence was on cisterns and wells. The citizens were in a pitiable condition. There was much sickness, mostly fevers and bowel trouble, and no medicines or remedies to alleviate the sufferings. Our boys soon fraternized with the "Johnnies," shared their tobacco and rations with them and proved that the "Yanks" were not such terrible creatures. The greatest relief to the inhabitants was the cessation of the cannonading and to feel that they could walk in the open once again. Vast quantities of guns, cannon and ammunition were captured and the Mississippi River was now open for navigation from the mouth to St. Paul. The Confederacy was cut in two, a wonderful achievement, but at a terrible cost.

For some time previous to the surrender, Gen.

Grant had laid an embargo on all boats going up the river from Vicksburg and those coming down from the North. In fact, all communication was closed with the army and the country could only guess at what was going on around Vicksburg. There were rumors that the War Department was about to remove Gen. Grant from command, or rather the military board composed of generals and other officers who conducted the war from their office in Washington, was opposed to Grant's campaign, in fact they were envious and jealous of his success. Dispatches had been sent ordering him to report to Washington immediately, but they could not be delivered, for all communication had ceased.[40] Gen. Grant said afterward that he proposed to finish his job before he quit. As soon as communication was opened, directly after the surrender, and dispatches sent announcing the victory, he received the belated orders and at once proceeded to Washington. The quiet, unobtrusive little

[40]Mrs. Hill's account of the difficulties faced by Grant after his victory at Vicksburg with his enemies in Washington is not supported by historical evidence. In fact, the President, the Congress and the people of the North were deeply grateful to him. There is no evidence that Edwin M. Stanton, the Secretary of War, had any intention of removing Grant from his command. There was no "board composed of generals and other officers who conducted the war from their office in Washington." There was a Joint Congressional Committee on the Conduct of the War which was composed of Senators and Representatives. The Committee sometimes caused some trouble for Lincoln and the generals but it did not run the war. Lincoln did.

man appeared there but he was a victorious, triumphant general and his enemies were defeated and silenced, for Grant was the hero of his country and his name and fame stand beside that of Lincoln. That ended the active enmity against Grant among his own people.

We had received the news of the battle of Gettysburg and were rejoicing over the victory, but it was fraught with sadness and horror, the loss of life, the bloodshed of our bravest and best had been so terrible on both sides.[41]

It surely was a battle of giants and we were dazed and did not realize that it was the beginning of the end and that Gen. Lee never recovered from that crushing defeat. And on the Federal side the losses had been so great and the men so exhausted, they were unable to pursue the advantage gained over the Confederates. Then word came of the surrender of Vicksburg and the great advantage gained. The country was electrified and went wild with delight. Gen. Grant was acclaimed a hero, and it was believed the Confederates had received a death blow.

At that time, the surrender of Vicksburg was deemed the more important event, and great was the rejoicing, but in the light of later events, it is now known that the Confederacy received its death

[41]The Battle of Gettysburg, which was fought on July 1–3, 1863 was a Union victory. But the casualties on both sides were appallingly high. 3,155 Union and 2,592 Confederate soldiers were killed and tens of thousands on both sides were wounded.

blow on the field of Gettysburg.[42] The advantage gained by the dearly-bought victory of Gettysburg was not as immediate as that secured by the fall of Vicksburg.

Gen. William Sherman and he established headquarters in Vicksburg and began a sanitary movement for cleaning up the town.[43] It was very hot weather. There was much sickness in the army as well as in the town. The rank and file of the prisoners had been disarmed and paroled and allowed to leave for their homes, and an effort was being made to reduce the confusion and chaos to living conditions. One little incident I give to illustrate how our boys had suffered for proper food. When the Engineers were marching in that hot July morning, E.M. was riding past a house in the suburbs surrounded by a high fence. He spied a large garden on the other side filled with growing vegetables and tomatoes. He rode up to the house and asked the lady

[42]Mrs. Hill's estimate of the effect of the Battle of Gettysburg is somewhat exaggerated.

[43]William Tecumseh Sherman, a West Point graduate was a businessman and a lawyer in San Francisco, in Kansas and in St. Louis.

On May 14, 1861 Sherman was appointed colonel of an infantry regiment, and fought at Bull Run. His gallantry in the battle of Shiloh won him a promotion to Major-General. He aided Grant in the siege of Vicksburg and was appointed Commander of the Army of Tennessee.

In May, 1864, Sherman began his march into Georgia which ended with the capture of Atlanta on September 1.

In 1869, when Grant became President, Sherman was appointed a full General, the highest rank in the U.S. Army.

who came to the door if she would sell him some tomatoes, that they were suffering for fresh food. She very graciously invited him into the garden and told him to help himself. He wrote me about it and said nothing ever tasted as good to him as those green tomatoes and onions and he filled his pockets to share with the others. He insisted on paying the lady for them. He wanted to make a good impression. As it happened, it was a fortunate move for the regiment went into camp beside her house and she sold the entire contents of her garden to them. It was the first U.S. money she had received in many months and it was most acceptable.

The Engineers were now set to work destroying the fortifications which they found very strong. There were three lines of them each stronger than the preceding one and they could not have been taken by assault without a tremendous loss of life. New fortifications were planned and started, and a fleet of gunboats patroled the river from the mouth to Cairo, Illinois. The probability was that the Engineers would remain there for several months, but changes soon took place. One battalion under Col. Bissell was sent to Memphis and Corinth to repair railroads and bridges and to destroy fortifications at Corinth, which was no longer a strategical point. The second battalion remained at Vicksburg under command of Major Tweedale. Soon after, Col. Bissell returned to Vicksburg and while there resigned very suddenly and his resignation was accepted and

General William Tecumseh Sherman,
Union Commander who led the famous "March to the Sea."
Courtesy Missouri Historical Society

he left for home. He was a fine officer and had made an efficient organization of the Engineers, but wherever he went it was usually a storm center. He had scant respect for his superior officers and often took the initiative, without orders, sometimes involving important movements in confusion.

Major Flad now commanded the 1st Battalion and was promoted to Lieutenant Colonel, a well deserved promotion. E.M. wrote me that as soon as the weather permitted, grew cooler, he wanted Georgie and me to come to him. He had engaged a room and board with the lady who had been so kind to him about the vegetables. The camp was close by and he could spend his evenings and nights with us, and he wanted me to see the town and the surrounding country, and thought I would enjoy the experience very much, but it would not be safe for us to come before the middle of September, and to be prepared to come then. Of course I was delighted with the opportunity and Mother was doing so well there was no reason why I could not leave.

After the railroad and towns in Tennessee had been abandoned (though later they were again occupied by the Federals), my brother-in-law and his wife found but little business in Trenton, and moved to St. Louis. We saw but little of them. After the surrender of Vicksburg, he decided to go there and open a shop for he had to live in a warm climate. He sent my sister home to Mother and he went down the river. We were so glad to have her, for, poor young thing, she needed her mother at this time. On the 9th of August her little girl was born. For a while we were greatly troubled about her, she was so ill. Mother and I were constantly with her and she soon rallied. As soon as she was able to travel her husband sent for her and she took her little baby less than a month old and traveled down the river alone to meet him.

About the middle of September, passage was secured for myself and my little son on the large side-wheel steamboat, *Queen of the West*, bound for New Orleans but stopping at Vicksburg. We started for St. Louis in good season, but on the way a freight train wreck blocked the railroad and we were greatly delayed. When we at last reached the station at the foot of Plum Street, we rushed to the levee landing and saw our boat just heading down the river. We were fifteen minutes too late. I had written E.M. I was coming on that boat and there was no telegraphic communication with Vicksburg. There was nothing to do but take the next steamer down the river. We found one that would leave the following day, a small stern wheeler which was loading far down the river and there would be no other for several days, so we went on board at once, not risking being left a second time. It was a long tiresome voyage. The weather was hot, the river was low and difficult to navigate. The boat was tied up to the bank at night and only traveled in the daytime and was so overloaded with freight, the

Mississippi River levee at St. Louis.
Courtesy Missouri Historical Society

progress was slow. The passengers were few and not pleasant or congenial, some "show" people going to New Orleans, flashy, vulgar people. A Jew and his wife were also on board bound for New Orleans, and she was a trouble maker and in the ten days of the trip she had everybody on edge who would listen to her. The captain did not come to the table or into the ladies' cabin and the clerk performed those duties. He belonged to the genus "Masher" and was a very unpleasant person.

It was a long and disagreeable trip in many ways, and it seemed as though we never would reach our destination, but finally one morning we came in sight of Millikens Bend, and there lying against the river bank on the East side, was the burned hull of a large steamboat, and we learned that three nights before, the *Queen of the West* had caught fire and burned so rapidly that they had hardly been able to make the bank of the river. A number of lives were lost by jumping into the river, among them a woman with her little boy clasped in her arms were drowned. I was horrified and distressed for we were only forty miles from Vicksburg and I knew the news of the catastrophe must have reached my soldier, but how thankful I was that we had missed that boat for it was a terrible experience to the survivors. Notwithstanding my anxiety, I was greatly interested in the approach to Vicksburg. I could readily locate points of interest and where the Engineer operations had gone on from the descriptions in E.M.'s letters. The batteries at Young's Point were still in evidence, but the cut levees were being rapidly repaired, and the river was so low at this time, the stream was comparatively narrow. At last Vicksburg came in sight, a series of huge bluffs facing the river, which made a sharp bend here. The town was built on and back of these bluffs, which were really immense clay banks of a tough stiff yellow clay, almost a soft stone. They came down in places sheer to the river, and these bluffs fairly bristled with batteries and cannon which made it a veritable Gibraltar for they commanded the river both above and below the town for a long distance. No wonder it was a hazardous undertaking for the gunboats to run past these bluffs. Many thrilling and dramatic stories were told of the attempts to do so. Several gunboats started one dark night to run past the batteries and join Admiral Porter's fleet on the Red River. All the lights were extinguished, perfect silence was maintained, no noise of engines, the boats were steered and drifted with the current. When just opposite the batteries a fireman on one of them unwittingly opened one of the furnace doors and the light flared out on the river. It was but for a moment, but it acted as a signal to the Confederate watchers on the bluff and boom went a cannon and immediately a heavy fire was directed at the gunboats. One was sunk and two others disabled, while the others hastened back, and there was considerable loss of life.

When at last we reached the landing, there was no E.M. to meet us. The other passengers started out to see the town, but I remained on board, uncertain what to do, for I did not know where to reach him. The boat would not leave till the next morning which gave me time for inquiries. The clerk found me a boy to carry a message to my brother-in-law, E.M.'s brother, who had a watch and jewelry store on the main business street. He was not able to come to the levee, but sent the messenger on to the Engineers' camp. It was not long till a couple of the young officers whom I knew came on board. I was surely glad to see them, and they seemed much relieved to see me, for they were still fearful that I had been lost on the *Queen of the West*. E.M. had been terribly distressed and had at once gone up to the wreck when the news had been received, fearing that the mother and child who had been drowned were us, but he had remained till the bodies had been recovered and knew they were not. It had been a terrible shock to him and he was still very anxious to know what had become of his wife and boy. His comrades had been most kind and sympathetic. He was unable to meet the boat because he was ordered to accompany Major T— on a tour of inspection of the new fortifications with Gen. Sherman, Gen. McPherson and several other distinguished officers. They had started early in the morning and would not be back till night. Anyway he was not expecting me till he heard something definite of the change in my plans. The "boys" wanted me to return to camp with them and wait for him there, but I thanked them, and said I would remain here till he came for me. We had a nice visit and they were still there when the other passengers returned. After looking them over one of the young fellows turned to me and said, "Gee! but they are a tough looking crowd. How have you stood them for so long? We hate to leave you here." I laughed and thought it could be but a few hours longer. At last they departed with the promise of sending E.M. as soon as he returned. Georgie was dreadfully disappointed and kept asking why his Papa did not come and we settled ourselves to wait as patiently as we could. It was growing dusk when I saw my soldier coming up the long saloon cabin toward me. Georgie rushed to meet him and we were gathered in his arms. I thought he would never let us go. Surely he was glad to see us. We were soon on our way to the place he had provided for us, up steep narrow streets cut through the bluffs which towered on each side. The streets seemed like canyons. Finally, we reached a plateau on which most of the city was built.

The camp of the Engineers was about two miles from the levee landing and was next to Mrs. Wilson's home where we were to stay. It was a large white house with spacious upper and lower galleries, such as are commonly seen in that section. It had suffered in the bombardment. Some of the rooms were badly shattered by shells and cannon balls and only part of the house was habitable. There were evidences of past wealth and that it had been the home of culture and refinement.

Mrs. Wilson was a Virginia lady of the old school and had been a woman of great charm. Her manners were exquisite, but misfortune had come into her life and she was much changed. Her husband and son-in-law were in the Confederate army in Virginia and she was alone with her two little motherless grandchildren and her old slave servants who had remained faithful to her. She met us when we reached her house with true Southern hospitality and graciousness and ushered us to our room upstairs, a spacious apartment, elegantly furnished with handsome old-fashioned mahogany furniture. The bed-stead was like you see in pictures, a great high four poster with a tester or canopy, a wonderful piece of fluted silk upholstery, and the draperies were of net and lace, a counterpane of antique lace over satin covered the bed, which was carefully removed at night and the covers of the bed turned down, and pillows placed by the maid in charge of the room who was placed at my service. A stool at the foot was the means by which we climbed into this magnificence. In the morning a huge tin tub was brought into the room and our bath prepared for us and plenty of clean fresh towels. It was real Southern living, luxurious for that time, and very comfortable. After the strenuous summer in

Carondelet, it was greatly enjoyed. The fare was good and was mostly supplied by the U.S. commissary. E.M. had also made arrangements to supply Mrs. Wilson with necessities, she paying for the same. She had a wonderful old Mammy cook who regaled us with the old-fashioned Virginia cooking, and it was delicious.

Now to explain why we had been so fortunate as to be admitted into this Southern home. After the incident of the vegetables and the Engineers who had camped beside the house, E.M. learning of her forlorn and lonely condition and also of her destitution, had taken pity on her and had seen that she and her home were protected, and she had become quite friendly with him. When he told her that his wife and boy were coming to visit him, she insisted on his bringing us to her house to be entertained by her. After much argument E.M. succeeded in placing the matter on a strict business foundation which was more satisfactory to all concerned, and the remuneration was very acceptable in her impoverished condition. Our being there was a great protection to her and she liked and trusted E.M. and grew to like me. Her two little grandchildren were darling, and Georgie and they soon fraternized and played happily together, their nurse including my little one in her care. Mrs. Wilson had the saddest face and seemed to live in the shadow of a great grief. Many misfortunes had befallen her. She belonged to a one time wealthy Virginia family and had come a bride to Vicksburg where her husband was a prominent businessman. They had lived here ever since her marriage. One daughter was born to them and she had grown up to a lovely young womanhood and had married a wealthy young New Orleans man and had died at her mother's home in giving birth to her second child. The shock and grief, it was thought, had mentally affected the mother, for her daughter was her idol and she had been different ever since. The two little children, a boy and girl, were left in her care by their young father. And now comes the gruesome part of the story. When her daughter died she had the remains embalmed and robed in her bridal gown and veil, with bouquets and wreaths of orange blossoms and laid in a white satin lined casket with a full length glass top, and it was hermetically sealed. A room at the back of the house was closed and darkened, the walls hung with white and the casket placed in it, with large tapers placed at the head and foot and kept burning perpetually. Each day she took those babies in to see their dead mother, always carrying fresh flowers as an offering. The room was a bower of blossoms always. Her husband and friends implored her to have the body removed to the vault in the cemetery, but she became so excited and distraught when the subject was mentioned that they feared for her reason should they persist. Each day the children were taken in to see their dead mother. The little things had become accustomed to the sight of their pretty young mother asleep in her bridal robes and there was nothing horrifying or gruesome to them, while to the poor mother it was a sacred shrine. When the woeful tale was told me my heart went out to her in a great rush of tenderness and pity.

Time passed and the war began. Misfortunes increased and the business failed. Mr. Wilson finally received an officer's commission in the Confederate army and was ordered to Virginia. She had heard from him but once since the battle of Gettysburg in which he had taken part. Her son-in-law had also entered the army and was in Virginia and now that the lines were cut there was no communication. They had lost all their property. Their Negroes were freed and left them except a few house servants, and they only had the house and that only partly habitable.

After the bombardment began, some of the city officials came to her and insisted on the body of her daughter being removed to the cemetery. She wept and implored them to be allowed to keep her dead. The next morning after their visit, a shell from the Federal batteries struck the corner of the house and tore a great opening in the room which she had made a mortuary vault. That convinced her, and the remains of her daughter were taken to the cemetery that day and placed in a vault. While she was away, another shell had completed the work of destruction and shattered the room into a ruin. It was left in a ruined condition, only sufficient repairs being made to insure the safety of the other part of the house. That was the most gruesome experience I ever heard of.

In our room there was a large round hole through the side of the house just over the bed and also one through the tester of the bed, both made by the same cannon ball, which dropped on the bed and was picked up and thrown out of the window by the houseman, fearing it might explode, but it was a solid shot. It was placed on the parlor mantelpiece as a memento. There was scarcely a house in the town that did not show the mark of shot and shell. Many of them were shattered ruins and many had caught fire and were destroyed. A book could be written filled with the thrilling incidents and experiences of the beleaguered inhabitants. E.M. had made friends through being able to grant some favors, and in their warm Southern fashion they were very hospitable, so that we had the pleasure of meeting and knowing some very delightful people. Then too, the sense of security and protection, the resumption of business, the opening of communication up and down the river, had reconciled them to the occupancy of the Federal troops. In their hour of dire need, when want and destitution stared them in the face, they were fed and cared for by those they designated their enemies, and many a proud planter carried his basket to the commissary stores and was glad to have it filled to satisfy the hunger of his dear little ones at home.

In the two months which had elapsed since the surrender, reconstruction along many lines had taken place. Confidence was being restored, business being resumed and the city assumed a more normal condition. Among the better class who had lost most heavily, poverty and want still pinched and they were the most difficult people to help. A large army commanded by Gen. Sherman was stationed here, and new and stronger lines of fortification were being constructed, employing a large force of men. Still it was a time of truce and every one was relieved and at rest, disposed to enjoy the good the Gods provided.

Many of the officers sent for their wives or families, expecting to spend the winter here. Several of the unmarried ones obtained leaves of absence to visit their homes and returned with brides, and we formed quite a gay and lively military social colony. There were also a number of nice Southern families who were disposed to be friendly with us and as there were several charming young ladies among them, our young officers lost no occasion to take advantage of their opportunity. For the next two months we certainly had a gay time. It was riding parties, exploring parties, dancing parties, card parties, something going on every day and evening. Of course, many were on duty but many were not, and anyway it was not steady strenuous duty. There was considerable play mixed in the work. It was really a breathing spell between two important campaigns, the one just ended and the other about to begin.

We explored the caves in the cliffs that had given security and shelter to hundreds of people during the days of the siege. When it was no longer safe to remain in their homes, caves were dug and excavated in the clay bluffs. They were extensive, and sometimes there would be three or four large rooms leading from one to another. One of our friends took us through his cave dwelling. He had excavated a tunnel or passage, curving so as to give two outside openings, thus insuring ventilation and air. Opening into this passage were four good sized rooms, comfortably furnished, and here they had taken refuge after their house was partially destroyed by cannon balls. They could do no cooking during the day because of the incessant firing and the danger. Of course they could do none in the caves. When night came they could more readily see the flight of the balls and shells, and avoid them. Most of the food for the day's use was prepared over open fires. Even then accidents occurred. Our host told of a neighbor who lost his cook. She was preparing the evening meal when a shell struck near and exploded killing her and scattering the fire, supper and cook in all directions. That was only one of many such incidents. The bluffs were perforated for many miles with these caves and they looked so weird and peculiar, they gave one an uncanny feeling, especially when you went through them. You thought of the ancient cave-dwellers and the catacombs of Rome, and were glad that you did not live in Vicksburg during the siege. We were invited to this gentleman's house to supper, dinner being the midday meal at that time. The wife and mother was a happy cheerful woman, disposed to make light of adverse circumstances and they had three or four half grown lovely children with charming manners. The house was a partial ruin, but in that respect no wise different from their neighbors. The dining-room was badly damaged, but the table service was perfect, the linen immaculate, the china and glass of the best, and the silver service and salver, solid, heavy and rich. On the sideboard stood a massive handsome coffee urn, battered and dented almost out of shape. I spoke of it and he said that was a memento of the siege and then he told us of it. They had just been called to breakfast one morning when a shell struck the side of the house upstairs, and as it went through the ceiling, it exploded and tore the ceiling to pieces right over the breakfast table. The breakfast was scattered and the coffee urn seemed to get the brunt of the splinters and plastering. If it had happened five minutes later, there would have probably been a dreadful loss of life. So Mr. C— said the urn would go down to his descendants as a memento of their narrow escape. They were an interesting family and told us so many thrilling incidents and escapes of the siege. I wish I could remember and relate more of them. The terrible straits they were brought to—no light, no water, scanty food, not even paper to print their newspapers on, and they had to use the back of wall paper to print the last issues. E.M. had sent me a copy of the last paper printed on the morning before the surrender, a piece of wall paper as large as a sheet of foolscap, and printed on the back of this in faint type, was a despairing article on the desperate condition of affairs, but still breathing a note of defiance against the Yankees. E.M. also sent me quite a roll of Confederate money, which did not differ in appearance very much from our "shinplasters," except that its purchasing power was nil, when the Yankees took the city.

E.M. frequently took me with him when he went out on the works that the Engineers were engaged on, and we had many delightful rides together. Of course the only means of going was on horseback, and it was very enjoyable after the nervousness of riding a strange horse had been overcome. We went all over the different lines of fortifications where mines had been laid and exploded, making breaches, which the Federals assaulted. But the Confederates had been too strongly fortified and the Federals had gained no advantage. He took me out to where some fierce battles had been waged and we rode over the battlefield and it was all visualized to me. The realization of what war really was. I saw these battlefields and the blood that had been shed on them, and I thought of the wounded and crippled boys in the hospitals at St. Louis that I had helped to tend this past summer, who had come from these same fields, and my heart swelled within me till I thought it would burst. It was all so cruel.

Col. Brewster (the title was an honorary one) was a typical Southern planter and gentleman, despite his slaves and possessions, a Union man at heart, but like hundreds of others, was carried by the current into the vortex of secession. He had to "stand by his state." He owned vast cotton and sugar plantations and his slaves numbered into the thousands. His home was in the suburbs of Vicksburg and was one of the few houses untouched by missiles during the siege. His family consisted of a semi-invalid wife, and one daughter, the light of her father's eyes. His sons were in the Confederate army. After the surrender, he reported to the general commanding the post, and asked for protection. It was given to him, after he had taken the oath of allegiance, and a guard was placed around his home to protect it from depredations. He became very friendly with the authorities at Headquarters. One line of the new fortifications ran near his house and the Engineers were working on it. In that way be became acquainted with several of the officers and showed them much attention and hospitality, inviting them to the house and introducing them to his wife and daughter. He was a charming man of culture and refinement, a man of education and wide travel, who had seen much of the world. He was delightful to talk with and a perfect host. His daughter was the bright particular star to our young officers and they needed no urging to accept the colonel's hospitality.

Pretty Molly Brewster, how can I describe her! As well try to describe a sunbeam or the perfumed zephyr that floats into your window on some balmy spring morning. She was so sweet and happy, such a simple unaffected genuine girl, and so uniformly kind and gentle to everyone. She captivated all hearts, and we women who had the pleasure of knowing her, were as much in love with her as the men. She was a rare character and yet in a way, an arrant little coquette, though she did not mean to be. Right here must be related what might have proved a calamity to a friend of ours.

Just before leaving St. Louis for Vicksburg, I called on a young friend who was engaged to Capt. D— of the Engineers, to see if she had a message or package to send to the captain. I found that she was in the midst of her preparations for the wedding. The day was set and the captain was expected the following week and was probably on his way up the river then. We discussed the wedding and her returning to Vicksburg with him, and she showed me her trousseau, even the wedding dress, and regretted that I could not be present for the occasion. After reaching Vicksburg, in talking with E.M. and other people, the remark was made that Capt. D— had probably passed me on the way down. "I think not," E.M. replied, "I saw him this morning. He was riding with Molly Brewster."

"Riding with Molly Brewster! Why the wedding is set for tomorrow. What do you mean?" I asked.

"Well, he is just daffy about Molly and is with her every moment he can get away from his duties. The boys are wondering if he is going to win out. He seems infatuated. You had better keep perfectly quiet about this. Do not speak of it to anyone. I will ask him to call. He probably would anyway. Yet I don't know, seeing that we are friends of Kittie's."

The next evening the captain called. He seemed a little distraught and ill at ease. No reference was made to his affair with Molly Brewster. I was supposed to be in ignorance of it. I spoke of my surprise in finding him here when his wedding was set for that very day, and Kittie's preparations were all made, told him of her trousseau and pretty dresses and how happy she was in the expectation of spending the winter here with her soldier boy, and what a disappointment it would be to have it deferred. I supposed he had been unable to get a leave of absence just then. E.M.'s face was so funny when I made that talk and I dared not look at him. The poor captain looked confused, turned red, stammered and finally made a clean breast of it.

"What will you think," he exclaimed, "when I tell you I forgot all about it? Don't you folks give me away and I will try to make it right. I have been living in a dream." He left soon afterward in a very uncomfortable frame of mind, and I know he had a bad night, for he had always been a quiet serious-minded young fellow, and the last person to get into such a situation. You never can tell! The heart of a man is a deceitful thing. A few days afterward E.M. told me the captain had gone to St. Louis on regimental business, so that all would be well with Kittie, for she was the one he really loved. We never mentioned this episode to anyone and Kittie never knew of the affair with Molly Brewster, unless he told her, or some kind (?) friend informed her when she came back with her husband.

Dr. Knower also went to St. Louis at this time and was married to Miss Mary Lesley, to whom he had been engaged for a long time. After the brides returned, many festivities were given in their honor.

Gen. McPherson, who was quartered in one of the finest houses there, with sun parlors, conservatories, fountains, and large spacious rooms, gave a grand ball, after the weather grew cool and comfortable for dancing.[44] It was given for the brides and the visiting wives of officers, and was a brilliant affair. We who were among the invited, donned our best bib and tucker for the occasion. The brides were decked in their bridal robes. It was *the* affair of the season and it was very gay and festive. Gen. McPherson was a perfect host, and his assistants, most of them distinguished men of military renown,

[44]General James B. McPherson commanded a Union army corps during the battle of Vicksburg.

ably seconded his efforts. Gen. McPherson became quite enamored of Mrs. Knower, who was a tall stately blonde, and looked very handsome in her wedding gown. He showed her much attention and danced with her a number of times, which the doctor did not fancy. Kittie and her captain were there, she looking very sweet and pretty and very happy in her bridal dress. Molly Brewster was easily the belle, for she had that self forgetful charm that is so attractive and flattering to men and she was surrounded by a bevy of officers striving to gain a dance with her. It was noticed that Capt. D— did not go near her all the evening, on the principle that a burned child dreads the fire. But it was a merry time and we danced to our hearts' content. The music was of the finest. The orchestra being picked of musicians from several regiments who had practiced together. The supper and refreshments were sent from New Orleans by a celebrated caterer and he sent the waiters to serve it.

Most of the dances were square or cotillions, very few waltzes which were not popular at that time. We danced the lancers and minuet and finished up with the old fashioned Roger De Coverly or country dance which almost degenerated into a romp, for many guests were feeling quite exhilarated by then. As the women say, "I had a lovely time" for I danced nearly every set and with a number of celebrities, Gens. McPherson, Mower and several others. It was the finest ball given that winter and

I am sure it was never forgotten by those who had the pleasure of attending it.

Another time a few of us were invited to Col. Brewster's for the evening. It proved to be a dark rainy night. It was two long miles from our camp over bad roads full of ruts and much mud. The prospect was not very promising for our reaching there and we hesitated, but the men were eager to go and they got a covered ambulance. E.M. sat with the driver and held a lantern, and the rest, eight of us, were packed into the ambulance and off we started. Many times we were almost spilled out, and it looked doubtful about our ever getting to the house, but we were a jolly crowd and a little thing like being tipped over did not count. Once the wheels went into a deep rut with a sudden lurch that threw us all into a pile. I was flung into Lieut. H—'s arms and I grabbed him tight exclaiming, "Oh! My dear!" That was enough. Everyone shouted and made all sorts of funny comments, and the rest dubbed him "my dear" and wanted the driver to find some more ruts so they could have their turn. In fact they nicknamed the poor lieutenant "Dear," and it was some time before the name was dropped. E.M. was rather annoyed. He did not fancy his wife being the cause for any silly jokes, but there was nothing to do but join in the fun, even at your expense. Those young fellows were irrepressible.

When we arrived at the Brewster's house, we were

a battered, disheveled crowd. We were the only guests and were warmly welcomed and it did seem good to reach the warmth and light and cheer of this hospitable home. Someone had just received a new game of cards and brought it with him. It proved to be a game of "authors," something entirely new, and was a novelty to us. Instead of music and dancing, we gathered around the big table in the dining room and played all evening. Midnight soon came and after a substantial supper, we prepared for our return to camp. It was still raining hard, and dark as an Egyptian darkness. Col. and Mrs. Brewster insisted on our spending the night with them and would not listen to our returning. The men had to return to camp, but we women gladly accepted the kind offer and remained all night. The next morning the ambulance was sent for us and we reached our homes more safely than if we had attempted it in the night. E.M. said the return was even worse than the going out had been.

The Brewster house was a large rambling structure of two stories, with innumerable rooms and galleries and verandahs extending round it on every side. The rooms were large and lofty, the furniture rich, solid and heavy, but there was a sense of bareness, and I noticed that was the impression most Southern houses gave a Northerner. There were few draperies or ornaments and scarcely any pictures except family portraits, no carpets and few rugs. The drawing room was handsome and very simple, the chairs being covered with beautiful brocaded satin and the tables and cabinets were hand carved. On the high mantel were the most magnificent silver candelabra I have ever seen. The floor had no covering but was polished till it was like glass. Labor was cheap and plentiful. The walls and ceiling were decorated with mural designs and executed by a celebrated artist, and most of the furniture came from France. In the dining room the furniture was solid mahogany and very massive. There were cabinets in this room filled with rare china and rich costly silver. The kitchen and servants quarters were detached from the house as the custom was in the South, and it was quite a sight to see the procession of little darkies coming from the kitchen carrying the covered dishes of viands and foods across the yard to the "big house," where they were received by the waiters, who took the dishes to the dining room and served or passed them.

The many delightful hours I spent in this hospitable home and with this lovely family is why I describe it more particularly, and the memory of those days and of sweet Molly Brewster is a very pleasant one. None of those who paid court to her at that time succeeded in winning her. Some years after the end of the war, she married a Northern man. I do not know whether he had been in the army.

Some changes were made in our regiment. Lieut. Col. Flad was promoted to colonel with headquarters at Corinth, Mississippi. Major Tweedale was made lieutenant colonel with headquarters at Vicksburg, and my soldier was promoted to major. Several lieutenants were made captains and there were promotions all along the line. When E.M.'s commission as major came, we had quite a celebration and gave a little party for our friends and comrades, Mrs. Wilson kindly placing her house at our disposal. We had music and played cards. My sister and her husband and their dear little baby girl came. My sister had a very beautiful and cultivated voice and was a fine pianist. She added so much to the pleasure of the evening with her lovely singing. The affair was quite a success. E.M. received many congratulations on his deserved promotion and we were able to acknowledge in a measure some of the social favors that had been shown us. A few days afterward a number of us went on horseback to see the grand review of the army by Gen. Sherman. It was an impressive sight to see those battle scarred, war worn veterans marching past their Uncle Billy Sherman. They broke into shouts and cheers as they passed, and showed how strong their affection was for him. There was cavalry, artillery, and infantry, an interminable line, not on dress parade but in every day war time marching order—real soldiers.

After the review, many brigades and regiments were transferred to other commands, but the movement was gradual and took months to accomplish.

In November, soon after E.M. had received his

promotion, he was ordered by Col. Flad to report to him for duty at Corinth, and to come at once. Thus our happy time in Vicksburg was at an end. We began making our preparations for leaving. The hardest wrench was for E.M. to say goodby to the men of his old company D. They had always been faithful and loyal to him, and as one of his men told me years afterward, "The captain never said 'Go boys!' but it was always 'Come on, boys,' and he would lead and they follow. He could always depend on his men for they had confidence in him and he treated them as men and human beings."

Our comrades and friends gave us a good by party and much regret was expressed at our leaving. That was our regret too, that we could not remain in such pleasant surroundings, still E.M. was glad to rejoin the colonel for whom he had a sincere and loyal affection. They had always been congenial and worked together in harmony and accord. There had been pleasant happy days in Vicksburg, but it was war time, and they were only interludes in the great drama that was being fought out, and which would result in the life or death of a great republic, the greatest the world had ever known. A number of our good friends went to the boat to see us off, and soon we bade farewell to the frowning bluffs of Vicksburg which had been the scene of such stirring events during the past few months.

We found a number of acquaintances and friends on the steamboat bound for the North, among them

Gen. Mower and his staff, who were friends.[45] He had been ordered to St. Louis and did not know then what his destination would be from there. He was a most interesting man, a graduate of West Point, and belonged to the regular army. He had seen much service on the frontier, especially in Texas, and was afterward commander of the division of Texas. We had delightful talks together. He was so happy at being sent to St. Louis where his wife and two children were, the youngest a baby boy of several months, whom he had not seen. He showed me their pictures and seemed so pleased to have a sympathetic listener, while he expatiated on the beauty and goodness of his wife and little ones. He was usually such a dignified reserved man, but on this trip he seemed like a boy from school going home for the holidays.

We were a happy and congenial party. Military discipline was soon relaxed, pleasantries exchanged, good stories and experiences told and enjoyed. There was a general unbending from formalities, the few days we were together. The journey was all too short, but the old boat chugged and puffed along up the river and Memphis was reached in a couple of days. The general and his party continued on to St. Louis, and we (E.M., the boy and I) went to the Gayoso House for a short time. We had to do some shopping, for E.M.'s wardrobe was in sad need of replenishing. Then we also had to

[45]General John Mower was a Union general.

decide what was best for me to do. E.M. wanted me to remain in Memphis till he went to Corinth and found what the conditions were and whether he was to be sent on detached service. He wanted us near him if it could possibly be arranged, but my recent letters from Mother had been of a very disquieting nature and evidently she was in trouble. My first duty at this time seemed to be to her, for she needed me and the country around Corinth was in a disturbed condition. There were frequent raids and skirmishes and the Engineers in their work frequently had to fight. E.M. would have less care and anxiety about us if he knew we were safe and mentally he would be in a better condition to perform the duties devolving on him. After much arguing he acceded to my plan, but with the promise that we would return to him if all was well with Mother and if he found conditions pleasant at Corinth. He secured us passage on a steamboat going to St. Louis and saw us off. Georgie was inconsolable at leaving his father and it kept me busy trying to pacify him.

The journey to St. Louis of several days was made without incident. On arriving there we went at once to the house in Carondelet. They were not expecting us and it was quite a surprise and evidently a pleasant one. A sad state of affairs was revealed. When getting off the train at the little station, I had noticed the shipyards were partially closed and very few men seemed to be about. There was no clink clank of hammers, no pounding of iron and steel, an unusual quiet seemed to pervade the place. I asked the station agent about it. He said the government had stopped building the river gunboats since the river was open to navigation and only kept a small force of men there to repair the boats of the fleet that were used as patrols. That meant trouble for Mother.

On reaching the house I found poor Mother and her four girl children entirely alone in that great barn of a place, Mother a cripple, unable to walk or even stand. She had injured one of her legs and it had become infected, but she kept on with her work, and had not taken care of it. She was without help and felt she must struggle on, but finally she had to succumb and send away most of her patrons. Then the works closed down. Those that had remained left, and there sat Mother unable to move. The older girls took devoted care of her, but could not make the living in a great empty house miles away from the city and their friends. As the saying is, we soon "got busy." There was no use remaining there. The gunboat business for the river was finished and it had finished Mother, and the next thing was something else.

Fortunately my little cottage home was vacant, the tenants having recently left it. Lottie and I went over and had it cleaned and put in order. It would make a comfortable shelter for the family till something else could be done and till Mother was better. We took enough of the furniture to make it cosy and pleasant, packed and stored what else Mother wanted to keep, sold the remainder and got Mother into a carriage and made the journey of twelve or fourteen miles without serious trouble, managed to get her into the cottage and installed her in a big easy chair with a foot rest, in a bright sunny room. I sent for our doctor and had him treat her leg and attend her. My! but I was glad that I had come home and the dear soul began to improve now the anxiety and worry were removed. We settled down very cosily for the winter. Our first duty was to take care of Mother and get her well. Overwork and worry had aggravated the trouble with her leg, which always troubled her more or less the remaining years of her life. The little girls were put in school. The older girls helped with the care of the house and Mother, and the winter days went quietly by.

E.M. wrote that the battalion was comfortably housed in winter quarters, the colonel and he occupying one house together. Mrs. Parker and several other wives were there, and there was a nice place for me if I would come. They were busy most of the time repairing railroads, building bridges and dismantling fortifications. Already there were rumors of their being sent to Nashville, which was now the base for the preparation of the next campaign, and their stay in Corinth might be of short duration.

The battalion remained at Corinth till December 26, 1863, when it was moved, under the command of E.M. to Nashville, to be consolidated with the 25th Missouri Infantry. They arrived at Memphis and were embarked on the steamer *America*. The trip was long remembered for the cold, hardships and exposure they endured. Six companies were crowded on a little boat, without fire or facilities for cooking. December 31, the boat reached Smithland, Kentucky, and the cold was so intense and the river so blocked with ice, that the men nearly perished. E.M. refused to go any farther till the weather moderated. The boat was made fast and quarters were found in vacant buildings where the men could have fire and shelter and cook their food. The battalion reached Nashville January 4, 1864, and went into camp there.

We who remained at home provided for our soldier's Christmas. We prepared and sent in good season, a large box of Christmas cheer which we knew E.M. would want to share with his comrades. There were mince pies, a plum pudding, a chicken pie, roast turkey, boiled ham, fruit and pound cake, doughnuts and cookies, home made candy. It reached them in good order and added to their pleasure for they were then getting ready to move.

Our Christmas was a very quiet one. We were all thankful it was as well with us as it was.

The winter of 1863 and 1864 was noted for its severity. Even as far South as Nashville and Memphis, many of our poor soldiers who were exposed to the inclement weather and not warmly clad were frozen to death. It was no unusual thing to find a soldier frozen on picket or guard duty.

That winter Mother and the girls were comfortably housed in the little cottage, and George and I were with them. Mother was quite a cripple from overwork, and for several months was unable to walk across the floor, so the care of the family devolved on Lottie and myself. We had an experience that winter which might have proved a serious matter. Just before Christmas it was bitterly cold. The Mississippi froze over solidly, so that teams were driven across the river on the ice and a regular road established, with booths lining each side where hot drinks and food were sold. It was before the day of the Eads Bridge and all passengers on the railroads which came to the Illinois side of the river were transferred by ferry to St. Louis on the opposite shore.[46] While the river was frozen they were brought across on the ice in great sleighs drawn by six and eight horses, and it was one of the sights to go down to the river and see the loads of people coming across in this way. In fact while it lasted, notwithstanding the bitter cold it was quite a carnival time for St. Louis, and one of the things to do was to drive across the river and back again, stopping for refreshments at one of the decorated booths which lined the way.

Two or three days before Christmas, there came a

[46]The Eads Bridge, a magnificent steel arch bridge, was completed by James Eads in 1874.

bright sunshiny day and sister Lottie and I decided we would go downtown and do some Christmas shopping. We lived about five blocks from the street cars and the grocers and market men did not deliver goods so far in the suburbs, so we had to bring home our own marketing, but we were young and strong and did not mind that. We started gayly off about noon, got downtown all right, went to the bank and got some money, then went to the market on Third Street and Broadway. We bought a few Christmas groceries and got the things for the Christmas dinner. As the poultry and game were all frozen solid and were selling cheaply, we invested rather largely in that. When we came out to the street, we had two baskets well filled and we found that it was getting very dark and snowing hard, and the wind was howling, and in fact it was a regular blizzard—one of the worst I ever saw. Well, how to get home was the question. The snow was already drifting and street car service was uncertain, especially out to where we lived. We made our way up to Fifth Street, but car after car went by and would not stop, for they were loaded, men clinging to the steps, and the horses with difficulty pulling them. We waited till we were nearly frozen, and then went to a shoe shop on the corner of Franklin Avenue and Sixth Street where we always bought our shoes. It was now quite dark and you could scarcely see across the street for the falling snow which was drifting into great heaps, and the street cars had already abandoned the line out towards our house. Mr. French, who was a friend of the family, counseled our going to a hotel for the night, but I knew how anxious and worried Mother would be about us and there was no way of reaching her with a message. So Mr. French got a carriage or hack and prevailed on the driver to take us home. He took us to the end of the street car line and refused to go any farther, and there we were dumped out in the storm and darkness half a mile from home, beyond street lamps or any means of getting farther except by walking and carrying two heavy baskets. The driver charged us five dollars and we could not remonstrate for we were two lone women, stranded in a very lonely part of the city, and we had to pay him what he demanded. He drove off and left us there. There were no houses near, and the road led past some dangerous rock quarries, then across a common and past the water reservoir. We started off cheerfully, making light of our predicament and got along fairly well till we got to the reservoir. There we had to take the full brunt of the storm. It was intensely dark and fearfully cold, and the wind blowing a gale, so that it was sometimes difficult to keep our feet. The snow was drifting in great heaps which made it still harder to get on. We kept hold of each others hands and went carefully past the stone quarries, for a misstep there meant a fall of thirty or forty feet on the jagged rocks below. Finally, we reached the common on the north side of the reservoir and were in sight of our home. But we were in the fierce grasp of the storm and floundering through the great drifts that threatened to bury us. I tried to sing and to tell Lottie of what we would do when we got home, and how pleased they would be with our marketing and shopping, but she, poor child, gave up and cried out, "Oh Sister, I can go no farther! I am so sleepy. Just let me sleep for a minute, I am so tired." I knew that meant death and I did not dare leave her and try to get help, for we might both perish in sight of home. I insisted on her making another effort, and we struggled on a few steps farther and then she fell and made no effort to rise. I knew only desperate remedies would be of any avail. I set down the baskets which I had been carrying after she had given up, and fell on her, pounding and belaboring her with all my might. She was in a stupor and only faintly responded. I was frightened and desperate, and beat her and rolled her, tried to lift her up, and finally commenced slapping her face, and that roused her. She cried, "Let me alone! Let me alone!" But I did not desist and she thought that I was really fighting her, which I was. She became angry and began to fight back, which was what we both needed at the time. I fancy we had a regular rough and tumble affair of it, but she picked up the basket and marched off with the remark that she would never speak to me again, and I followed breathless and spent. We reached home in a few minutes and when the door was opened, fell into the room and fainted away from exhaustion. They had to tear the gloves from our hands and rub our hands and faces with snow. We were badly frost-bitten and were in bed for a couple of days, but got over it all right and we saved the baskets of provisions. The next day Lottie said, "I was so angry with you, sister, I could have killed you for beating me and not letting me sleep, but you saved my life."

St. Louis was completely shut off from the outer world for nearly a week. All street cars and traffic were stopped, and if we had remained downtown, we could not have reached home for several days.

During the Holidays in the last days of 1863, E.M.'s regiment was ordered to move to Nashville from Corinth, Mississippi, where they had been for several months, building fortifications and earthworks, but the fall of Vicksburg and the opening of the Mississippi River had rendered Corinth of no importance any longer as a strategical point.

The government was massing troops at Nashville, preparing for an advance into the heart of the enemy's country, and was dependent solely on the Louisville and Nashville Railway for forwarding supplies to the great army gathering there. This line was easily cut and damaged by raids and guerrillas and it took a large force of men to guard it. The Cumberland River was not navigable to Nashville for steamers and transports. It was sixty miles from Nashville to the Tennessee River, through a rough wild country, a primitive back woods region. The government decided to build a railroad through this strip, connecting Nashville with the Tennessee River, and transports could always go up this river guarded by gunboats. The Missouri Engineer regiment was detailed to build this road. The Missouri Engineers had been in active service since 1861. It was a regiment of skilled mechanics, and its officers were men of skill and attainment in all engineering matters. Many of the officers and men had been detailed and transferred to staff and special duties, and since they had been in a number of battles and sieges, their number was greatly depleted. Two of the companies had never been with the regiment, being detailed for special duty. So the regiment was ordered to Nashville and went into camp about two miles from the city in a beautiful suburb. Then they were consolidated with the 25th Missouri, Col. Van Horn's old regiment. The regiment thus consolidated, consisted of three battalions of four hundred men each, making a regiment of twelve hundred men. E.M. as Major, commanded one of these battalions. They were to remain in camp for six weeks or until the spring opened and they could begin operations on the railroad. In the meantime, the men drilled and the officers studied. Of course there was much to do in the amalgamation of the two regiments in order to have matters run smoothly. Luckily most of the engineer officers had been retained. Col. Flad and Lieut. Col. Tweedale still were the commanders, and E.M. was made the ranking battalion commander. The other two were commanded by two of the 25th Missouri officers. As soon as they were fairly settled in camp and knew they were to be there some time, several of the officers sent for their wives and of course E.M. immediately sent for George and me to come at once. He said we could not be with him in camp, but he had arranged for a room and board with a very nice family, who were glad to take one or two officer's wives in their home for the protection it afforded them. Their home was quite near to the camp and he wanted us to come at once, and here begins the tale of my adventures.

About the second week in January a letter came from E.M. urging that we should come to him at once (little George and I), as they were to be stationed some time at Nashville, and I could be there near him. The weather had grown warmer. The ice and snow from the great blizzard had melted and gone. Mother was better and she and the girls were comfortably provided for and could be left without anxiety concerning them.

How to reach Nashville was the question, for I did not hesitate a moment about going, but Nashville was the base of military preparation for a big campaign, and it was a difficult matter for a mere woman with a child to get through the lines. Military matters came first and when you started for a point where war preparations were going on, there was no assurance when you would reach it. Fortunately, as we thought at the time, a friend of the family who was in government employ was ordered to report at Nashville by a certain day, and he was to take forty men with him from the machine shops that he was superintendent of. It was some special and important work to be done in Nashville and he was detailed to take charge of it. Mr. Gordon was an old friend and dear friend, a loyal and staunch old Scotsman, tall and gaunt and in many matters simple as a child. He came out to the house to bid us good by and when he found I was making ready for the journey, he proposed that we (George and I), should go when he did, and he would help me through. The difficulty for me was to get through Louisville. All persons going through the lines were required to have a pass, and they were strict about issuing them. Then, too, you could only buy a ticket to Louisville, and then get one from there to Nashville. The government trains came first and the other trains for civilians and ordinary purposes were very uncertain. You might wait for days before an opportunity came to get through. I was only too glad to accept Mr. Gordon's offer, for it relieved me of so many difficulties, and Mother was better satisfied, for you must know that I was only twenty-four years old and George was a little past four, not more than a baby. But he was a bright, sensible little fellow and was a protection to me during the many perilous trips we took through those stormy years.

All went well until we reached Louisville. Mr. Gordon had his forty men in charge. He had to see to their lodging and food for the night and to secure transportation for them the next day. It was dark and rainy when we reached Louisville, and he sent us to the Galt House and he went with his men to care for their needs, saying he would see me later in the evening when we could arrange about the pass and ticket, so that we could go on in the morning on the same train which left at seven A.M. The little boy and I prepared to make ourselves comfortable. I managed to secure a room, for the house was crowded with officers and people who had been recalled from furloughs and leaves of absence and ordered to report at Nashville. After supper we went into the parlor and there I met Col. and Mrs. Palmer of an Illinois regiment. He was a friend of E.M.'s and I was very glad to meet them, for I was feeling rather forlorn and wondering if I should have to go back. He wanted to know how I was going to get through the lines and where I was going. He had been ordered back to his regiment and had brought Mrs. Palmer along and they were going on the same train as myself in the morning.

Then Chaplain Mason came in, a dear old friend of whom E.M. was very fond, and whom I knew. Our little group had a pleasant visit together and they assured me they would see me through, as it was uncertain about Mr. Gordon helping me very much. The routine and red tape to be gone through with to provide transportation and rations for his men would keep him busily occupied. They were very kind and pointed out many distinguished officers and generals, and stayed with me till after nine o'clock. Still Mr. Gordon did not come, and it was after ten before he came. He was having a dreadful time with his men. Some of them were insubordinate and he had been obliged to remain closely with them till they had been secured for the night. He had managed to get my pass for me and would get my ticket in the morning at the train. I told him about Col. Palmer and Chaplain Mason, but he decided it would be better for him to get my ticket as he had promised my mother to see me safely to E.M. I gave him my purse with my money and he put the pass in it, for that had to be inspected before they would sell a ticket. We did not know how much it would be, so I left plenty in the purse to pay for the pass and for a message which he was to send to E.M. in the morning. I kept out enough to pay the hotel bill and a few dollars for change. I had plenty of money with me but it was in the form of drafts and certificates of deposit and only took enough currency for my needs.

He promised to meet me at the Galt House and go with us to the station in the morning. If he should not be able to do so he would surely meet me at the station. After he left, I took my little son to our room and put him to bed, but I could not sleep. My mind was full of foreboding for it did seem a serious undertaking to reach E.M. Affairs were in such a disturbed, and to an onlooker, chaotic condition. The air was full of rumors of battles and attacks and a great onward movement, and everyone seemed to be rushing to the front, and how was one woman with a little child going to get there. The woman had no thought of turning back. She was going to reach her husband if it took her a week to do it. There was but a faint possibility of Mr. Gordon coming to the hotel in the morning, as I well knew, for if he had a squad of insubordinate men to get started for the front on that early train, they would tax all his resources, and the care of a woman and child was an outside matter that he ought not to have undertaken, and would not if he had realized the condition of affairs.

We were called the next morning at five o'clock, a dark cold rainy morning. Chaplain Mason took us to breakfast. We found the room full of people who like ourselves, were going to Nashville. At a table adjoining us the Chaplain, who was well known, pointed out to us Gen. Grant and Gen. Sherman and members of their staff. Then there were many other generals there, but we were more interested in those two. After breakfast we went into the parlor. I paid my hotel bill and had only three or four dollars in change left in my bag. Still Mr. Gordon did not come and I was beginning to feel a little sick with fear and anxiety. Col. Palmer and his wife came in and asked how matters were. He said,

"Never mind. You come with us and we will get you through to the Major." So I shut my eyes and chanced it.

When the bus came I got in with them and we went to the station where everything was bustle and confusion. We found the train and the car that we were to take, and guards with crossed muskets and bayonets fixed at the entrance, allowing no one to enter the car till they showed their pass or passes. Col. Palmer kept George and me with his party. Chaplain Mason was right behind us. Col. Palmer drew out his passes and told the guards this was his party and it was all right. The officer in charge said, "All right, Colonel, get on quick. There is such a crowd." We climbed on and the colonel told Chaplain to take charge of me and see me through.

The car was packed with people, but the Chaplain found a seat for us near the front end of the car. The Palmers were seated farther back and I may as well remark that I saw no more of them till some days after I reached Nashville. E.M. and I called on them to thank them for their kindness, and found the colonel had already been ordered to the front on the Chattanooga road with his regiment, and Mrs. Palmer was alone and preparing to follow to Chattanooga. We had a good laugh over our adventures that rainy morning, and how the colonel had carried the matter through, and she was interested to hear of my subsequent good fortune that day.

But to return to my story, the question with me

was how I was going to pay my fare, for I had not enough currency to pay about fifteen dollars for a ticket and a half, and I did not know enough about business to realize that my drafts were good money. Everything was in an unstable, uncertain condition. The conductor might refuse to receive a draft and anyway, I had no pass to show him. However, I thought, "sufficient unto the day is the evil thereof." As I looked out of the window watching for Mr. Gordon, and George was seated on the Chaplain's lap prattling to him, I saw Gen. Grant with some of his staff who were much more imposing looking in their uniforms than the general who wore a plain blue coat with old tarnished shoulder straps designating his rank. He came into the car where we were and stood and looked down the whole length of it. There was not a vacant seat. Chaplain Mason sprang up and said, "Have this seat, General." He (Grant) looked at me and said, "I shall be crowding the lady." I assured him to the contrary, and the pleasure it would give me to have him take it. He hesitated and the Chaplain introduced me and told him who my husband was. He asked, "Major Hill of the Missouri Engineers? I know him well," and sat down. He asked if it was Major Hill's son and took little George on his lap.

Well, this was a new situation. Just then the train started and as I looked out of the window, who should I see racing down the platform but Mr. Gordon, with his hat on the back of his head, his coat tails flying and waving my pocket-book frantically above his head. I pounded on the window and tried to raise it and was greatly excited, but it was too late. Mr. Gordon was left behind waving the unfortunate pocket-book, and doubtless wishing I was in Tophet before he had ever undertaken to chaperon a woman through the lines, when he was on military duty. I turned to Chaplain Mason who was standing by our seat, and asked him what I should do about it. He advised telling the general. I hated to do that, but finally made a clean breast of the matter, after the general had asked me what the trouble was. He asked me a number of questions, and my answers were frank and truthful. He became convinced that I was honest and sincere and the Chaplain's guarantee was worth much. At that time there were so many adventuresses and worse forcing their way through the lines, that a woman traveling alone was looked upon with suspicion. The general finally smiled and said, "Well, you know women have no business at the front, even if their husbands do send for them." I had shown him E.M.'s letter telling me to come. "You have got this far. We will have to see you through." I did not ask him how, but began to talk to him about mutual friends in St. Louis, and he was greatly interested in George.

Presently the conductor came in to collect the tickets. When he reached the general he saluted and took his ticket and reached for mine. Gen. Grant said, "This is Mrs. Major Hill. You will please pass

General Ulysses S. Grant,
Commander-in-Chief of the Union Army.
Courtesy Missouri Historical Society

her. Her escort, who is on the train following this, has her ticket and pass. Major Hill will make the matter right with you after we reach Nashville." "Certainly, certainly, General," and the conductor passed on and I drew a deep free breath and felt that I was alive once more. I thanked the general for his kindness, but was careful not to be too effusive. The Chaplain who was very relieved also thanked him, and went back and told the Palmers about it.

Now I was prepared to make the most of my opportunity and enjoy the day, for he was already a renowned man. I found him delightful to talk with. He was modest, simple and unassuming, but not at all reserved and talked well. We found we had many mutual friends in St. Louis. He had just come from there and had been to visit his son, Fred, a lad of fifteen who was very ill with typhoid fever, contracted while in camp with his father. Mrs. Grant and the boy were staying with Rev. Frank Morris and his wife, the latter a cousin of Mrs. Grant. The Rev. Morris, son of Bishop Morris, was my father's pastor, and they were beloved friends. The general told me about his family and how he liked to have some of them with him whenever it was possible. He also spoke of the service E.M. had been able to render Mrs. Grant at one time. And then he talked freely of the engineer regiment and the good service it had done during the siege of Vicksburg, and said many nice things of E.M. He called Col. Bissell of the engineers a thorn in his side—that he did not obey orders and went on unauthorized expeditions, and finally he had become so exasperated that he had sent for the colonel and ordered him to write his resignation then and there. In newspaper parlance that was a scoop, for it was not really known in the regiment why Col. Bissell had resigned, but it was surmised that he had been made to. You may know I tried to be tactful and pleasing and the general unbent, and really seemed to enjoy the conversation. He did most of the talking and he found me a good listener. He told George all about the battle of Chickamauga and Missouri Ridge. His boy, Fred, was under fire there, and he was very proud of him.

Congress was discussing at that time the question of making him a full general, creating the position for him. Also the matter was being agitated of nominating him for President, as that was the year for the election. I asked him if he would rather be a full general or the President. He thought for a while, and said, "I do not think I would make a good President. I prefer the Generalship. That is for life and my family would be provided for. There are too many things to consider in the Presidency, anyway, I am going to stay with the war until it is ended. I think no farther than that now."

His description of the battle of Missouri Ridge was very vivid and interesting, and also many scenes and incidents in the siege of Vicksburg.

Several times some of his officers would come to him to know if he wanted them or had any orders to give, but he assured them he was having a very pleasant day and he really enjoyed the little boy, and they chatted together, and he would laugh heartily at some of Georgie's sayings, for he was a bright precocious child. He (the general) turned to me once and remarked, "Mrs. Hill, you have not asked me to do anything for the Major yet. That is usually among the first things that women do." I told him he had done enough for the Major's wife and the Major could rely on his own merits. The reply seemed to greatly please him, and he was more cordial than ever.

When the train stopped at the station for dinner, he invited George and myself to join him, but I thought it better to decline for several reasons, and thanking him for his kindness, I assured him I had lunch in my bag. When he returned I thought he might change his seat, but he came back, bringing a cup of milk for George, and a couple of warm buttered biscuits, sat down and took the boy on his lap, and began to feed him, saying that was better for him than crackers or cakes. The afternoon passed all too quickly and we reached Nashville about six P.M. It was raining hard and the streets were rivers of mud and slush.

Such a dark dreary night and no E.M. at the station to meet me and no Mr. Gordon in sight. After we left the train the general remarked to me that the major was not there and "What are you going to do Mrs. Hill? You had better come to the St. Cloud with me and we will send an orderly to the camp for the major." I might have accepted his kind offer, for he was so simple, kind and sincere, and he had taken quite a fancy to the little boy, but I happened to see two of his officers look at each other, smile and wink, and I looked at Chaplain Mason and he slightly shook his head and indicated disapproval, so thanking the general very much, it seemed better to wait for awhile at the station, that my husband might be on duty and delayed, and Chaplain assured him that he would see me safely to the Major. The famous man, famous even then, kissed little George and bade us good by and left with his staff of officers, and I never saw Gen. Grant again till many years afterward, on the rear platform of a Pullman car in Hutchinson, when he was on his way to California. His son, Fred, whom he had talked so much about on that memorable day in my life, was with him, and the old veterans crowded up to the car to shake hands with their beloved leader. One would cry out "I was with you at Vicksburg, General," and another would say, "I helped you at Fort Donelson," and "General, I fought at Shiloh," and he said, "God bless you boys," the tears running down his cheeks. E.M. and I stood back watching the scene, but it made our throats ache and the tears came; old memories crowded in fast.

Well, to return to Nashville and our plight, Chaplain advised our remaining in the station till he found some place we could stay, and found means of communicating with E.M. The little boy was hungry, cold and tired, but he was so happy in the thought of seeing his father that he did not fret or worry. After waiting some time Chaplain Mason returned. He had been unable to get a room at either of the better hotels. The town was simply jammed, but at the City Hotel he had found a room that was occupied by a woman and as it had two beds in it, I could occupy it with her for the night. At any rate we could go there and get supper, and he could institute inquiries for the engineer camp.

We bumped and lurched and splashed over rough muddy streets in an ancient and broken-down cab that threatened to fall to pieces every minute, and finally reached the hotel, but my heart went down when I saw the dirty disreputable looking place and the worse looking men loafing in the hall. George wailed and cried, "My Papa don't stay here. Let us go with the general, Mama. Will Papa come here?" But we had to make the best of the most adverse circumstances in those days. We did get a warm meal of corn bread and bacon and eggs with coffee, and the world did not look such a gloomy one when our hunger was appeased. We were shown to my, or rather the room I was to share with the unknown woman, and who called herself Miss Stevenson, sister of Gen. Stevenson, Chief of the Commissary Department at Nashville.

Chaplain Mason then started out to find E.M. or get a message to him. The room was unoccupied when we entered, but was roomy and comfortable, with two double beds in it, and I was glad to find shelter for my little one from the stormy inclement night. We proceeded to make ourselves comfortable with pictures, papers and I entertained the boy till he grew sleepy. He tried so hard to keep awake to see Papa, but finally I undressed him and put him to bed and laid down beside him till he slept. Then a woman burst into the room, laughing loudly, and two or three officers with her. They stopped when they saw me and one of the men said, addressing the woman, "What does this mean? You said we could come tonight." She asked me if I was the woman who had been put into her room. We talked a little about the matter, and I explained my being there. I paid no further attention to them and went on with my reading, but it did not look good to me and I felt timorous and wished E.M. or the Chaplain were there. After a whispered conversation with the men they went away and she remained. Then she tried to explain herself and get acquainted with me, but it was soon clear that she was no sister of Gen. Stevenson, and that she was not a good woman, and she was anything but pleased at being disturbed in the occupancy of the room.

To make a long story short, Chaplain Mason had the woman and her companions moved to another room. He then found Col. Innes of the Michigan Engineers and brought him to me. The colonel immediately volunteered to send an orderly to the

Missouri Engineer camp, about three miles out of the city, and inform E.M. of my being in Nashville. The night was pitch dark and raining steadily, and the roads almost impassable with mud. It seemed dubious about his orderly reaching the camp. After they left I settled down quietly to wait, when I was disturbed by what appeared to be a terrible quarrel between the occupants of the adjoining room. A man and woman who seemed almost to come to blows. I looked out of my door to see if there was anyone passing to notify, when there close by the door sat dear Chaplain Mason. He said he thought it better to wait there till the Major arrived. He had learned that the house was a very disreputable one, that it was the only one where he could get shelter, and his being there would be a protection to me till my husband arrived. He explained the noise in the other room. It was John Wilkes Booth and his leading woman, who was also his mistress, and they were rehearsing some of their scenes. It was very realistic and sounded more like a drunken row.

About midnight E.M. arrived, wet and cold and splattered with mud, but how glad we were to see each other, and my troubles were over. The next morning, bright and early we started for the camp in an ambulance. E.M. had engaged a room and board for me and the boy in a very nice German family, who was glad to have us there as a protection for their property. The old gentleman, whose name was Buddeke, was a wholesale merchant in the city, and he had this beautiful home in the suburbs. Just now he was surrounded by the camps of the Union Army, and if he filled his spacious house with the wives of officers, who were taking this opportunity to visit their husbands, during the lull of warlike operations, it afforded him a protection from the depredations of the soldiers.

For the next two weeks, while the consolidation of the two regiments was being made, we had a gay time. Little George made friends with the ladies of the house and they were devoted to him. He was a friendly little fellow, bright and obedient, and people liked him. The family was a musical one and it was there I met and heard the famous Father Ryan, the Poet Priest of the South. He was a charming man, very witty and had a wonderful musical talent. His improvisations on the piano were most beautiful, while his playing of the harp and singing of Irish songs, which were impromptu, and composed as he played, were never to be forgotten. He was a wonderful man of great magnetic force, and how he loved the South and her cause.

It was a household of women except Mr. Buddeke and his son, who was a youth. Officers were not allowed to spend their nights away from camps, but when there was time, we had some delightful trips, always on horseback. A party of us went one day to the Hermitage, Andrew Jackson's old home. Just a comfortable Southern home, very quaint and primitive, and already showing signs of neglect and decay. Another day we went to the beautiful Acklin home, a perfect fairyland. It was far in advance of the period, and there was quite a romance connected with the owner of it. She was a beautiful girl, going to school in Nashville. Her parents were poor but refined people. One day as she was returning from school, she passed the hotel, and a man sitting on the verandah saw her. He was twice her age, and very wealthy, in fact was a slave trader and had just returned from a trip to the South. He sought out her parents and was introduced and then met her, and they were soon married. He was desperately in love with her and was most lavish in the outpouring of his wealth on her. They went to Europe, and on their return, he laid out and built this beautiful home, after plans that had been made abroad.

The house was two stories and built around a large inner court which was glassed over, making a perfect sun room. It was this immense room with its oriental rugs, Turkish divans, easy chairs and the most luxurious furnishings which was the living room of the family. It has always been an ideal room to me. There was an immense musical box that played the sweetest music the day we were there. To go back, this adoring old husband had every convenience and comfort known at that time installed for his bride. Their furniture, draperies, hangings were brought from abroad. He also brought landscape gardeners from Italy to lay out and care for the grounds. A large water tower was built (an unusual thing at that time), to furnish the necessary water for the house and grounds. A palm house and extensive conservatory was also built. In fact it compared favorably with some of the magnificent estates you so often see in Europe. I wish I could describe the place as I saw it that bright winter day. The crocus and jonquils were already showing their green leaves in the gardens. The grounds were very beautiful, laid out in terraces, sunken gardens and statuary and fountains here and there. A series of terraces led up to the house, a large two story white marble residence with Doric pillars and stately porticos, giving an appearance of harmonious dignity. On one side of the building was a suite of rooms held sacred to Andrew Jackson, who had spent much time there. In one of the rooms which had been Jackson's sitting-room were many of his little personal belongings just as he had left them. I noticed several pipes and an old fashioned Japanese tobacco box.

Not many years after the marriage the old slave trader died, leaving a young widow and an immense fortune, hundreds of slaves and one little child. Among her childhood friends was a boy playmate and neighbor. He had grown up and become a struggling young lawyer, bright and clever but poor. To him she went and placed her business and the care of the estate, for everything had been left to her. In the course of time they were married and he took up his abode there and the place became known as the Acklin place. They were very happy and she had four children, and fortune smiled on them, and their home was the center of a beautiful family life and gracious Southern hospitality.

Soon after the war broke out, Mr. Acklin died very suddenly and she was bereft. When the Union forces occupied Nashville, she went to the commanding general and asked for a Federal guard to protect her property, and it was supposed that she had paid a large price for the protection. A captain and company of soldiers were placed on guard. Many of her servants were sent South and she gathered up her children and many of her valuables and went to France and stayed there for several years.

The following year after we visited the place, the battle of Nashville was fought in that vicinity, and part of the desperate battle raged over the beautiful grounds. Negro soldiers bivouacked in the marble halls and the sumptuous inner court and the priceless tapestries and draperies and rugs from the famed looms of the far East were used for blankets and horse coverings. After the battle, there was little left but ruin and desolation of the once stately home. I learned years afterward that Mrs. Acklin subsequently returned and married the captain who did at one time guard her property. They built a modest home on the ruins of the mansion and settled down to pass the remaining years in quiet and peace, after a troubled life of much romance and adventure.

Another trip we made was to the noted Belle Harding horse farm or plantation, where blooded and thoroughbred race horses were raised, famous in the racing annals of the ante-bellum days. The house was a great rambling, two story structure, with double galleries all around it. A great hall went through the center of the house, hung with trophies of the chase and hunting field. Every room had an open fireplace and in the drawing and dining rooms, the mantels were handsomely carved. There were twenty bedrooms and in the palmy days, open house was kept all the time. When we saw it only a few old Negro servants were there as caretakers. The family had fled to Europe and many of the rooms had been dismantled of much of the handsome furniture, paintings and draperies. Both the house and the many stables and barns and the race track were falling into decay, and already had a dilapidated look. It gave one a feeling of melancholy to see a once celebrated and beautiful home deserted and neglected. Afterward, during the battle of Nashville, when the fight raged in that vicinity, it was burned down, and nothing but a few chimneys looking like spectres remained of a home that was once celebrated throughout the South.

While the consolidation and reorganization were going on, we took advantage of every chance for pleasure because long and serious work lay before the regiment. We made up a large party one night for the theatre, and saw John Wilkes Booth in

"Shylock" and "Taming of the Shrew."[47] His Shylock was very fine and he seemed to lose himself entirely in the character of the Jew. Afterward, he played "Petruchio" the same evening and made it very realistic and frolicked and fumed around the stage. Both he and the actors seemed to enjoy it as much as the spectators. During the banquet scene, he sent the dishes of viands flying over the stage. One of the property hams bounced and hit one of the orchestra in the face and started his nose to bleed, and a loaf of bread landed in a woman's lap, who sat near the front. I thought then, and still think, he was under the influence of liquor, for he had such a reckless devil-may-care manner with him. Finally, the curtain was rung down before the end of the scene. He was a very handsome dark man, but my impression of him was that he was of a wild undisciplined nature and inclined to dissipation, that he liked to pose and was theatrical.

The following Sunday the regiment had its only full dress parade while in the service. If I remember rightly, they never had been all together at one time before. Now they were twelve hundred drilled and seasoned veterans, who had just been equipped and paid off and were ready for work wherever they were sent, either with a gun, axe or shovel. It was a gay and impressive sight. Several generals and their staffs in full uniform were there and the regiment

[47] John Wilkes Booth, an actor, assassinated President Lincoln in the Ford theatre in Washington on April 14, 1865.

was reviewed by them and declared very fit for their new duties. It was the last time they were all together. The next morning early, they broke camp and began the march in rain and mud to the scene of their new duties. The regiment was broken into battalions and companies along the line of the proposed railroad. E.M.'s battalion was placed at Section 57, and the headquarters of the regiment was at Waverly, Tennessee, about fourteen miles nearer the Tennessee River, while still another detail was at Johnson City on the Tennessee. The city at that time being composed of a few log huts and the camp of the engineers.

After the regiment left Nashville, several of the wives returned North to their families. Two or three, with myself, remained where we were so much nearer our husbands. After the pleasure and gaiety of the preceding weeks, it was very quiet and dull, and the deserted campground was a forlorn and desolate place. In about two weeks after the regiment had reached its destination and the different details had gone into camp and settled down to their work, E.M. sent for me. Major Nichols sent for his wife and Capt. Gieseke sent for his wife and little boy. We were the three women who had remained at the Buddeke's. And so one dark cloudy morning in February, we began our journey into the unknown. We managed to get on a construction train that would take us as far as the road was built, about twenty-five miles from Nashville. An ambulance would meet us there and take us the rest of the way, about forty miles. We could only take our handbags and had to leave our trunks to be sent for at some future and uncertain time. The spirit of adventure was strong within us, and we started blithely and without any misgiving of the difficulties of the way. We were all day reaching White Pine, the end of construction, shut in a freight car. Fortunately there were some boxes to sit on and there was a stove and a good fire. The workmen made coffee at noon and shared with us, but paid little attention to us. They knew we had no business there, but the foreman had received the order to pass us along and had no comment to make.

We reached White Pine by dark, to find there was no ambulance awaiting us. We were hungry and cold, and it was beginning to rain and growing colder. The only building there was a temporary one, for the use of the construction gang. A man and his wife were in charge of it, who did the cooking and looked after the wants of the men. It was a rough plank house with a living room, dining room, and kitchen downstairs and a large attic upstairs. The only way to reach the attic where the men slept was by a ladder from the living room. The man and his wife slept in the dining room, and the men sat and smoked and played cards in the living room when not at work. They took us three women and two little boys in, for it was the only shelter and when we were fed and warmed we felt more comfortable after our day's rough experience, and began to devise some way to put the children to bed. A corn shuck mattress was brought down stairs and laid on the floor in one corner of the room and the superintendent of the gang loaned us some blankets. We soon had the children in bed and sound asleep. The noise and talking of the men did not disturb them for they were tired out. When it came time to retire, the men filed up to the garret. Another corn shuck bed and some blankets were brought and laid on the floor and we women slept as best we could, but we were soldiers' wives and Mrs. Nichols and myself were old campaigners. It was Mrs. Gieseke's first experience of roughing it and she was rather dismayed and would gladly have turned back if she could. In the morning the men came down and went to the kitchen before we were up, and remained till we got up and dressed. Our toilet conveniences were of the crudest, and conspicuous by their absence. We had to wash in the kitchen and use the one tin wash basin and one coarse towel that was for general use. During the night there was a fierce storm of wind and rain which had turned to sleet, and it was a wonderful world that we looked out on, every tree and shrub was covered with a thick coat of ice, and still sleeting. It was a fierce storm, the like of which had never been known in Tennessee, and it lasted for three days. Everything was covered with glare ice; great limbs and even trees snapped off with the weight of ice on them and it was dangerous to attempt working or walking out of doors. We were all storm bound in that railroad shanty. Fortunately we had enough to eat, such as it was, and we could keep fairly warm, for wood was plentiful even if it was wet. We piled our beds in one corner of the room and kept the children on them during the day. The young superintendent and his men were kind and considerate as much as they could be in the awkward circumstances, for it was as unpleasant for them as for us, to have the care of three women and two children thrust upon their hospitality, and we had to stay there until the ambulance came for us. It was here that the engineers had bivouacked the first night of their march. Their colonel had issued stringent orders against depredations or the destruction of property. The order greatly interfered with the comfort of the men, for they were not allowed to gather wood to make fires, and the night was very cold. After several officers had pleaded with the colonel, he relented and gave the order permitting them to take the top rail of the fences which were on both sides of the road, but only the top rail. The boys soon had good fires and hot coffee, and savory smells of cooking meat became apparent.

One of the officers found some men cutting up a freshly killed pig. He wanted to know where they got it and one of the men, a ready witted Irishman said, "Shure, sir, I killed him in self defense. He came at me in the dark, and I thought he was a wolf and didn't know at all that he was a pig. Shure, Captain, we'll send you over a slice of him for your supper." I do not think the captain refused. In the morning the colonel was astounded to find all the fences within reach of the camp gone, and only piles of ashes and half burned rails left. When questioned, all the men insisted they had strictly obeyed the colonel's order, and only taken the top rail each time, which was a fact, and the affair ended a huge joke on the colonel.

We were storm bound for nearly a week. The roads were in a fearful condition; the rivers and creeks overflowing and out of their banks, and the prospect for continuing our journey rather a doubtful one; but all things come to an end, and one day about noon Sergeant Anderson drove up with two powerful gray horses attached to an ambulance. He was a sturdy, reliable old Scotsman, honest and trustworthy, rather a character in his way but level headed and sure. The colonel had sent the best man and team for us at his command, but had to wait till the storm was over, and they were all very anxious about us at camp. We had to start directly after dinner to make a tavern or road-side house where we could get accommodations for the night. Gladly we piled ourselves into the vehicle after our weeks confinement and roughing it in the shanty, with nothing but the contents of our handbags in the way of cloths and necessities. Mrs. Nichols was almost ill with a cold and neuralgia. Mrs. Gieseke was hardly coherent, the experience was so new and strange to her, and more primitive than she had ever known. I had to do the cheering up for the crowd. The two women and little boy sat on the back seat well wrapped up in blankets, and George and I sat on the front seat with the sergeant. The memory of that forty mile ride is like a nightmare. It was terrible. The roads were almost impassable, and the horses, strong as they were, would only go in a walk. Trees and great branches had fallen in many places across the road which was only a narrow country road through the woods and over rough rocky hills, and across rivers and creeks where there were no bridges, only fords or ferries.

Many times we had to drive over obstructions in the road, it being too narrow or the bank too steep for us to avoid it. Many times the ambulance would sink into a rut or hole, and we all expected to be thrown out. The good old sergeant would say, "Now don't you women get frightened and screech. I will get you there all right. I promised the Major I would, and I will."

At nightfall we reached the banks of a wide rushing river. On the other side the lights of a house twinkled and gleamed. It was the roadside tavern where we expected to spend the night. The sergeant looked at the river and grew very grave. He said it had risen much higher during the day, that he had forded it easily in the morning but feared we would have to swim for it, but there was nothing to do but try it. He made us gather ourselves up on the seats, and told us whatever happened to keep quiet, the wagon and seats would float. So we obeyed his instructions and prepared for what looked like a very serious undertaking. I gathered my baby to me and held him tight. I was on the front seat and could see all the terror of the situation. The sergeant drove down into the water which was icy cold. The current was very swift and the river full of debris, whirling limbs and branches of trees. The horses were reluctant to go on, but he talked and coaxed them as though they were children. I shall never forget how one horse turned his head and looked at the sergeant with almost a human appeal and terror in his eyes. Soon the water was over the backs of the horses and covered the floor of the ambulance. Very slowly and carefully they stepped, deeper the water became and then they were beyond their depth, and began to swim and the wagon to float. The water reached the seats and we were submerged to our waists in the icy water. The sergeant remained cool and collected, talked to and encouraged his horses. Mrs. Gieseke began to whimper, when he growled, "Stop that, you'll scare the horses." We other women kept quiet. Only once my baby said, "Mama you hurt me," and I realized I was crushing him to me in my terror. I had an insane desire to sing, and the only song I could think of was "Jesus Lover of my Soul!"

The current was so swift, we were being swept far

below the ford and feared the horses would become exhausted and not be able to make the land. It was rapidly growing dark. The brave horses swam on with their precious loads of human life, while the brave sergeant cheered and encouraged them, gave them their heads and gave them their own way. After what seemed hours, but was probably only minutes, for we women were almost senseless with terror and exposure, the horses reached bottom and found their feet. The banks were very steep here, but they managed to land and drag their heavy load up the bank to level ground. They were trembling and almost exhausted, and as they rested, the old sergeant looked over the raging whirling river and exclaimed, "Thank God we are on this side of it and not in it." We made our way to the house and hailed the inmates. It was quite dark now, and as the river had risen so rapidly and become unfordable, they had not expected us. They could hardly believe it possible that we had crossed it. We were taken into the house and the women got dry clothing. We had been in the icy water almost to our shoulders, and were numb with cold. The kindly women soon had our wet clothes off, and dry ones put on. There was a generous fire blazing on the hearth and they got us hot coffee and life once more looked brighter. How good the warmth and shelter were and how delicious the hot supper of corn pone, roasted sweet potatoes and fried pork with rye coffee without sugar tasted. We had milk for the children.

We were a thankful party of people that we had passed safely through a great peril. We went to bed in clean warm beds directly after supper, worn out with the fatigue and excitement of the day, and too, our good driver wanted to start by daylight so as to reach number 57, or rather the Porter farm, by night, which was about two miles from E.M.'s camp, and where we would remain for several days.

Mrs. Tremper, our kindly hostess at the tavern, had our wet clothes dried and ready for us in the morning, a hot breakfast prepared, and a generous lunch put up, as there was no house on the road where we would be likely to procure food. In the gray dawn, rested and refreshed, we started on what we hoped would be the final day of our journey. Our road, which was the main traveled one, led for quite a distance through the river valley, with fertile farms on each side of the road, and we were able to travel more rapidly, though it was still very muddy. We made good progress and by noon had reached the broken hilly country covered with forests, and where the traveling would be slower, and where there was more danger of attack and capture by wandering bands of guerrillas. We stopped for lunch and to feed and rest the horses, but our driver was very anxious to get us to a place of safety. We soon entered the dense forests and our troubles began. The country was very rough and rocky with steep hills, and rushing creeks greatly swollen by the recent rains and storms. The roads were washed into deep gullies and holes, and in places almost impassable. We had to turn off of the road quite often and make a detour through the woods to avoid the trees and limbs which had fallen during the recent storm and which choked and filled the road. Sometimes we drove on through the debris; sometimes the ambulance went on two wheels and we expected to be spilled out on the road-side. That terrible ride! It has always remained vivid in my memory. We were jounced and bumped and thrown from one side of the wagon to the other. Poor Mrs. Nichols was thrown against the wooden frame of the cover and her head was badly hurt. She lost consciousness for a while and we had to stop to revive her. Once the sergeant turned down the wrong road and we went several miles before discovering our mistake. We found we were getting further into the forest, and the road was growing wilder and more broken. We had to turn back and retrace our way to the road we had left. The weather had changed and was growing colder and cloudy, and looked like rain, and the afternoon was fast waning. It looked very much as if we would have to remain in the woods all night without food and shelter except what the ambulance afforded.

We reached the right road at last, and then plodded on. Darker and darker it became and there was no gleam of light or break in the forest to show that we were approaching a clearing. The children were tired, cold and hungry and fretted continually. It took all our fortitude to keep our own spirits up, and we told funny stories, jokes or sang. We were bruised, beaten and banged up generally, sore all over from the rough riding. Night was coming on, and it was beginning to rain. I strained my eyes to see if the woods were becoming thinner. Finally I called the sergeant's attention to a lighter looking place in front of us but on the left. He started his horses faster and we bumped and jolted on and soon reached a clearing and found we were at last out of the woods. Back in the clearing, some distance from the road, stood a log cabin, with another smaller one behind. There were openings for light and going in and out, but neither doors or windows, not even the customary wooden shutters. A forbidding looking place, but there was some one there, for we saw the light of an open fire in the house. Our good driver was quite reluctant about turning in there. He had passed the place when going for us, but thought it deserted, and now feared danger from some roving band of bushwhackers. It was miles to another house. It was raining and would soon be pitch dark. We could not travel in the night over those uncertain roads, and food and shelter for the children were imperative. After much arguing and doubt he drove up to the house. We hailed several times before anyone made an appearance. Finally, a woman showed herself with three or four children clinging to her skirts. Both she and the children were barefooted, and their clothing consisted of a single garment made of coarse homespun, called osnaburg, and the inevitable snuff stick protruded from the side of her mouth. She was very sullen and hostile, and when we asked her to take us in, she refused and drawled, "You all had better drive on. We don't harbor Yanks. My man is not home and I can't feed you." The old sergeant told her we would have to stop there, for neither we nor the horses could go any further that night. She would have to give us supper and breakfast and we would pay her well. So we just took possession. They were the poorest of poor "white trash," and we thought the men were probably hiding in the woods nearby. The sergeant attended to his horses and fed them. There was no barn or shed on the place. Fortunately he had filled the bottom of the ambulance with hay for our comfort, so that he had something to feed them with. He tethered them to the back of the ambulance, which he placed under a large tree in front of the cabin for shelter, and where we could watch them. We were glad for even this poor shelter from the inclement weather. There was only one room with two beds in it, and the furnishing of the sparest and most primitive kind. The adjoining cabin had only the one room. There were two beds in that, but the cooking and eating was done there.

The sergeant made up a big fire on the hearth of the first room and we were soon warmed and comforted. Very reluctantly the women prepared supper for us. We found, on going into the kitchen, that there was an old woman there; evidently the mother or grandmother of the swarm of children. Our supper was meagre but probably all they could give us. It consisted of corn meal hoe cake, sorghum molasses and milk and a vile concoction they called coffee, but it was hot and we were not disposed to quarrel with our bill of fare, especially when it was served to us under compulsion. But it took the pangs of hunger to make us swallow the distasteful food, cooked in such filthy squalid surroundings. When we had fed the children and eaten what we could ourselves, we returned to the other cabin which they gave up for us for the night.

The sergeant was very uneasy and anxious, for he feared we might be without horses and ambulance and himself a prisoner before morning. There was nothing to hinder one of the children from going to the woods if the men were hidden there and bringing them to the house to capture all of us. We had noticed two or three boys among the children. They were like little wild things of the forest, and we also had noticed the women in consultation and their taking one of the boys apart and giving him a message. The sergeant wanted to know where he was going, and the woman replied that he had gone for the cow to have her near to milk in the morning. We were greatly worried and decided not to undress or go to bed. Our driver would watch his horses and care for them. He had just been out and looked after them, fastening blankets over them and putting up a blanket at the door to keep out the wind and rain for us, when looking down the road, he saw a man on horseback approaching. The man was so disguised with a covering to shield him from the rain, and in the dark was so undistinguishable it was impossible to tell who he was. The sergeant hastened into the house and warned us not to show fear. The man rode up to the house, dismounted and walked around the ambulance and horses examining the latter closely, lifting the blankets and feeling them. Then he came toward the house and we thought our time had come. My heart was in my throat and I could hardly breathe. Little George stepped forward, and by the dim light of the fire peered up into the stranger's face, when he cried out in his shrill childish voice, "Why, it's my Papa! It's my Papa!" and rushed to him and sure enough was clasped in his father's arms. How glad and thankful we all were, but he was so disguised with his ponca, it took the love of his little child to penetrate it. The sergeant was relieved of his responsibility, and E.M. took charge of affairs.

They had become very anxious about us at the camp, for we were long past due. E.M., his orderly and Capt. Gieseke started to meet us, expecting soon to see us coming, but after several miles they realized they were getting a long distance from camp, and E.M. sent the orderly back to report his absence and Capt. Gieseke decided to return with him, but E.M. kept on for he said he was going to find us before he stopped if he had to go to Nashville. The sergeant had been absent nearly a week and no tidings of him or his team had reached them. So E.M. rode on alone in the dark and rain and his relief can be imagined when he found the horses and ambulance, and his joy when he knew we were safe. His presence gave us a sense of safety and security we had not felt. He ordered the women and children to bed, and the sergeant to roll up in his blankets and lie down in front of the fire and rest. The poor man needed it for he was almost worn out with anxiety and care. E.M. stood guard and he kept a constant march and watch outside all night. Once during the night he caught one of the boys slipping away to the woods and tied him in the ambulance. There was little sleep among the women, and we were glad and relieved when morning came. It had cleared in the night, and the morning was bright and warm. We started by sunrise and did not wait for breakfast, for there was an inn about four miles farther on where Eben had expected to find us the night before. There we had a warm bountiful breakfast and started on the remaining ten miles of our journey, reaching the Porter farm by noon, where we were to remain for several days before going to the camp which was two miles away in the woods, where the railroad was being built. Mrs. Nichols was to rest a day or two and then go in to Waverly with the sergeant to join her husband, the major.

How good that homely farmhouse looked to us poor beaten, battered women and babies after the experiences of the past two weeks. Mr. and Mrs. Porter were Union people, thrifty, kindly and hospitable. They had a fertile and large farm, and several of their slaves had remained with them after their freedom was declared. They welcomed us and took us into their house and hearts. How luxurious and delicious the dinner was after our coarse fare. Platters piled high with fried chicken as only a Southern cook can fry it, biscuits white and flaky, corn bread like pound cake, sweet potatoes baked in a rich syrup till they were translucent, cream gravy, sweet clean butter and real coffee with rich cream and sugar for it. It was a feast fit for the gods, and we starved people did it full justice. It certainly seemed good to sit down to a clean, well served and deliciously cooked meal. After dinner, E.M. left us and returned to camp. He could not stay longer because he was in command. He had taken a risk the day before in going to meet us, but his suspense and anxiety were greater than he could bear.

After dinner we gave the children a good bath and put the little fellows to bed, then we women went through the same process. Mrs. Porter had her maids wash and iron our clothes and we also went to bed while that was being done. We were stiff and sore and bruised, and it was heaven to get into the clean beds and between the sweet smelling white sheets. We certainly were spent and weary pilgrims. We remained there a few days till Mrs. Nichols was well enough to go on, and till E.M. could prepare for us. It had been the intention for us to remain with Mrs. Porter till the engineers had finished their work and E.M. had engaged room and board for us, and he would visit us when he could. We should be near him, but a very strict order had been issued forbidding officers from being away from their commands overnight.

We were now in the enemy's country, a country infested with wandering bands of guerrillas, not connected with the army of the South. Constant tidings were coming in of the depredations they were committing on plantations whose owners were suspected of Union proclivities. In a short time we went into camp, and just in time, for hearing that a party of Union officers and their wives were staying at the Porter's, a raid was made on them one night. The Porters barely escaped with their lives. They hid in the woods, but their house was burned to the ground, their provisions destroyed and their horses and mules driven off, but fortunately no Yankees were found there to be murdered. The Porters came to our camp in the morning and told of their misfortunes. We wanted them to remain with us, but they decided they would not be troubled any more, and they had better go back and stay by what was left and try to plant a crop. That is just one instance among many of what the Union men in the South had to undergo.

Now, I must tell you a little of our life in camp where we passed several months, and some of the incidents connected with it. The headquarters of the regiment was at Waverly, the county seat of that county, a little primitive backwoods town about twelve miles from the Tennessee River, and our battalion, the 2nd, was at No. 57, about twelve miles on the other side of Waverly. We were camped on the side of a hill in a pine woods. The forest was dense all round us, and our camp was compact and close for safety. E.M. had two tents erected adjoining each other. The back tent was his personal one. We used it for a bedroom. There were two cots and a small bunk for George, a camp table and stools and our trunks, when they came, also furnished seats and a board floor. The front tent was a large one, a hospital tent. At one side we had an open fireplace and chimney built of sticks and mud, such as was common in the country. The ground was leveled and smoothed and covered with a heavy tarpaulin, pegged down. We made a couch of boxes covered with blankets, and we had camp chairs and tables, and though simple and primitive, it was quite luxurious for soldiers on active duty.

Our tents were pitched a little back from the officers, for the sake of privacy. Our family consisted of the members of E.M.'s staff, Dr. Knower, the surgeon lieutenant, Lyle the Quartermaster, and Lieut. Lancaster the adjutant. They, with us, formed the mess. There were two servants, one a cook and the other a sort of valet or general utility man. They were Negroes.

Nearby were two tents—one used for a kitchen and the other as a dining room. Officers were not supplied with rations, but had to buy all their provisions, and the high price of living today is nothing as compared to the prices of those days. I know we had to pay $1.00 a pound for coffee, and $5.00 a pound for tea. Butter 60¢ to 80¢ a pound and other things in proportion, so that the slender salaries paid at that time did not go very far. We all put in a fund, and every month divided the expenses. The cooking was done on open fires with covered pots and pans, and later we arrived at the extravagance of a portable sheet iron stove. But all those domestic matters troubled us but little as long as we had enough to eat.

The second battalion at No. 57 had just fairly settled when smallpox broke out in camp. The doctor and E.M. had a large hospital tent erected some distance away in the woods for a pest house, and removed the men stricken with the disease at once. There were five or six cases. They were made as comfortable as possible under the circumstances. Some of the men who had had the disease and were immune, were detailed as nurses, and a strict quarantine was established. No new cases developed with us, but two of the men died.

Smallpox was very prevalent that spring in Nashville, and throughout the army stationed around that vicinity. The Negro regiment had a number of cases and several deaths, and for some time a strict quarantine was maintained. Dr. Knower sent to the government Medical Department for vaccine and when it came vaccinated most of the men, but some of the vaccine was impure and a number of the men were made ill, with symptoms of a dreadful nameless disease. There was great indignation, but there seemed no redress, and it was worse than the smallpox.

A tragic incident occurred in the 13th Negro regiment. After the quarantine had been lifted, several from our camp went over to call on a young lieutenant and his wife. It was a beautiful Sunday afternoon and there was quite a large party of us. The lieutenant's wife and two children, a little boy and girl, had arrived from the North the day before. They had to remain in Nashville at a hotel for several days till the lieutenant could send a conveyance for them. The children, six and four years of age, were beautiful and very attractive, and much attention was shown them and they were greatly petted by the people at the hotel. They were unusually bright and pretty children, and were well trained. The mother was a lovely young woman and we all welcomed her and the little ones to our social circle. We greatly enjoyed the afternoon spent with them and invited them over to our camp for the next day. Instead of their coming they sent a message saying the children were not well, had some fever and thought they had better remain at home. The next we heard was that both the children had the smallpox, and the father and mother had gone with them into a deserted log cabin in the woods. In a week they were both dead, and the poor father dug a grave in the woods and both the little ones were buried in one grave. Then the mother had the dread disease, and it was feared she would die, but she slowly recovered, and when she was able to travel, her broken-hearted husband resigned his commission and took his poor wife home. They were a wrecked and doubly bereaved couple. It cast a great sadness over both camps and their loss affected us all deeply.

Now began a very busy time for the engineers. The railroad was graded, but in front of us was a great ravine which had to be bridged. It would take a trestle work 1200 feet long and in the deepest part, 80 feet deep. E.M., with his men, were ordered to build that bridge and have it completed so trains could cross it in two months. The timbers for it stood in the forests. The trees, oak, hickory and pine were cut down and hewed into beams. Even the spikes and bolts with which it was put together were made in the blacksmith shop of the camp. Four hundred men with their officers worked six days a week from dawn till dark. Little by little that great gap was filled. Timber hewn down one day was dragged and put in its place in the bridge the next day, every man in his own place, doing the work required of him, and when the time was up, a train rolled over the completed trestle. It was the most important piece of work on the road, and so well built and solid was the structure, it remained in use for twenty years after the war till it was replaced with a steel and iron bridge. In these days of labor strikes, short working hours and high wages, I have often thought of those men of the engineer regiment, most of them skilled artisans and mechanics, toiling and laboring from dawn till dark, far away from their homes and families, at times enduring incredible hardships while facing many dangers, for they were the men who prepared the roads, bridged the rivers and cleared the way for the infantry and cavalry. For all this work they received the munificent sum of thirteen dollars a month and rations of food of the plainest and simplest. There was something in their patriotism and devotion to their country that was praiseworthy.

Spring was now coming, the storms were over, the days were growing warm and balmy and we spent most of our time in the open. A number of the officers both at headquarters and in the different battalions sent for their wives. The 13th Colored Infantry was stationed upon the hillside across the ravine, about half a mile from our camp. They were supposed to guard the Engineers who were building the trestle, but really they were being drilled and made into soldiers. When their freedom was declared, the Negroes swarmed into the Union camp till it was difficult to know what to do with them.[48] I think it was Gen. Butler who suggested organizing them into regiments and drilling them for soldiers, which was done.[49] The officers were all white men, chosen for their efficiency and service in the army. Several of the officers of the 13th had their wives visiting them. We exchanged friendly calls and formed quite a pleasant little social circle. Only three officers in our camp had any leisure during the day, the doctor, Lieut. Lancaster, and Lieut. Lyle. All the others were on the work. The only way to get about through the wood paths and over

[48]Mrs. Hill's observations about the newly formed black regiment, whose officers were white are accurate and of interest. Responding to the pressure of radical Republicans and to the dire need for fresh troops, President Lincoln and Secretary of War Edwin M. Stanton agreed to the recruitment of black soldiers.

In time, about 170,000 black soldiers served in the Union army and fought with valor and distinction in many battles. Shortly before he was assassinated, Lincoln advocated that blacks, especially those who served in the army, be given the right of franchise in recognition of their contribution to the Union's victory.

[49]General Benjamin Butler, commander of Union troops in Louisiana welcomed, as Mrs. Hill writes, Negro slaves who escaped into the Union lines and allowed them to perform services for the Union army. President Lincoln unofficially supported Butler's policy.

the rough hills was on horseback. Several of us enjoyed horseback riding and rode every pleasant day, escorted by the two young lieutenants. The doctor did not often go for he had his hands full with his smallpox patients. We took long delightful rides through the beautiful woods now bursting into leaf and bloom, and down into the valley of the Harpeth, past rich and fertile farms or plantations which yet had not felt the devastating hand of war. We would stop sometimes at the houses on foraging expeditions, hoping to procure supplies for our scant menu in the way of fresh eggs, butter, cream and chickens, but we seldom succeeded. We would be received with cold hostility and they seldom had anything to sell to us. They had no more than they needed for their own use, they said.

There were a number of fine musicians in camp and we formed a glee club and an orchestra. The orchestra consisted of two violins, a flute and guitar. A young surgeon of the 13th played the latter and made the finest music I have ever heard from that instrument. We had a quartet. Mrs. Wells, the wife of the surgeon of the 13th, was the soprano, and I was the alto, Sergt. Carlton tenor, and Capt. Patten bass. Then there was a chorus of half a dozen. We really gave and received more pleasure from that glee club than from any other diversion we had. We would gather in front of our tent and give impromptu concerts in the evenings, reading from our notebooks by the light of pine torches. We sang only the old songs and the newer patriotic ones, songs of home and mother which touched many a homesick heart. The boys would gather around us and beg for "Annie Laurie" and "Home, Sweet Home" and "Just before the Battle Mother," and we usually finished in a grand flourish with chorus, orchestra and everybody, in "The Star Spangled Banner" and "Three Cheers for the Red, White and Blue" till we would make the woods ring again. E.M. said those little concerts at night, after a hard day's work, cheered and heartened the tired men and helped wonderfully.

Till the bridge was completed, there was little time for pleasure or recreation, and at night taps were sounded and all lights out by nine o'clock. After supper E.M. would receive the reports of the officers in charge of the work, and they would confer and lay their plans for the next day and talk over the day's problems and difficulties. Often when E.M. would go to the woods to search for and select trees to be used in the work, he would take me with him. We would leave the trail and make our way through the unbroken forest over fallen trees and logs, climbing hills so steep, I would have to lie flat on my horse's neck and grasp the mane to hold on, while he climbed like a cat. E.M. thought I could go anywhere he could and would call back, "Follow me. Don't be afraid. Charlie will bring you through. Give him his head," and I would shut my eyes and let him take me.

I must give a word to my horse. He was a stray animal that had wandered into camp. He had the U.S. brand on him so we knew that he belonged to the government. He proved to be a thoroughbred and a fast traveler, not very large and just right as a lady's horse, and E.M. secured him from the Quartermaster for my use. He was the one thing I enjoyed more than anything else that summer, and we became great friends and comrades. He was very intelligent and showed quite an affection for me, which was returned, and I felt perfectly safe on his back, whether climbing the mountainside or curled up on his back swimming a river, or flying over logs and high fences or running from a hidden foe. I became quite an expert horsewoman, but it was largely owing to the confidence I placed in my beautiful horse. Two tricks he had which occasioned annoyance at times. After he had become attached to me, he would let no one else ride him. Sometimes he was needed by or loaned to some officer, but woe to the unfortunate who tried to mount him, and if that was accomplished, he would buck and plunge and kick and prance like any young bronco, and could not be made to go till the mount would gladly give up the struggle. Yet he was as gentle as a kitten with me and all the months I rode him never gave me any trouble. The other matter was, he would lead. Of course in the army precedence meant much, and when on our rides, the colonel and his lady rode in advance. We smaller fry had to fall back in line according to rank, but Charlie defied precedent, and was going to be in first rank, and I could not hold him back. It was suspected at first that I was the cause of it, but when they saw me struggle with him to keep him in place, they absolved me of blame. Finally the colonel said, "Let him come on, and you ride with me." He was greatly amused, and there was much fun and joking about it, but when Charlie got in the front rank he went peaceably as a lamb, except that he would not let the horse back of him come too close. His heels would fly out in warning to the fellow behind to keep his distance, but he was a splendid horse and a good friend.

At this time we were not much troubled with bushwhackers. There were frequent excursions from Waverly, supposed to be tours of inspection to see how the work was progressing, but there was a good deal of fun and pleasure mixed with them. Sometimes we would ride back with the colonel and his party in Waverly and spend the night in Waverly. We usually spent most of it in frolicking and dancing, and then we would return the next morning. We were mostly young people and we got all the pleasure we could out of our surroundings. I remember on one occasion the colonel and a large party came and inspected the work. They remained to dinner. E.M. and I were the host and hostess. After dinner we all went six miles farther to Col. Thompson's camp of the 12th Colored Infantry. We had refreshments there and then returned to No. 57, taking him with us. We got little George, who rode in front of his father, and we all rode back to Waverly, making a twenty-four mile horseback ride for me, and thirty-six miles for some of them. When we reached headquarters, there was a wonderful supper spread for us. After supper, we women rested a little and then went to the Court House to a grand ball which some of the young officers were giving for the belles of the little town. I tricked George into bed at the colonel's quarters, then E.M. and I were ready for the fun.

It was very primitive and simple. The music consisted of two violins played by old darkies who were perched on a table on the platform at one end of the room. The dances were all cotillions, for the girls would not waltz with the Yankee soldiers, and one old darky would call the figures in a sing song tone and make a regular song of it. There were very few men there other than those connected with the army. Nearly all the men belonging in the town and surrounding country were in the Confederate army. But it was a great ball and we danced till sunrise the next morning forgetful of war or rumors of war. Then E.M. and his party had breakfast, and we rode back the twelve miles to our camp, reaching there in time for the day's duties. There were a number of pretty girls at Waverly, of good family, and who had received many advantages in the way of education and accomplishments. They were past masters in knowing the ways of flirtations, and led some of our young officers, who had become very much infatuated, a merry dance. One young widow received five proposals of marriage that evening from five different men. They certainly were charming women, with few aids to beauty except their own radiant health and good looks. Most of them were dressed in coarse cotton and linsey dresses, spun and dyed from the cotton and wool which they raised and wove on their own household looms. Their stockings and gloves were knitted from cotton thread which they had spun themselves, but that did not prevent them from being charming ladies and proud of the sacrifices they made and the poverty and deprivations they endured for their "Beloved Cause." No matter how they might flirt and coquet with the young Yankee officers, they were loyal and true to their country, and many a bit of information was cajoled from their admirers, sometimes of great importance and forwarded to their own generals.

Lulled into fancied security by the absence of attack and the report that the guerrilla bands had been called in, we had grown rather careless, till one dark night we were wakened by the pop pop of muskets on the picket line and then a fusillade of shots. The celerity with which E.M. dressed I never saw equalled. As he slipped into his clothes he said, "Stay right here. Do not make a light, and keep perfectly quiet. They are after the horses and commissary stores," and he was gone. When he reached the company quarters every man was out armed and in line and officers ready for orders. I heard them marching by our tents, and I gathered my baby in my arms with my heart in my mouth, waiting for what would come next. The firing seemed to approach nearer as though the pickets were being driven in. Crowded there in the dark there was no way of knowing how large a force had attacked us and what the outcome would be. The suspense was terrible. Soon there was a sharp exchange of shots when our men reached the picket line, and it did sound fearsome. Gradually the sound of the firing receded and I knew the enemy was repulsed. E.M. took two companies and pursued through the woods and sent the other two companies back to guard the camp and stores. There was no more sleep that night for any of us.

Two of our men were wounded, and after daylight, our men found one dead and three wounded of the enemy. It was a small squad that made the attack, and they scattered and fled through the forest. Toward night, E.M. and his detachment returned tired and hungry after their fruitless quest. It was an exciting incident, but we had to be prepared for such alarms.

A short time afterward, E.M. had to make a report at Headquarters about the progress of the work, and the boy and I accompanied him. We did not take an orderly. E.M. had many times impressed me with the necessity of keeping cool if we should be attacked while on the road, and to make no effort to help him, but to ride to the nearest camp as fast as my horse would travel and have assistance sent him. We had rehearsed such a possibility several times when out riding together. He had taught me to use a revolver, and to fire over my horse's head, and he had fired unexpectedly so that the horses would not frighten.

This day we were riding back to our camp very leisurely. George was in front of his father, and very much of a man because his father had him straddled in the saddle with him. His shrill little voice was piping away asking baby questions which amused us. E.M. leaned toward me and remarked we must hurry to get to camp before dark, then he said under his breath, "Ride up, faster, faster." By that time our horses were in a gallop. A couple of shots rang out behind us, and we put our horses to a run and never stopped till we reached camp.

E.M. immediately sent out a squad in pursuit and by morning they returned with two prisoners. As we were riding along, E.M. had caught the glint of a gun aimed at us over the top of a log and knew there was an ambush. What he thought strange was that they did not fire at once. The next morning the prisoners were brought before him. Little George was standing beside his father. One of the men spoke up. "You all may be thankful you had the little one with you. We aimed to kill you and your woman, and had a lead on you, but we could not fire on the baby," so that our little lad probably saved our lives. E.M. wanted to release them, but the orders were very strict and they were sent to Nashville.

Little George was the most popular person in camp. He was a lovable, friendly child, bright and intelligent, and a great favorite among the men, many of whom were married and had families at home. He quite attached himself to his father's old Co. D, and they claimed him and elected him a corporal. I made him a little uniform with the chevrons on his sleeves, and how proud he was of it. He would spend hours with the men, and they would tell him of their boys at home and show him their pictures. He was a great pleasure to them and I felt perfectly safe to leave him in their charge. His chief chum and pal was Bill Rehoe, an ambulance driver and blacksmith helper. He was a very profane man, but the little lad was fond of him and spent much time with him, for he loved to hear about Bill's little boys. One day when the air was blue with Bill's oaths, George pipes up, "Bill Rehoe, I am not going to play with you anymore. You cuss so much. My Papa don't cuss and I don't like you when you swear so hard." That brought Bill up standing and from that time he tried to reform for the little child's sake. George had a miniature musket that someone had given him, and the boys of Co. D. drilled him and taught him the manual of arms and how to clean and take care of his musket, and on

Sunday morning he would go on inspection with the rest of the company and stand in line and wait his turn with the gravity of a man. One time they had him on guard duty for an hour and he paced up and down with his gun as seriously and faithfully as any sentry. It was all real to him. E.M. encouraged it for he saw the men enjoyed it and the discipline was good for the boy.

About that time a very welcome guest came, the Paymaster. The men of Co. D insisted that George should stand in line and be paid off with them. The captain humored them and gave the Paymaster a hint of the matter. He was a jolly old fellow, and saw the humor of it, and E.M. said he would make it all right with him and refund whatever he might give the child. After the boy had dressed in his clean well-brushed uniform, had stood patiently in line for what must have seemed an endless time and had seen most of the men paid off and Bill Rehoe had shown him his roll, his name was called and he marched into the tent and stood at attention, saluting first his father and then the Paymaster. He was required to sign the payroll and marched up and printed his name, then was handed a small bundle of currency, several fifty, twenty-five, ten and five cent bills. It was all paper money at that time, and called "shin plasters." He was required to sign his name to a receipt, which he printed, and then he saluted and marched out. His comrades gathered around him and were very interested in what he received. E.M. wanted the receipt, but the old Major said it was well worth what he had paid for it, and he was going to send it to his wife. He was greatly impressed, and told the story many times in his travels, and it was published in the newspapers at the time. When George came to me and showed me his money I asked him what he was going to do with it. He said he was going to send half of it to Bill Rehoe's little boy to buy some shoes, for "Uncle Sam" had been so long paying the soldiers, Bill's little boy had to go barefoot to school in the winter time. Bill sent the money to his boy, a dollar and a half, which was half of what he received.

The country was now beautiful in its verdure. The woods and fields full of flowers, the hillside covered with the pink blossoms of the mountain laurel, the orchards laden with bloom, and the air was full of fragrance. We had long delightful rides through the beautiful Harpeth valley, following the main roads as being safer than the wood paths, where danger often lurked in ambush. Many of the farms were deserted, the men in the army, the women gone to the towns and villages for safety and protection, the Negroes freed, and many of them in the black regiments. It was such an isolated back woods country. The plantations were unmolested and it all looked so pathetic and lonely, especially at this season which usually was the busiest time of the year. From these rides we would return laden with flowering shrubs and fragrant branches till we looked like the woods of Dunsinane and we would decorate our tents till they were bowers of beauty. There were but a few sick at that time in the hospital, but we always shared our good things with the sick men who were far away from home and family.

While we women were enjoying all this beauty and the lovely outdoor life, the work on the trestle was approaching completion. Already construction trains could cross it, and the track laying was being pushed rapidly toward the river, and the strain and tension would soon be over for that time.

One hot morning in the early part of May, a messenger from Headquarters galloped into camp. He was greatly excited, and his horse was in a foam of lather and sweat. He yelled, "Where's the Major! Where's the Major! I have dispatches for him. Forrest is marching on 57 to destroy the trestle!" He rode over to the bridge and found E.M. and delivered his orders. Word had just been received that Gen. Forrest was making a raid to destroy the railroad and burn the bridges. They were not certain where he would strike first, but he was headed for 57, and the Major must defend that point with his men. All the women and children both in the Engineers and the 13th Colored Infantry must be sent to Nashville, also the sick that could travel. There was great excitement for a short time, the men rather enjoying the prospect of a fight. The first thing was to get rid of the women and children.[50] There was a train at the end of the bridge unloading supplies and commissary stores. In half an hour after the receipt of the order, the women and children from the two camps and the three or four sick men from our hospital were loaded on to that train and started back for Nashville. We took only what we could put into valises and put up such food as was prepared for a lunch, expecting to reach Nashville by three or four o'clock. There was so much excitement and everything was in such a hurry and rush, we women were a minor consideration only to be gotten out of the way to a place of safety. Already E.M. had a force of men at work, raising earthworks and preparing for the defense of the bridge, and he deputed the Quartermaster to put the little boy and me on the train and see us started. We were put into a freight car that had just brought beef cattle to be killed and dressed for the men's rations. The car had not been cleaned out, but five or six women and three or four children, with five or six sick soldiers were piled into it, to do the best they could. The engineer was ordered to get away from there at once, and the train started back to Nashville in a short time after the message reached the camp. It

[50]It is indicative of the fear and terror that General Forrest inspired that merely a rumor of his impending raid caused the immediate evacuation of women and children from the camp. This episode confirms Mrs. Hill's description of the cruel treatment of prisoners which she made during Forrest's brief occupation of Trenton, Tennessee.

was a dreadful situation. The floor of the car was in a terrible condition with the droppings of the cattle, and there was no way to clean it out. The only men with us were too sick to sit up, and we took their blankets and spread them in the driest corner of the car and had them lie down, not a very easy bed, for it was a springless freight car, and we bumped and jounced over the rough road. It was a hot and sultry day and altogether the conditions were almost insufferable. The filth of the car, the moans of the sick men being jolted from side to side, the crying of the children, and the fretting of some of the women, made the situation almost unendurable. Every little while the train would stop for some purpose and we would manage to get water for the thirsty men and children. We expected to reach Col. Thompson's camp by noon and knew he would help us out, but it was about four o'clock before we reached it. The filthy car on that hot day was our worst trouble, and when we finally stopped at Col. Thompson's camp he came down to the train and was surprised to see a party of refugees on it and learned then of the scare. The train stopped for only a few minutes, but he had the car cleaned out, a bucket of drinking water brought us, and loaned us three or four camp stools. In our hurry at leaving 57, we had neglected to bring any seats, and had been sitting on our bags and valises and holding the children. He also got us some crackers and cheese for the children to lunch on, as our lunch, which was meagre had been consumed at noon. We still expected to reach Nashville in time for supper. We were a grateful lot of women to our good friend and started on again, more comfortable. We moved but slowly and stopped often for no apparent cause. It was hot and sultry, the children cross and hungry, the sick men moaning and groaning and we women doing the best we could. Mrs. Wells and I started to sing to cheer the situation, but one of the sick men told us to "stop that infernal noise." Another one said he would sooner have Forrest take him a prisoner than endure what he was undergoing. I told him if he had seen the way Forrest treated his prisoners, as I had, he might change his mind. Then I told him of Forrest's raid on Trenton, Tennessee, and how brutally the sick soldiers were treated when taken prisoners. We then told stories of our most exciting experiences and I told the children fairy stories and so the slow hot hours passed. The train would chug along for a few miles and then stop, with us penned up in that filthy cattle car. Even when the train stopped there was no way for us to climb in and out, or to get any relief and we all suffered with the stench and stifling heat and at times almost smothered. No one came near us or paid any attention to us, and I really suppose the train men forgot us. We reached Nashville about nine P.M., but were held on the long trestle leading into the town. We waited and waited, and finally we began to call for help. It looked as if we were to be held there all night. About midnight the train of empty freight cars (ours was the only one occupied), moved into town and stopped in the yards, did not go to the station, and we scrambled down as best we could with our children and baggage. We helped the sick men down and made our way in the dark to the station which was closed. We managed to find a place for the men to lie down for the rest of the night. In the morning they could be taken to a hospital.

The next thing was to find food and shelter for ourselves. We went to the St. Cloud Hotel, which was but a short distance, and called the night clerk. He had no rooms for us. The house was full, and many sleeping on cots in the dining-room. I told him he would have to shelter us, we could go no further, and would pay him liberally for accommodations. After arguing and persuading, for I was determined to remain there, he said we might use the ladies parlor for the rest of the night. Then I demanded food, but he said that was impossible, the kitchen and store rooms were closed and locked and all the servants gone for the night. He was very indifferent and cold-blooded and we were furious. We were all famished and the little ones crying with hunger and exhaustion. Mrs. Wells and I started out to find food. When we reached the street, all the shops were closed and dark, but far down we saw the glimmer of a light and made our way to it. We found it was a cheap little eating place, the only one open on the street, rather disreputable looking, but we were desperate. We entered and disturbed several men who were drinking and gambling at a table. They stared at us in bewilderment, but we took our courage in our hands, and stated our want and need of food, for which we would pay well. The proprietor responded very kindly and said he would give us what he had. The place did not look very clean or inviting, but we were not disposed to be squeamish. He made us some ham and beef sandwiches, went into the back room and made a big pot of coffee. How fragrant and good it did smell. We added crackers and cheese, and also a can of milk. With these we made our way back to the hotel, the man going with us to carry the coffee, milk and cups. Some of the women were so exhausted, they cried when they saw the food. We soon had the poor little children fed, and then attended to our own wants. We were really in a serious way and when the man saw our condition, and realized what we had endured that day, he berated and swore at the hotel people. We felt as he did, even if we could hardly express ourselves as forcibly. We were soon fed and satisfied and thanked the man for his kindness. We paid him generously, and he soon gathered up his dishes and left us. How I wished we could have shared our good fortune with the poor sick men at the station.

Then we made the little ones comfortable in the sofas and in big chairs, and they were soon asleep.

Some of the women sat up and slept, but I stretched myself on the floor, with my arm under my head for a pillow. It was almost morning and we slept but little, for it was an intensely hot night. The air was close and sultry and it was difficult to breathe. But all material things have an end, and morning dawned at last. When it was daylight we roused, but we were stiff and sore from our rough experience. We decided we would not remain to breakfast at the hotel, but each go her own way. Mrs. Gieseke decided she would return to Missouri. She had had enough of camp life anyway. She was a little German hausfrau and could not fit into the unconventional way of living in the open, so we bade her good by. Mrs. Wells would go to some friends, and I got a carriage and went out to the Buddeke home, where I would remain awaiting events. We called the clerk and told him we would not remain for breakfast, and asked for our bill. He had the grace to apologize for his brusqueness and refused to make any charge, and was very desirous that we should remain. I told him he had his chance to play the good Samaritan, but he was like the Levites. He had passed by on the other side. We reached Mr. Buddeke's house in time for breakfast and were warmly welcomed, and all the miseries and discomforts of the previous day soon vanished. It really seemed good to sleep under a roof once more, and be surrounded by the comforts of civilization.

The morning papers were full of the raid Forrest

was supposed to be making, and troops were to be rushed out to defend the railroad. I decided to remain with my friends till I knew what the result would be.

The next day a note from E.M. stated that the reported raid was a false alarm, that Forrest was really trying to join forces with Hood, and that everything was safe and quiet along the railroad, that he would send for me in a few days.[51] Two days afterward, much to my surprise, his orderly appeared one morning with the message, or order, for an immediate return. I asked him why he came. He replied that the Major sent him to help me and the little boy. I was disposed to wait till the next day but he had to return that afternoon and we were to accompany him. We made the train in time and were soon returning over the road we had traversed before in such misery of mind and body, for we had all been very unhappy at leaving our husbands to the dire mercies of Forrest and his men.

At last we reached the end of the road that was open and found a construction train loaded with ties and iron just ready to start out on the remaining ten miles to camp. We clambered up on a pile of rails and were soon off. The orderly, who was usually quite talkative and always ready to relate camp news and gossip, was very silent and noncommittal and seemed under some constraint. I

[51] John B. Hood, Confederate general, fought at Gettysburg and in other campaigns.

could not ask him why he was sent so suddenly, for his place was to obey orders, and mine not to question him. Still, it was perplexing and irritating. When we reached 57, Dr. Knower was there to meet us. That seemed strange and I asked him where the Major was. He replied that he was busy and had sent him. Still no suspicion of the true state of affairs touched me. The orderly had gone on down the hill with the boy, the doctor and I following, and I was grumbling and the doctor silent. We passed several groups of soldiers in earnest conversation and they looked strangely at me as we passed. A light flashed in my mind and I whirled on the doctor, "Doctor, why didn't E.M. come to meet me?" I cried. "Because he could not," the doctor gravely replied. "He is badly hurt." "Is he dead?" "No," he answered.

I turned and fled up the hill and never stopped till I reached our tent. There lay my soldier, ghastly and grey, eyes sunken, cheeks drawn with great suffering, but he was alive and knew me and held out his dear arms to me. The doctor soon came and I was ready to nurse and minister to him, and after we had done what was necessary for his comfort, he suggested our leaving him with the orderly. I was anxious to hear how it occurred and how seriously he was hurt, and consult with the doctor about attending him, but E.M. would not let me leave him, kept tight hold of my hand and looked with such pleading at me, I just kissed him and sat down beside him and waited till he went to sleep, which he soon did, the first time, the doctor said, since the accident. Then I slipped out to attend to my boy, but found his friends had already done that.

Then the doctor related how it all happened. He was on the top of the trestle looking over some of the work and stepped on one end of a board that tipped and let him fall before he could save himself and he fell through the timbers. It was at the highest part, and half way down he struck a beam and fell astride of it and hung there. After much trouble they reached him and got him down. They thought he was dead, for he hung there like a dead man. They got him to his tent, and after the doctor had worked over him a long time, he discerned a flutter of the heart, and he soon began to breathe, but he did not regain consciousness. They examined him and found no bones broken, but he was frightfully injured and bruised. How badly he was hurt internally they did not know. He suffered intensely and all that night when he partially regained consciousness, his cry was "Send for Jennie. Send for Jennie," and they had started the orderly early the next morning, but forbade him telling me what the trouble was. They feared he might be dead when we reached there.

His brother officers and his men were most kind and considerate and helped to care for and nurse him, for it was the first severe accident that had occurred in the building of the trestle. Though there was abundance of willing help in nursing him, I scarcely left his side till he was out of danger. He seemed less restless and better able to bear the pain when I was near him. When I saw how severely he was injured, I was frightened. It did not seem possible that he could get well, and in fact he never was a sound or strong man after that. But he really recovered rapidly, for he was such a healthy clean man with a good constitution. He suffered intensely for a long time with internal bruises, but he never murmured, and was an ideal patient. His room became the gathering place for the telling of stories and jokes and the latest gossip from the different camps. Many of the officers were young men, bright, alert, quick-witted, and full of fun and jokes which they loved to play off on each other. To hear the roars of laughter at times, it would be difficult to realize that it was a sick room. One young Irishman, Lieut. Murphy, was the soul of the fun. He never seemed to take anything seriously, and no one escaped his witticisms, though they were always kind and good natured, but he could hold up all the little foibles of the others to ridicule. No one escaped, for he had no reverence for the man higher up, till he would have us shouting with laughter. He was a general favorite and we all knew wherever Lieut. Murphy was, there would be fun, and he was very welcome at this time though he did poke fun and joke E.M. unmercifully about his agility in walking ties and jumping, and the new horse he had found to ride. With all his fun his heart was as tender as a child's, and no one nursed E.M. with more care than he. They were all so good, and were such true men and friends. My heart grows warm and tender when I think of them and what they were to us in that time of anxiety and trouble.

My soldier was soon convalescent. The work of the engineers at section 57 was nearing completion and there was more leisure. The trains would soon be running to Johnson City. It was an important achievement, but in the light of the tremendous affairs taking place, little notice was made of it, but it opened up a very necessary feeder for the armies, both in the field and gathering at Nashville.

The engineers were proud of their work, as they had reason to be, and the trestle at 57, considering the primitive materials and appliances they had, was quite a piece of engineering skill. I can only speak of our own battalion. They were dropped down in the dense woods and told to fill this deep ravine with a bridge or trestle work. There was the timber in the woods, and the wagons hauled the iron rods from Nashville, with which the bolts and spikes were made to fasten it together. As I said before, it stood and was in daily use for twenty years after the war. In the other engineer camps equally as skillful and efficient work was done, but which we were not as familiar with as in our own.

The master mind and guiding spirit of the whole

work, in whom officers and men had implicit confidence was Col. Henry Flad, who afterward was chief engineer in the building of the Eads bridge at St. Louis across the Mississippi River, a noble monument to his skill and ability as an engineer.

In early summer, the road was turned over to the Government and opened for traffic. Now I must tell you of the big junket which took place. An excursion was planned to Johnson City, named after Gov. Andy Johnson. It was to be quite a celebration, "the wedding of the Cumberland and Tennessee," they called it. There was to be a banquet with toasts and speeches. The engineer officers and their wives were invited and a few of the officers of the colored regiments, Col. Thompson being one, for he had a large circle of friends in the army and was very popular and a general favorite. The train bearing the party from Nashville reached 57 about ten o'clock one hot summer morning. About a dozen of us got on. We found a large party of distinguished men at that time, Gov. Johnson[52] and his staff, a number of generals, among them was Gen. Sickles, and their

[52]Andrew Johnson, Senator from Tennessee before the Civil War. He was the only Southern Senator who remained loyal to the Union. When Tennessee was freed by the Union forces, Johnson, who then held the rank of Major General, was appointed Military Governor of Tennessee. This is the time that Mrs. Hill saw him in Johnson City and in Nashville.

Johnson was elected Lincoln's Vice President in 1865 and then served as President, after Lincoln's assassination on April 14, 1865.

staffs, who were stationed in and around Nashville at that time.[53]

It did not take long to discover that they were bent on a "day off" and having a frolic. Liquid refreshments were being passed freely, and by the time we reached the river some of the men were quite hilarious. The train stopped and picked up the other engineer officers, and we formed quite a party, and we found we were the only women of the party, so we kept together. The banquet was spread on rough board tables in a shed that had been built to store freight. No table cloths or napkins, the seats rough planks on boxes and nail kegs. The materials for the feast had been brought from Nashville. There was not much to eat, but much to drink.

We women, there were half a dozen of us, were treated with great distinction, and were placed on each side of Gov. Johnson according to our husband's rank. The dinner was quite a rough and primitive affair. It was really more like a picnic. Champagne flowed like water, and when the toasts and speeches began, everyone was feeling happy and brotherly. Andy Johnson, as everyone called him, had about all he could carry, and when he rose to make his speech, was almost incoherent. He mumbled around for a while, and became lachrymose and shed tears, and then turned to a big black Negro standing behind him, threw his arms around

[53]General Daniel Sickles, Union general, commanded the Third Corps at Gettysburg.

his neck and hailed him as a brother. That disgusted us and Col. Thompson came to us and said, "Let us get out of here. This is no place for ladies. It is degenerating into a drunken orgy."[54] To give added zest to the speechmaking and drinking going on in the shed, the Confederate sharp shooters kept up a constant "pop pop" from across the river, but they were too far away to do much damage. But, oh, that celebration was a disgraceful affair!

Andrew Johnson had been nominated for Vice-President on the ticket with President Lincoln. He was then governor of Tennessee and I had heard of him as a very able and wonderful self-made man, but by the time we reached 57 on our return, my illusion was shattered and I never had any respect for him afterward, and I think his subsequent career as Vice-President and President proved the correctness of my diagnosis of the man. After that day, I saw him as he was on the train going back to Nashville. It was a regular drunken crowd. Johnson was so drunk he was stupid. He sat a few seats from me, and one of the generals going past him yelled, "Wake up, Andy, wake up. The bushwhackers are coming," then mashed his tall silk hat down over his eyes. The hat was smashed, and they finally got it off. Another wag opened the car door and

[54]Mrs. Hill's description here and in the subsequent pages of Andrew Johnson as a man addicted to heavy drinking is in contradiction to the assertions of most historians and history textbook writers who say that Johnson was a moderate drinker.

Andrew Johnson,
Military Governor of Tennessee and later
Vice-President and President of the United States.
Courtesy Missouri Historical Society

shouted, "Down! Down, guerrillas are here!" It was a sight to see those people slide down under the seats and crouch on the floor, and our future President slid down under the seat in a drunken heap and it took three men to drag him out and prop him up in his seat. Dirty, dusty, disheveled, a pitiable spectacle, he lost many a vote that day.

After we left the shed E.M. and Col. Thompson accompanied us women to the train and we remained there. One of the young officers came in with a couple of bottles of champagne, which the Lieutenant Colonel's wife took from him. They bantered about it, but she would not let him have them. She was holding one in each hand, when he caught her wrists and struck the bottles together swiftly, smashing them, and the wine flew all over her and those near her. That was the climax in our party and I thought for a moment there would be a free fight with men and women mixed in it, but it had the effect of subduing and sobering our crowd, and we were quiet on the way home.

Some of our men were overcome that day, men who in all the years they had been in service, had never before been intoxicated, and they were really very funny. We were glad to reach 57, and our own camp. When we got off the train, Dr. Knower, who was very proper and very good and who never forgot his sense of propriety and dignity, found that his legs refused to work properly, and his knees to bend when they should not. He would giggle at us and say, "What is the matter with my legs? They won't work right. My knees won't stand." One of the boys told him he was drunk. He looked up so astonished, and said, "Is that how it feels to be drunk?" He was helped to his tent and we saw no more of the doctor for two or three days. The loss of self-respect and the pangs of remorse for his slip were almost more than he could bear.

The whole affair left an unpleasant memory and I only set it down as one of the incidents of those days. Johnson was very polite and complimentary, though effusive with us women, but he was not really a gentleman, rather a coarse-fibered, common sort of man, stubborn and narrow-minded. He had shown great native ability and was a self-made man.[55] He was a drunkard and a drunkard he remained and it was the habit that he evidently never mastered, that made him unfit for the duties of the office that he was called to fill after the death of our great President Lincoln. This happened at a critical time in the affairs of our country, and he antagonized both friend and foe. He was unfit for the position he occupied, because he was a slave to drink.

Soon after we were ordered to move our camp to section 51, which pleased us, for it had grown very hot where we were, surrounded and hemmed in by

[55]Mrs. Hill's judgment of Andrew Johnson seems very harsh. Johnson's biographers are sharply divided in the assessment of his personality and his record in the White House.

dense forests. Our camp at 47 was placed on the top of a hill, with a fine view of the surrounding country and the Harpeth Valley. The change was beneficial to all of us. Georgie was sick with measles when we moved, but we bundled him up and put him on his little cot, and loaded it into the ambulance, and Bill Rehoe took charge of him. It was a long drive of ten miles for the little fellow, but he took it like a soldier. We, his father and I, rode ahead and had the tent pitched and ready to receive him when he arrived. The trip never hurt him.

The Headquarters of the regiment were moved from Waverly to 51, and the other battalions were moved nearer so that it was more compact. There was still much to do and several details were spread along the road to build block houses. We bade good by to our friends of the 13th Colored Infantry with regret. It was the breaking up of a pleasant little coterie and we should lose some of our best musicians. They expected to remain at 57 and go into winter quarters and the men would continue to guard the railroad.

We were soon settled at Camp 51, and realized it was only temporary, but we enjoyed the passing moments. There was more leisure, and the headquarters people were always planning some pleasure. There were six of us women in camp. My friend, Mrs. Nichols, was now near us, and we all liked her. She was bright and clever with a keen wit, quick at repartee and had a great sense of humor.

Mrs. Parker was more popular with the men, because she was very lively, rather loud and boisterous and would do and say daring things and was good company at all times, warm hearted, and generous. If one of the men was sick, whether an officer or private, she would be the first to help take care of and nurse him. She was just a sister to everybody.

We formed a whist club for amusement and a reading club. Our friends and relatives kept us well supplied with reading matter from home, and we would procure new books. Some one would read aloud, usually one of the young officers, and we women would busy ourselves with our fancy work and sewing. We read *Adam Bede* and *Mill on the Floss* which were new at that time. We liked Thackeray better than Dickens and we also had Charles Reade and Wilkie Collins, and I must not forget Miss Evans, with *Beulah* and *St. Elmo*. Then, too, we liked Shakespeare and read and discussed him. E.M. had been quite a student of Shakespeare, and could recite several of his plays from memory. He had a pleasing voice and good delivery, and we would prevail on him to recite *Othello* or *Macbeth* for us.

We made several excursions to Col. Thompson's camp. Most of the officers of that regiment were young men and unmarried, so there were no women there. The colonel and his major had just completed what was quite a pretentious log house, for their quarters. They expected to spend the winter there. There was a living-room, a dining-room and two bedrooms. The kitchen was detached. A party of us was invited over for a house warming, and we gladly accepted. Col. Thompson had formerly been the First Lieutenant of E.M.'s Co. D. They had slept under the same blanket the first winter in the service. They had formed a close friendship for each other and were like brothers. Every one liked Charlie Thompson, and at New Madrid he showed such fine qualities while under fire that Gen. Rosecrans detailed him to serve on his staff. His promotions were rapid, and he always won praise on the field of battle for conspicuous bravery and courage.

We were delighted when we found that he was to be our neighbor, and renewed the old friendship, and he certainly enjoyed his former brother officers. E.M. and I visited back and forth quite often. Thompson was every inch a gentleman and soldier, a college bred boy who had left college to serve his country, and he had maintained and kept his ideals. He was a very handsome young man, clean and wholesome, perfectly fearless, and the ladies named him Apollo. And yet, with all his success and popularity he was unspoiled. While I am on this subject, I will finish the story of his record. In the fierce battles around Nashville the following winter when Gen. Hood gave battle to Gen. Thomas, the three colored regiments were formed into a brigade and Col. Thompson was given command of them.[56] In

[56]George H. Thomas, a Union general, fought in the Kentucky and Tennessee campaigns.

the two days of fighting they were in the thickest and fiercest stage of the battle. The colored men fought like seasoned veterans. The slaughter of them was tremendous, for no Negroes were taken prisoners. Charlie Thompson led his troops to victory and won his brigadier's star on the blood-soaked battlefield of Nashville.

To return to the house warming, we rode over on horseback, a merry crowd, and we found great preparations made for us. The rooms were decorated with green boughs, and although the dinner was served in the usual simple camp style, the table was covered with spotless linen, and the furnishings were all quite luxurious, while the dinner was abundant and deliciously cooked, for our host had a famous Negro cook for his servant. After our usual simple menus of fried or boiled salt pork, beans, rice and bread very often sans butter, roast duck, fried chicken and roast beef with all the vegetables that accompany them was a feast indeed, and also in honor of the occasion, he served a light French wine called Bouzey, and that came near my undoing. It was a sweet sparkling wine. Around the table was kept up a constant flow of badinage and repartee, a good many puns were made on the name of the wine and the effect it would have on us. It certainly came near making me boozy. I was seated at the colonel's right hand, and E.M. sat nearly opposite, laughing and talking with the others. I would take a sip or little drink of the wine, my glass being between the colonel and me. Happening to glance at E.M. I saw him wink at the colonel. Looking around I saw him refilling my glass. I had wondered why my glass was so full. They all thought they had the joke on me, and I fancy they did, for I certainly felt dizzy and could appreciate how Dr. Knower felt. E.M. always declared that it took his and Col. Thompson's united effort to put me on my horse, but that really was not so. As it was part of the fun, no harm was done to anyone and we made merry over it. We were not a drinking, carousing crowd. In fact the whole regiment was noted for its strong temperance sentiment.

While at 51, the only occurrence of note was an expedition of the regiment commanded by Col. Flad. Small bodies of rebel troops were very troublesome in the neighborhood of Johnson City, on the other side of the river, and Col. Flad with his men went on a scouting expedition and cleaned out the marauding parties. The post at 51 during their absence was left with only Dr. Knower, the few sick and the women and children. It was quite a deserted camp for a week and was very lonely, and our returning soldiers were gladly welcomed. Though there was little accomplished of military importance, they had many good stories to tell of each other's prowess or lack of prowess.

In July our battalion was moved to section 28, at Kingston Springs, which before the war had been quite a favorite summer resort and watering place for the people of Nashville. The Springs and hotel and cottages were about a mile from the railroad, and were used as post headquarters while we were there, and our battalion was camped at the railroad. We went from 51 by train, while our tents, baggage and camp equipage went by the wagons and did not reach us till the following day. That night was my first real experience of sleeping in the open. The ground selected for the camp was in a beautiful grove of hickory and oak trees with no underbrush but a thick growth of penny royal covered the ground. It was dark when we reached there. The men were in marching trim and had their blankets and three days rations, and we had, if I remember rightly, some hard tack, and cold fried salt pork for our supper. We did manage to get some milk from a house nearby for George, but otherwise we fared the same as the men. Our servants were with the wagons. We had no lights or fire, and when bedtime came we spread our blankets on the ground and with little George between us, we slept, or rather E.M. and George did, with nothing but the stars overhead for a covering. In the dark where we had spread our blankets, was a thick bed of penny royal, and the pungent odor was almost overpowering. That, and the hard ground and the little spice of danger from snakes and creeping things kept me awake, and I laid and watched the stars and was glad when morning came.

Our wagons got in that day and the camp was a

busy, bustling place and we were soon very comfortably settled. Our large tent was pitched for a living-room as before, then a passage was roofed over with green pine boughs, which made a pleasant shady porch, and then our smaller tent was our bedroom. Next to us on one side was the Adjutant's tent, and on the other, the Quartermaster's and then the doctor's tent next to that. Back a short distance was our mess tent, furnished with mess chest and camp stools and the kitchen tent beside it, and the servants' tent at the back of that. The ground was smooth and level, covered with large trees, making a beautiful shady grove, and in front of our row of tents, spread the companies' tents, laid out in regular streets. It really was a very pretty camp. Military regulations were followed and military discipline enforced.

From the report of the Adjutant General of Missouri for the year 1865, I quote the following from the History of the lst Missouri Engineers, edited and compiled by Dr. Neal:

"The 1st Regiment Missouri Engineers remained at Nashville during the month of January, 1864, and part of February to perfect the re-organization of the regiment. It was then ordered to complete the western portion (20 miles) of the Nashville and Northwestern Railroad. During the following two months the regiment constructed several large bridges and trestle work, among others one seventy-five feet high and nearly one thousand feet long, laid the track and constructed platforms, switches, turnouts, etc. At the same time, small forts were built at

Waverly and Johnson City. After the completion of the road, the regiment commenced the construction of block houses for the protection of the numerous bridges and trestleworks, and had nearly completed them from Johnsonville to Kingston Springs, when about the middle of September it was transferred to the Department of the Tennessee and ordered to report to Major Gen. Howard before Atlanta."

Now followed busy yet quiet days. The work on the Nashville and Northwestern R.R. was completed, and we all knew that it was a question of short time when they would be ordered on some new and arduous work. The men having little to do became restless. The three years for which they had enlisted would soon expire, and many of them would be mustered out. Of course there was more or less friction, little jealousies and heart burnings, but as a whole the officers and men were very loyal and true to each other, and all upholding their regiment as the finest and best in the service.

There had been a little undercurrent of murmuring about "petticoat government," because of the women remaining so long with the regiment. There was nothing to it, but in connection with this matter, I must relate an incident which was difficult for me, but had a good effect and cleared the atmosphere caused by the presence of women as far as our battalion was concerned. One evening, E.M. was conferring with several officers in the living-room tent. I happened to come in while they were talking, but have forgotten just what the subject of their conversation was. From what followed, evidently the subject of "petticoat government" had been spoken of. Some statement was made and I disagreed with it. We had all been so friendly and such good comrades that I felt as one of them, but that was the wrong time to speak. E.M. drew himself up, and his face changed. His eyes looked like steel or ice. He turned to me and said in a voice that might have traveled over miles and miles of Arctic ice fields, so cold and hard it was, "Who commands here, you or I?" He had never spoken to me in that tone before, and I looked at him and wilted. "You," I murmured in a weak tone. "Then remember that in the future," and turned to the conversation.

I whirled on my heel and fled to the woods, outraged and humiliated, for the offense had been so trivial for the punishment meted out before those officers. A very bad two hours followed for me in the solitude of the forest. Finally E.M. found me and explained why I had been made the scapegoat, and why he had been so severe. I could see that he was right, but I did not enjoy the experience. The next morning those who were at the conference the night before, were especially kind and considerate to me and seemed sorry that it had happened, but nothing was said, and they saw that all was right with E.M. and me for we rode together to Headquarters. But the incident, painful as it was, had a good effect among our battalion officers and men, for E.M. had demonstrated there was no "petticoat government" in the regiment.

While at Kingston Springs I lost my good horse, or rather the owner of him turned up. We were riding one day and stopped at a camp of Tennessee Cavalry that had recently moved from Waverly. As we stood there talking, one of the men was eyeing and looking over my horse very closely. He turned to E.M. and said, "I believe that is my horse that strayed away from me last winter. I thought some bushwhacker had got him." He turned to the horse and said, "Hello, Trotter, old boy. Don't you know me?" Charlie pricked up his ears and looked at the man and in his horse's way, showed pleasure. Then the man talked to him, and asked him to shake hands and Charlie held up his forepaw for him to take. Then he said, "There's something in my pocket for you, Trotter," and the horse nosed in his pocket for the piece of hard tack. He rubbed his head up and down against the man and whinnied with pleasure. The man proved indubitably that the horse was his and had been a pet and plaything for him. He had taught him many tricks, for he was very intelligent. After talking with the captain of the troop, we were all convinced that the horse belonged to the trooper, and told him to come for him the next morning. I shed some tears when I bade my pretty horse good by the next day, and I hoped he was sorry to leave me, for we had become good friends and comrades and he had taken me safely through many dangerous places.

Just one more incident before the marching orders came. The weather had been extremely hot, sultry with frequent showers. Everything was damp, sticky and mildewy. This morning the sun shone hot and clear and the men took the opportunity for house cleaning. They had their blankets and clothing hung in the sun to dry and air. Dr. Knower was also giving his tent and medicine chests an airing. He had his bottles and boxes and flasks spread out in front of his tent. The Quartermaster was busy going over his stores and the Adjutant was cleaning up and re-assorting his papers. As the morning was very still, the work was done out of doors. E.M. and Capt. Hudson had gone to Col. Thompson's post on business. Some of the men had made George a little waterwheel and were showing him how to manage it, in a little ditch nearby. We were shut in by the grove of trees and could not see the distant sky. One of the men came to the doctor and said he believed a storm was coming because there was a very black cloud in the West. Just then Sam, the cook, called us to dinner and we all thought we would have time to get through the meal before the storm reached us.

We had scarcely begun, when a fierce gust of wind came and scattered things. Then in a moment the hurricane in all its fury was upon us. The doctor, Adjutant and Quartermaster flew to save their goods, but too late. They were scattered far and wide. For the next few minutes it is difficult to tell what did occur. Everything came with such a roar and bang and so swiftly. I caught George to me just as the tent came down on top of us, and the canvas of the roof and the tent pole fell in such a way as to afford a little protection. There was a regular cloudburst and I feared we would drown, for quicker than it takes to tell it, we were standing in water over ankle deep, the wind roaring and playing havoc, lightning striking near us continually. I could only hold on to my boy and pray for life and E.M. It was a perfect pandemonium for a while. The Quartermaster at last came and lifted the tent off George and me, expecting to find us dead, for a great tree had fallen in such a way as to partly crush the tent. It was still blowing and raining fiercely, and in the midst of it here came E.M. and Capt. Hudson. They both rode powerful horses, but the horses were nearly exhausted. They had seen the storm coming and had started at once for the camp, thinking they would reach there before it, but it overtook them, and the last mile they rode through falling trees. In some places trees would be bent to the ground, and they would ride right into them, and the wind was so strong it almost carried horse and rider away. The horses were terrified and needed no urging to go on. When E.M. found that George and I were unhurt, he gave a very fervent "Thank God," which I fervently repeated the blessing for his safety. Capt. Hudson and he never forgot that wild and fearful ride through the heart of the storm, and it was marvelous that they were not hurt or killed. When we were disentangled from the tent, a scene of wild destruction and confusion met our gaze. The whole camp was lying flat. Men were clinging to trees and shrubs to prevent being blown away. The only tents left even partially standing were ours, and they leaned at a sharp angle, but the shelter between the tents had acted as a brace and so kept them from falling down. The stores of the doctor and Quartermaster were gone, as also were many papers of the Adjutant. Our mess provisions were gone or ruined with water. We had recently bought a five pound chest of tea for which we had paid twenty-five dollars. We never saw any of it again. Also a sack of coffee which had cost a dollar a pound was gone. We found the sugar sack caught on a bush, but the contents were washed away. We afterward found knives and forks and many small articles, a half mile from camp. The greatest havoc was in the beautiful grove. Many of the trees were blown down, great limbs torn off and branches and limbs covered with fallen tents. Several of the soldiers were hurt, but fortunately none of them were killed. The loss to the camp was great in clothing, supplies and stores. Many articles of clothing were picked up miles away, caught in trees and on bushes. The storm swept on and over Nashville, within a few minutes after it had passed us, and did great damage, killing several people. It rolled up the great lead roof of the State House as though it had been a sheet of paper and deposited it in the street below. A messenger was immediately dispatched to Kingston Springs to ascertain if the post was damaged or anyone hurt and to report our own mishap. The road was full of fallen limbs and trees, but since the post had been outside the chief brunt of the storm, little damage was done. A detail was ordered to clear and clean up the road and that night a party of us rode over in an ambulance and danced in the large pavilion till daylight. A ball had been planned as a sort of farewell affair for the summer. Many from neighboring camps had been invited and we were anticipating a gay wind-up. We supposed after the storm, it would be postponed, but a little thing like that did not trouble seasoned veterans, and the colonel sent word to come on and we would have our dance anyway. After the day's experience, we all enjoyed it with greater zest. There were many thrilling incidents to relate of the storm and we were all thankful there was no loss of life in our vicinity. We laughed at the doctor and told him he did not throw physics to the dogs, but to the winds. The Quartermaster, too, was busy gathering clothing from trees and bushes a mile away from camp, but there was more that he never found.

About this time Mrs. Nichols, Mrs. G— and I went to Nashville on a shopping expedition. Talk about the high cost of living! Among my purchases was a beautiful calico dress for which I paid seventy-five cents a yard, similar to what costs seven cents a yard now. I paid eighty cents a yard for cotton cloth to make some shirts for my husband; twenty-five cents a spool for thread, and other things in like proportion. Gold and silver coins had disappeared from circulation. Nothing was used but paper money, down to the lowest denomination. We used to jokingly remark that we would take a basketful of money and bring home our purchases in a small parcel in our hand.

Rumors were now rife that the regiment was to be ordered to the front, and the women of the party were busy putting their husbands' clothes in order and preparing for our return to the North. All was now a bustle of preparation. A number of men whose three year term of enlistment expired were mustered out and returned to their homes. The paymaster came, and clothing was issued to the men, preparatory to the change. The colonel was absent several days in Nashville, conferring with department commanders and officials. He returned jubilant with the news that the regiment was to go to the front and take part in the siege of Atlanta. On the 15th the orders came for the regiment to move, on the seventeenth. The baggage, supplies and camp equipment was loaded on the cars and the second battalion (ours) marched by road to Nashville. There, after turning over all surplus baggage supplies, stores and tents, and placing the sick in the general hospital, the regiment was loaded on cars in light marching trim and started for the front, reaching the Chattahoochee River bridge the morning of August 25th, marched three miles to the front taking several siege guns with them to put in place.

When we broke camp at Kingston Springs, as the men had to march to Nashville, the accumulations of camp furniture had to be disposed of. Some of the men had made me two beautiful rustic chairs and an oak table which were highly prized, and which I was anxious to keep and take North, but no excess baggage, express or freight other than government supplies could be transported, and E.M. said they would have to be left, and with great regret they were given to a family who lived near the camp. George and I went to Nashville on the train, E.M. going with his battalion by road. We were in Nashville a day or two. That last night can never be forgotten. On the morning of August 20, E.M. took us to the train and bade his wife and boy good by. We were going to Louisville and he was going to the train that was to take them to Chattanooga. Some of our little female band had already left for the North, and some were going to remain a few more days in Nashville. Thus ended an eventful and memorable summer, replete with stirring experiences and incidents and containing much of pleasure. Many of the women I never saw again, though I frequently heard from some of them. Our lives developed along such different lines. But we greatly enjoyed each other and our happy-go-lucky life in camp, and it was a privilege and joy to be near our husbands and share in the dangers even in a slight measure. We had always been treated with kindness and consideration by both officers and men. There was a great charm about the outdoor life and freedom from conventionalities, and the spice of danger from guerrilla bands only added zest to the enjoyment of it.

E.M. desired for me to go to Dayton, Ohio, to be with his brother and family for a while. It was nearer to Atlanta than St. Louis, and when Atlanta was captured, if they remained there any length of time working on fortifications, he wanted that we should come to him. We could reach him more easily from Dayton.

After leaving my soldier it was a sad journey to Louisville, and when I reached the Galt House that night I was quite ill and had to call the services of a chambermaid to care for my little boy and get me to bed. The next day I was too ill to leave my bed and was in a panic for fear of an attack of fever. Fortunately I resumed my journey the next day, and reached my brother-in-law's house in safety.

Daily letters came from my soldier boy telling of their journey to the front and the hardships they had to endure, but it was such a busy life and they were so glad to be in the thick of it. They were set to work planting siege guns, building fortifications, repairing roads and bridges. The regiment was assigned to Gen. Howard's Corps and reported to him during the campaigns that followed.[57] One time the regiment marched forty-eight hours without a halt. At another time there had been a severe fight and they had been hurried to the front, the men marching continuously thirty-six hours without removing their knapsacks. The teamsters and some of the officers, marched sixty hours without sleep. The men slept well after coming to a halt, tired out, not noticing the heavy artillery and small arms firing that was kept up all night, some of the shells coming near the camp.

E.M. wrote me often, and when he had the time, quite fully of the work his regiment was engaged in. On that dreadful march he was so worn out that the last miles he slept on his horse, as it moved along with the others.

Sometime about September 1st occurred the battle of Jonesboro in which our boys were subject to a heavy fire from the enemy's batteries while they were throwing up earthworks for our army, and

[57]General O. O. Howard, a West Point graduate, was a Union general who fought at Chancellorsville and in other battles. A native of Massachusetts, he was deeply religious and never swore or drank. He earned the nickname of the "Christian General." General Howard was given command of black regiments which fought with great courage under his command. After the Civil War, General Howard became the head of the Freedman's Bureau, and established many schools for the children of ex-slaves.

Howard University in Washington, D.C. was named to honor its founder, General Howard.

were exposed without guard or shelter. They stood their ground bravely, but several were killed.

About October 1st the whole regiment went into camp in Atlanta and spent the month there building and strengthening the various fortifications. When Sherman went North with his army after Hood, the regiment was left cooped up in Atlanta. Because the railroads to the North were torn up, there was no way for supplies to reach them. At one time, it seemed as if Gen. Hood would annihilate Sherman and his army, and our regiment was in a perilous position for weeks. No letters reached us, and only reports sifted through of the dire straits of the men left in and around Atlanta. There were no rations except hardtack and an occasional little fresh beef. Since there was no feed for horses, many of them were slaughtered for food. E.M. frequently shared his meal of hardtack with his horse, Snorter, a magnificent great gray stallion of wonderful endurance.

They did not dare go outside the lines to forage, as roving companies of the enemy were constantly on the move around them, and it was at this time that E.M. nearly lost his life. They heard of a place where they might get feed for their horses. E.M., a brother officer, and an orderly started for the plantation, which was outside the lines. Riding through a strip of woods, and turning a sharp corner, they came right on two rebel cavalry men riding toward them. The rebels gave a yell, drew their sabres, and charged the three Federals. One of them had his sabre descending on E.M.'s head, when the latter fired and the fellow dropped, badly wounded. The other whirled around and fled, pursued by the others. They did not get their forage for their horses, but they returned to camp with two prisoners and two horses, while E.M. retained the sabre which so nearly took his life, and that sabre is in the family now, a trophy of the campaign around Atlanta.

While these events were taking place around Atlanta, the wives and mothers in their Northern homes were suffering tortures of suspense and anxiety. Mails were very uncertain. Sometimes there would be no letters for days, or even weeks, and then they would come in bunches. Rumors of dire disasters to Sherman and his army crept through the lines, and the country was in a state of suspense. Terrible fighting was going on, and our brave and good friend, Gen. McPherson, was killed in one of the battles. He was a brave and gentle soul, greatly beloved by his men. His untimely death caused great grief to us who had been counted among his many friends.

One package of letters I received told of the hardships they were enduring and how serious the problem of food was becoming, and the last one written told of their tightening their belts till their stomachs touched their backbones. As usual, E.M. made light of their troubles, but he gave their bill of fare that day. Some moldy and wormy hardtack, for animal food they knocked the worms out, and for beverage they did have good spring water. He spoke of how good a cup of coffee would taste, and even a dish of beans would be fine. There were no odors of frying bacon and boiling coffee in the camp. He had not been able to eat the horse or mule meat, though some of the men had tried it. They were becoming faint and weak with hunger, and I would scarcely recognize my gay and debonair officer friends in the pallid spectres who were suffering the pangs of hunger. There would have to be relief very soon, and the colonel and some others were talking of taking chances and sending out a foraging expedition that day. They might be killed or captured, but they would die trying and it would be better than staying in camp and starving.

Then there were no more letters for a week and I was wild with anxiety and grief. What could one woman do but just suffer. There were hundreds in the same case. When I would go to the abundant and bountifully spread table I could not eat. The food choked and nauseated me. I could see those poor starving boys in that dreadful country. At night I could not sleep and could only picture them in their distress. We stood ready to send a great box of provisions, but the roads were torn up and the enemy was strongly entrenched between Atlanta and Chattanooga and the government was unable to afford any relief at that time. After the tension had almost reached the breaking point, another package of letters came and I knew my soldier was still alive. I tore open the first one, which had been written a couple of days after the one which described the starvation. In it he said he knew I would pity them for they were suffering from the agonies from too much food, just as two days before they had suffered from hunger. Their foraging party had been successful and they had returned to camp with several wagon loads of provisions, and he said,

"You ought to see the cooking going on. The men can scarcely wait for the food to be properly prepared. Sam, our cook, was in his element again, and he surely got us up a good meal and plenty of it; fried chicken, ham and eggs, hot biscuits and *butter*. What do you think of that for luxury? Sweet potatoes and onions. I did not know onions could taste so good, and like the children in the story, we ate and ate and ate, till now we are fairly groaning with overloaded stomachs, and the boys are in almost as bad a state as they were when their stomachs were empty."

At the first reading of the letter, we thought it must be the result of the mind—wanderings of a starving man, but my brother-in-law suggested my opening the others and reading them. They had been successful in their foraging expedition, and all the men in their camp had been fed, and the worst was past, for the railroads had been repaired and supplies were being rushed to the front.

The last of October, about five hundred of the men whose term of enlistment expired, were mustered out and returned to their homes. By this time the regiment was reduced from thirteen hundred to six hundred and they were consolidated into a battalion of five companies, Lieut. Col. Tweedale commanding, and E.M. as Major. Many of our old friends dropped out and left the regiment at this time, and those that were left were old veterans by now. E.M. wrote of the campaign that was being planned, through Georgia, that they were busy building boats of canvas and wood for a pontoon train to accompany the army, so that pontoon bridges could be quickly thrown across the rivers for the army to pass over, and that their regiment would probably be in command of the pontoon train. Capt. Poe, chief engineer on Gen. Sherman's staff, and Col. Tweedale, a skilled engineer, made the plans that were so efficiently carried out later by the officers and men under them.

E.M. also wrote of the evacuation and burning of Atlanta, a beautiful and once prosperous city. It greatly saddened him to see the destruction of the beautiful homes. All the inhabitants were ordered to leave and the torch was applied, and at the end of three days and nights, little was left but a smoking and smoldering pile of ruins and ashes. Surely, as Gen. Sherman said, "War is hell." Then about Nov. 15th, Sherman and his army burned their bridges behind them and started on their march through Georgia into the unknown. They went in light marching trim, each man carrying his own baggage and they were to subsist off the country.

During the three years of the war, Georgia had suffered but little, except for an occasional raid in the Northwest portion. Cotton planting had almost ceased. The planters devoted all their time and labor to raising supplies for the army around Richmond, and it was a "Land of Canaan flowing with milk and honey."

E.M. wrote that there would be no communication with the rear, and the next letter I received from him would be by way of the coast or somewhere else, to have no fear, there was a large army in front of them, and no way for a Confederate army to reach them and give battle, and they were prepared for any contingency. Then silence, and the whole country wondered where Sherman was going and what he was going to do when he got there. No word seeped through. He had a magnificent army and some of the best generals in the service were with him. Gen. Thomas, of the army of the Cumberland, had Gen. Hood in the toils, so that the latter could not follow Sherman.

When it became known that the Missouri Engineers would go with Sherman, E.M. wrote that it might be a long time before we could be together again, and I had better go to my mother in St. Louis and remain there till he could come. I was far from well and needed my mother's care, and was glad to go to her, for I was very desolate and forlorn and filled with anxious fears for the safety of my soldier.

Mother had sold some property in Wisconsin the

previous summer and was able to make a few collections and had taken a small house downtown. She and the girls were very comfortably settled and gladly received the little boy and me after our wanderings of the past year, and quietly we waited, a household of females, for news of our dear ones. I did it with what fortitude and patience I could muster. There was always the thought of death and imprisonment lurking in my mind. Never for a passing hour was the thought of my absent soldier away from me, and at night in my fitful slumbers I constantly dreamed of him, and I was only one woman of many thousands who were undergoing the same experience with regard to their dear absent ones in the terrible war.

While on the subject of Sherman's march to the sea, I will give a series of extracts from the *History of the Missouri Engineers*, as concerning E.M., for while he was only one among others who were more prominent, yet we are chiefly interested in him:

Dec. 7, 1864.—

Arrived at Jeneks bridge about 10:30 A.M., a march of five and a half miles. As the enemy held the opposite side of the river, we were ordered to launch boats and ferry over troops, which we did under cover of our fire without accident, but on the other side quite a number of the soldiers of the skirmish line were killed before the enemy was driven off. The First Missouri Engineers then proceeded to lay the bridge which was done at 1 P.M. The bridge was 231 feet in length, the water twelve feet deep. In the evening, the surplus boats of the pontoon train were ordered to report to Corps Headquarters at 5:30 A.M. the following morning. Major Hill and sixty men were detailed, and worked all night repairing the boats and covers.

Dec. 8—

Major Hill and detail started at 5:30 A.M. at Corps Headquarters. A staff officer was sent with them. After marching all day they went into camp one mile south of Eden Court House.

Dec. 9—

Major Hill continued on with his detail to the Canonchee River where he launched his boats, ferried troops across and put the old bridge in repair, making up the deficiency in the center with pontoon boats, using for this three boats, and for ferrying, two boats.

Dec. 10—

Very bad roads. We arrived at Dillon's Ferry near Fort Argyle, an old fort of Revolutionary times, about noon and found the road approaching the river impassable. One company was sent to repair it and the train was sent into park. As the First Division had the right of way, the Second Division did not get across until 6 P.M., and as the roads were very bad, the regiment went into camp till morning. Marched seven miles. Major Hill took up their bridge and reported back at Dillon's Ferry about noon.

Dec. 12—

At 4 A.M. under orders from Headquarters, Major Hill and a detail of forty men from Company C, took four boats with the necessary balks, chesses, etc., and returned to the Canonchee River by way of Fort Argyle with Kilpatrick's Cavalry. During the night worked details of forty men relieved every two hours. Major Hill returned about 10 P.M. from the Canonchee River.

Dec. 13—

Bridge ready for crossing at 6 A.M. Whole length of bridge seven hundred feet. Depth of water at low tide, fourteen feet. The tide rises from six to eight feet. Major Hill and a detail from C company worked putting a side rail on the repaired King's bridge. Progress was slow on account of troops crossing.

Dec. 19—

Company C was sent to Fort McAllister. Balance of regiment at work on wharf and getting out and hauling timber. Major Hill was sent with detail to take up bridge at Fort Argyle.

Dec. 22—

It was found that Savannah had been evacuated during the night. The pontoon train with companies A and D marched into Savannah.

Dec. 25—

The Headquarters and the balance of the regiment marched into Savannah and went into camp.

The above brief extracts are made to illustrate the work of the regiment, and also some slight idea of the arduous labor required of the men, as well as the part of the duties to which E.M. was assigned. Comment has been made on the Engineers not being a fighting regiment. They were a very necessary body of men, and no one could impugn their bravery in the face of danger. Their work required them to be in the front, exposed to fire and the attack of the enemy. It was they who had to build the fortifications, throw up earthworks, build and lay bridges always at the front, while infantry could lie behind the shelter of the earthworks that the Engineers had built. Cannon balls and bullets were flying around them, with no means of defending themselves. This demonstrates that they were a superior class of men of great moral as well as physical courage, for when a man is attacked his impulse is to fight back. They fulfilled their duties with coolness and bravery and while being made targets of by the enemy showed they were men of fine quality. I could relate many stories of their bravery and coolness in trying situations, but will relate only one incident that came to our knowledge later, and in which my own soldier was concerned.

After the close of the war, we were in Augusta, Georgia, and while there boarded with a family named Wheeler. It developed that Mr. Wheeler had been a sharpshooter in the Confederate army and was with Gen. Wheeler at the time the general harassed and disputed the crossing of the rivers by Gen. Sherman and his army in Georgia. Wheeler's men usually had to be driven out before the bridge could be laid. This evening there were several present and they were relating incidents and stories of the war in which they took part. E.M. was silent, for he was the only Yankee present, and while they knew he had served with the Northern army, they did not know he was one of Sherman's men, and he thought it the better part of wisdom not to tell them.

Mr. Wheeler was telling about Sherman and his men and how, though Gen. Wheeler was not strong enough to attack them, they made the laying of bridges and crossing of rivers a dangerous job. He told of the pontoon train with Sherman's army and of the men who had charge of it. Gen. Wheeler had given orders that his sharpshooters should especially single out these men at the crossings and harass them and pick off their officers as often as possible. They would hide on the opposite bank and shoot at these men till compelled to retire by the fire from the infantry. He told of the coolness and indifference these bridge layers manifested in what was often a very dangerous situation, and how they tried to cripple them before the other part of the army came up, for these men were always in the van. Then he went on to relate about one officer who seemed to bear a charmed life. He was often in charge of the work, was very active and nothing seemed to daunt him, had fine command of his men and did not spare himself. If there was a danger point, he was right there. He had taken aim and fired at this officer many times, hoping to wound or disable him or even to kill him, but he had never been able to hit him, and he thought he was a pretty good shot too. E.M. looked up and quietly remarked, "So you were the chap that tried to pot me." The look of amazement on Mr. Wheeler's face was ludicrous. "Was it you?" he said. "I guess it was," E.M. replied, "and I thought you were a mighty poor shot not to be able to hit me, but I did not have time to think about it." They shook hands and became warm friends and had many stories to relate on either side of that memorable campaign.

That famous March to the Sea was the last and greatest blow to the Confederacy. Their main source of supply was cut off and Lee's army was narrowed to a small part of Virginia. Sherman really dealt the death blow. His seasoned veterans marched through a defenseless country and laid it to waste. Little was left but the bare land and an occasional home. The Negroes were freed and left their old homes following the army like irresponsible children, the women tugging great bundles of clothing, many of them with babies in their arms. The Exodus was a frenzy with them. "Massa Linkum" had freed them and they were going to him. He was going to give them land and money.[58] They would reveal to the foragers where the family silver was buried and where the contents of the smoke house were hidden.[59] Many plantations were left without a Negro or servant on the place, the mules and horses all confiscated and driven off. The cot-

[58]Sarah Hill's rather unsympathetic comments about the freed slaves are probably a reflection of the changed feelings about the Negroes in the North in the 1880's and 1890's. In those years, following the failure of Reconstruction, the Southern, ex-Confederate states passed the Jim Crow laws with the tacit approval of the North.

[59]Contrary to Mrs. Hill's assertion, historians find the restraint of the freed slaves in not avenging their long sufferings quite remarkable.

ton, sometimes a two year accumulation—ginned and baled ready for shipment, was burned, and if the planter made himself obnoxious and was rebellious, his mansion would be burned to the ground. Many families had to go to the deserted Negro cabins for shelter, the only refuge left them. Railroads were torn up and destroyed beyond repair, great fires being made of the ties, then the iron rails laid on them till they were heated, then twisted and bent till they could never be used. It was a fair country laid waste and despair was the lot of those who dwelt in it. Many unnecessary outrages were committed by the foragers and by irresponsible "bummers" as they were called. Nothing was saved from them. Cherished heirlooms were carried off, and the deserting Negroes often dug up the family silver that they had helped to hide, and carried it with them. Buckets of molasses would be emptied into a piano, costly draperies and rugs taken for horse blankets, priceless china smashed, cups strung on ropes, hung around mule's necks for necklaces and every kind of wanton destruction that could be carried out, was indulged in. The looting was deplorable, and regretted by many of the officers and men, but these were the fortunes of war.

One thing must remain to their credit. I never heard of a woman being assailed or molested and I lived in Georgia right in the path that Sherman's army marched over.

Sherman's army reached Fort McAllister about

December 19th and by the 22nd the news from Sherman reached Fortress Monroe and was telegraphed over the country. Sherman had reached the sea, and was in communication with Washington. Savannah had yet to be taken, but that was a small task for a victorious army to accomplish. The country was wild with joy and acclaimed Sherman as a hero, and gave him a place beside Grant, which he has always retained. Many anxious hearts of waiting women were relieved, especially in the West, and there was great rejoicing.

It was a glad day in our little family and I remarked to Mother that we would have a letter in a day or two. I knew there was a letter for me among those dispatches that had been hurried to Washington. Mother thought not, for mail communication had not been opened and we should have to wait till Savannah was taken. The dispatches sent by Sherman were special and intended for the government, but I was confident. On Christmas morning I received a letter from my soldier. It was written in pencil on a leaf torn from his note-book. It was written while he was on horseback in front of Fort McAllister, while he was under fire with his men. Shot and shell were falling around him, and his horse was very restless under the fire. There were only a few lines and they were almost illegible, with the constant prancing of his horse, but they told us he was safe and well and would write later. That little note came with Gen. Sherman's special dispatches through the kindness of the aide who had charge of the dispatches and who was a friend of E.M.'s. I was certain my man would find a way to send me word of his safety. That was a joyous day for us and we celebrated Christmas with glad and thankful hearts.

In a few days letters came telling of the evacuation of Savannah. E.M.'s regiment had spent Christmas in Savannah. They remained at Savannah for several weeks, and then the march was resumed through the Carolinas. Sherman hoped to reach Virginia in time to take part in the capture of Richmond. It was terrible weather, rain and mud most of the time and their way was through much marshy country where miles of corduroy were built to enable the army to proceed. The Engineers went through incredible hardships at this time, long hours without sleep, and when they could go into camp, they would often wake in the morning lying in pools of water, drenched to the skin. It was a very hard campaign, but they pushed on. There was a pronounced feeling of resentment toward South Carolina and when the army went through that state, they were not sparing in their work of destruction.[60] A number

[60]South Carolina was one of the first states to secede from the Union. It was one of the staunchest supporters of the Confederacy. In fact South Carolina wanted to leave the Union in 1831, thirty years before the Civil War.

On April 12, 1861 the guns of South Carolina opened fire on Fort Sumter to start the hostilities between the South and the North.

of men in the engineer regiment were greatly embittered. They were from Southern Missouri and during Price's raid through that country their homes were destroyed and their wives and parents despoiled, homes burned and the last crust and covering taken and many atrocities committed. These men took reprisals in going through South Carolina, especially at Columbia, where they largely assisted in the conflagration of that beautiful city by throwing bunches of burning cotton into the houses. The names of the engineers who did this were never known.

Amid all the horrors and tragedy of war, there were at times incidents that caused mirth. The following was one that convulsed the men of both sides with laughter. The engineers were to lay the pontoon bridge across a river. On both sides were bluffs and the wagon road was at the foot of the bluff along the bank nearest the Union Army. The Rebels were in some force on the opposite bluff disputing the crossing. The Union men were shelling them to dislodge them so that the bridge could be laid for the army to pass over. Just then an eight mule team and wagon was coming along the road, van of the wagon train. The teamster had to obey a call of nature and left his team and went into a fence corner. Just then the Rebels on the opposite bank spied him and began to pop at him and also to throw some shells. The team became frightened and ran away. The man also became frightened and started to run. He became tangled in his trousers and stumbled, throwing up his hands and gesticulating violently, frantic with fear. The men on both sides of the river saw him and began to shout and yell and the popping of the enemy's guns was kept up. At last he freed himself from his nether garment, flung it on one side and fled down the road in his bare legs and his shirt tail flying, till exhausted, he flung himself down and rolled over and over till he found a fence corner overgrown with weeds, and burrowed into it like a panic stricken rabbit. Meantime, the men on both sides yelled and screamed with laughter. E.M. said it was one of the funniest things he ever saw. The man was not hurt and the soldiers returned to their business. The enemy was dislodged and the engineers proceeded with the job of laying the bridge.

To give a faint idea of what was required of our men during this march a quotation from the History of the Regiment will come in place here.

"For many days, owing to the wearing out of the roads, they were mostly corduroy, camp was reached late—at 10 and 12 and sometimes after one o'clock at night. The next morning the call was frequently at 3 and 4 A.M., oftentimes giving but three or four hours in camp to eat and sleep, and nineteen and twenty hours on the march. The temper was frequently tried, especially in bad weather."

In Savannah several of the officers resigned, and a number of the men were discharged and returned to their homes. This reduced the Engineers still more in number. They realized that the war would soon be over and their work was now almost completed and they were anxious to return to their families. E.M. applied for a furlough to Gen. Howard who was his commanding general. The general refused to grant it. E.M. very much desired to be at home and I was very anxious to have him come and could not understand why his request was not granted. Only once during his almost four years of active service had he been granted a furlough, and that was a sick leave after the capture of Island No. 10. Finally one night he went to the general's quarters and asked for a private interview which was readily granted, for they knew each other well and were friendly. E.M. urged his case and asked why he could not be permitted to go. The general was most kind and said many complimentary things to him. He spoke of the coming campaign and what would be required of the Engineers and of the shortness of their force. Gen. Howard said that neither Col. Tweedale nor he could be spared. It was absolutely necessary that he should remain on duty. Then E.M. gave his reasons for being so insistent, that he desired to be with his wife during her approaching confinement, that she was far from well and had endured much during the past months of suspense, to give her courage for the hour of her trial. Poor E.M. pleaded with him and begged him to let him go. The good general was considerably affected, and showed much sympathy, but did not yield. They talked man to man, and E.M. who was always so reserved and reticent, bared his heart to Gen. Howard as he rarely did to anyone, and showed the depth of affection he had for his wife.

Finally, the general said, "Major, you are a Christian. You believe in God's goodness and protection; let us take it to Him. He can take care of your wife better than you or I can. Let us ask his blessing on the brave little woman who is patiently waiting for the coming of the little one that is going to be a blessing to both of you. Let us pray over it." The two men knelt in that dimly lighted room and the Christian general prayed long and fervently for the woman who was little more than a girl, far away in her Northern home, and for the husband, whose first duty at this time was to his country; that He would give him courage and patience to go on the way appointed for him. When they rose from their knees, tears were on the cheeks of both men and they were greatly affected. They grasped each other's hands in a warm clasp, and the general said, "Major, if I could grant your request, I would, but we will have to leave the matter with our Heavenly Father, who is able to care for and protect your wife. Be of good cheer. All will go well with her." E.M. returned to his quarters and spent the rest of the night writing to that loved wife. It was a wonderful letter, and it brought such a sense of peace and resignation to my soul. All fear and anxiety left me, and I felt that all would be well with me. E.M.

said he never heard such a prayer. The general seemed inspired, and talked as though in the presence of the living God, and he felt sure the petition would be answered, and it was, for E.M.'s apprehension left him and a serenity and confidence came to him that he had not felt for months. Ever after that the good general was very close and dear to us. He was truly a consistent Christian.

On a cold wintry morning in February, 1865, our little daughter was born. She was a fine healthy child and thrived from the first and Gen. Howard's prophecy regarding her has been fulfilled, for she surely has been a blessing. Is it any wonder that she more closely resembles her father in feature, character and disposition than any of his other children, when you consider the circumstances under which she was born. Her father, in those long months before her birth was never absent from my thoughts, and while telepathy, psychology, thought transference, and all those other new theories were not thought of then, yet there were many times in the silent watches of the night when I would sit by my window sleepless and brooding. My mind or soul would go out to his and I would feel that he was very near me, and that we were in communion with each other.

Telegraphic communication was impossible and it was weeks before E.M. received Mother's letter telling of the baby's birth and my well-doing. The regiment reached North Carolina after the march through South Carolina, and when the message finally reached him, they were at Goldsborough. He immediately took the letter over to Gen. Howard and they rejoiced together. The general congratulated him on his little daughter, and E.M. wrote that it was the first happy moment he had experienced in many months. He was very proud and happy over the news and there was quite a little celebration that night over the event, among the friends whom I had known the previous summer while in Tennessee. And now we settled down to wait for the end of the war, which was fast approaching, before seeing each other again.

A rather singular circumstance happened during that winter which was always an unsolved puzzle, but which I have never laid great stress on for I am not a believer in the mysterious or occult. One evening I received a call from Dr. Knower, who was then living in St. Louis, practicing medicine. I was not going out or seeing anyone outside the family, but he very much wanted to see me and I received him. I thought it strange he did not bring his wife for we were very good friends, but thought he might have some message for me from E.M. We talked and talked about mutual friends and the previous summer, and I wondered what he had come for and was a little embarrassed, and he seemed to grow so too. About ten o'clock, time to go home, he said, "Well, Mrs. Hill, what can I do for you?" I looked at him in amazement and asked him what he meant. He replied, "Didn't you send for me?" "No. I had not thought of doing so." Then he explained that a man had come into his office that afternoon and asked him to come and see me that evening. I asked him if he knew the man, and he replied he had never seen him before and supposed he was some relative, for he gave my address and said I was living with my mother. The doctor asked him his name and he said, "George Full." I jumped at that. "Why doctor, are you sure?" "Yes," he said, "Very sure, for it was such a peculiar name I asked him again and he repeated 'George Full,' and seemed very anxious and worried and I thought from his manner, you must be ill so I promised to come and see you this evening." "Doctor, do you know that George Full is the name of my father, and he has been dead and in Bellefontaine cemetery for three and a half years?" We were both bewildered and aghast. I asked him to describe the man and he said he was a man of middle age between fifty and sixty, clean shaven face, blue eyes, was rather thin and of medium build. "In fact, Mrs. Hill, you very much resemble him and that was why I thought him a relative." That was my father's description, and we gazed at each other in some consternation. At last I said it surely could not be a joke. He thought not. The man seemed so evidently in earnest and very anxious, and his age and manner would preclude the idea of a practical joke. I knew the doctor was such an earnest serious-minded man who never joked and was always honest and upright. I told him it seemed as though my father had been to see him, because he was a friend, but it was all beyond me. I did not understand it. Neither did he, and it has always remained an unsolved puzzle, one of the things past finding out. It left a deep impression on my mind and I thought much about it for a while. Of course I explained to the doctor I had not sent for him and was as much confused about the matter as he was. He made considerable effort to trace the man, but never saw or heard of him again. There was no George Full in the directory and no one of the name of Full in St. Louis except my mother and her family. It was very mysterious and I tell of it here because it was so unusual.

When the baby was a week old we received a message from my sister in Vicksburg telling us of the death of her husband, E.M.'s brother Elihu, caused by consumption contracted while he was in the army. She was bringing him to St. Louis to lay him in the Bellefontaine cemetery. They reached St. Louis about February 20, and the funeral was from our house. My recovery was very slow and there was much grief and sorrow in our little family, and we all mourned with the young sister and her baby girl who had been so sadly bereft, and who had been so alone in her bereavement.

Letters came frequently from my soldier and we knew he was safe and well and that the Engineers were still effective in their work and that the army was making its way towards Richmond. My sister returned to Vicksburg to settle up her husband's affairs and left her little girl with us. Then in April came the fall of Richmond and the surrender of Gen. Lee at Appomattox, and the North went wild with joy, still I could not help having a feeling of sorrow for Gen. Lee.

Our boys in North Carolina were now hastening North and made some record marches. The Engineer regiment arrived at Manchester opposite Richmond, Virginia, on May 9, 1865, crossed the river and marched through Richmond May 11th. They arrived at Alexandria in sight of Washington May 19th. They took part in the grand review of Gen. Sherman's army, May 24th, and remained in Washington until June 4th. In the march from Raleigh, North Carolina, to Washington, some very rapid marching had been done. At one time, they marched with the pontoon trains of sixty wagons, forty-four miles within twenty-four hours.

Another quotation from the History may here be in place:

> "The campaign in the Carolinas may be called the climax of this colossal war. The movement of Sherman, which commenced on May 1, 1864, and ended with the surrender of Johnson's army and all the Confederate forces from the Chattahoochee to the Potomac on April 26, 1865, extending through almost an entire year, was but one campaign, was but the carrying out of the plan of Sherman when he marched from Chattanooga—a campaign that has no parallel in the annals of history."

Some of the results of this campaign were fourteen cities captured, hundreds of miles of railroad track destroyed, thousands of cotton bales burned, eighty-five cannon taken, four thousand prisoners and twenty-five thousand animals. It was truly a conquering and never defeated army! But think of the ruin, poverty, and desolation left in its wake. Sure, Gen. Sherman knew what he was talking about when he said, "War is hell."

The grand review of Sherman's army took place at Washington May 24, 1865, and was a proud and culminating event to the men who had marched and fought over a thousand miles through the heart of the enemy's country, who had so crippled the enemy's resources that there was nothing left for them but surrender. Sherman's men were well aware of what their march had accomplished, and as they swung up Pennsylvania Avenue, with their free and easy stride learned in their long marches, it was with a satisfied air of proud accomplishment. They were ragged, unkempt, and travel worn, and certainly looked the name that had been given them in derision, Sherman's "Bummers" and "Do-boys." They were reviewed just as they had marched through Georgia and the Carolinas, a sturdy set of seasoned and war-worn veterans, who felt invincible, for they were a never defeated army. They had accomplished so much. The Missouri Engineers were a small part of this grand army, yet they had contributed their share toward the success of the colossal undertaking, and as they marched up the Avenue past the reviewing stand, they were loudly cheered. E.M. as he rode at the head of his men on his great gray horse, Snorter, that had borne him so many hundred miles, was a very proud and happy man. Mrs. Stanton called him to the reviewing stand and presented him with a beautiful bouquet of flowers, which he carefully preserved and then brought home to me, and which we kept for many years till only the dust remained. Many marks of appreciation were shown the men, for they were all heroes, and much jealousy evinced by the Potomac soldiers over "the fuss made" as they expressed it, "of Sherman's bummers."

After the review, much friction developed between the army of the Potomac and Sherman's army, and several personal encounters took place regarding the achievements of the two armies. Sherman's men certainly carried a "chip on their shoulder," inviting some of the Potomac "fellers" to knock it off. As one of the men told me, they felt decidedly "cocky," and weren't going to take anything out of the "fellers" they had pulled out of a hole. After the review, Col. Tweedale left for his home and E.M. was appointed the Lieutenant Colonel in his place, for E.M. had decided to remain with the remnant of his regiment till they were mustered out. Most of the Western army was ordered to Louisville, Kentucky, and our regiment left Washington June 9th, and reached Louisville and went into camp there awaiting orders for their disbanding. E.M. had very much desired that I should meet him in Washington and see the review, and share in the entertaining and the many nice attentions shown the officers, but my young baby came first this time, and I quietly remained at home with her, and waited for him to come to me. The waiting would not be long now. It had been ten months since he had bade me good by that August morning at Nashville, and our baby girl was four months old and had never seen her father.

After reaching Louisville and seeing his men settled in camp, for it would take some time for the final preliminaries to be gone through with, there was a large amount of property to be turned over to the government, and much "red tape" to be untied, E.M. applied for a leave of absence, and at last he was allowed a week's leave. He came flying home to St. Louis, and it surely was a happy meeting for all of us, too sacred to say much about. He was like a boy with the baby, and could hardly bear to have her out of his sight. Although he was almost the first man she had seen, she took to him at once and cuddled her little head into his neck. He would gaze at her till his eyes would fill, and he would gather her to him with a world of love and tenderness in his embrace. That was a very happy week. It was an end to all the suspense and anxiety as regarded ourselves. My soldier looked so well, lean and brown and toughened with his experiences during the past year. At the end of the week in which he had scarcely left us for an hour, he returned to his duties at Louisville, but we knew it was only for a short time till he would be home.

The Southern prisons were being emptied and our poor men who had been confined in them were sent as fast as possible to their homes. Many of them were taken to Vicksburg from Andersonville and sent North on steamboats to St. Louis. It was about this time that the *Sultana*, a large steamboat with over three thousand returning prisoners on board, was blown up at Memphis and twelve hundred lives lost. The survivors were placed on other boats and sent up the river to St. Louis. The Soldiers' Aid Society was still in existence and a committee of women of which I was one, went to the boat landing to meet them and serve them with soup and coffee and refreshments, for we knew in their journey up the river they had suffered untold hardships, many being rescued from drowning and many badly injured. When the boats tied up and the men began coming off, and we saw what the South had sent back to us from their prison pens, a groan of horror broke from us, and even after the lapse of almost half a century, the thrill of horror goes through me as I recall those poor creatures, hardly the semblance of men, just spectres and wraiths. It broke our hearts and for a few moments we were overcome and wept in grief and rage. Words cannot express the horrors of their condition, poor starved diseased creatures, and then when home and freedom were in sight, to be drowned, slaughtered and slain in so terrible a manner. It was all too horrible. I have always held that against the South, the treatment of Yankee prisoners, and to this day my heart burns with resentment. When memory recalls the scenes of that time, when we welcomed the return of our poor boys who had been the real martyrs, for many of them there was little left in life, when I thought of the stalwart brave strong boys I had seen march away four years before, and saw how they came back to us, my heart filled to bursting, and it has remained a nightmare in my memory.

Many regiments, or what was left of them, were returning and going out to Benton Barracks to be discharged. Four years before I had watched the Eighth Wisconsin march by our house on their way to the front, so gay and certain of success, a magnificent body of young men, many of them beardless youths, but fine specimens of American manhood, clean and wholesome looking, full of enthusiasm and eager for the fray. Their band playing, banners flying, and Old Baldy, their war eagle, on his perch carried beside the flag, they greeted us as they passed, for we had flags waving and words of good cheer for them which was not a usual occurrence in St. Louis at that time, and they shouted they would soon be back, for the war would not be long. The next time I saw them was in the review at Vicksburg after the surrender of Gen. Pemberton. There were fewer of them. They were stern lipped, grim visaged men and they marched grave and serious, their battle flag torn and bullet-riddled, but Old Baldy was still on his perch. When his regiment was engaged in a battle he would soar aloft with wild screams as though urging them on, and after the engagement would return to his perch. The last time I saw this famous regiment there were just a handful of men marching by, war worn veterans. Their flag was torn and tattered and stained with the life blood of the noble men who had given up their lives in defense of it, and Old Baldy was still there and he looked tired and war worn, too. He clung to his perch, but his wings drooped and head hung down and he had lost the fierce aggressive look of four years before.

Then, too, there was the Sixth Iowa that made a distinguished and enviable record for itself. Iowa was settled by a very fine class of pioneers, intelligent and superior men, and the state had sent the best of its sons in response to the President's call for volunteers. The Sixth Iowa was made up of young men; strong, stalwart, and of invincible courage. Its commander, Major, afterwards Colonel and General, Corse, had perfect command of his men. He was very small physically, in fact, I believe was the smallest man in his regiment, but he was a giant in intellectual attainments, in courage and ability, tenacious as a bulldog and full of resources. He proved his efficiency in many trying and doubtful positions and greatly distinguished himself in the campaign with Sherman from Chattanooga to Atlanta. I speak of these two regiments because they were typical of the material that composed the most of the Western Army, and also because of their distinguished record, and then too I knew many of the officers and men and always followed their career with interest.

Daily now regiments were arriving and going out to Benton Barracks. They marched out on the street within a half block of our house and we were greatly impressed in noting the difference in the return of our men. Grim and quiet they marched, no bands playing, an occasional shrill fife and drum, and those were but few. All the gay military trappings conspicuous by their absence, but the work they started out to do was successfully completed. Our country was saved and was one, undivided, and they had given the best years of their manhood to accomplish it.

E.M. had written me the Engineers were to go to Benton Barracks for their discharge, but he hardly knew when. They were very busy turning over the U.S. property to the government, and closing all accounts. He had received his commission as lieutenant colonel and been mustered in. Also, he had received his commission as colonel, but could not be mustered out as such. There was no longer a full regiment and he supposed the colonel's commission was in the nature of a reward of merit. Still it was gratifying to have that recognition of past services.

At last, E.M. wrote that they were starting for home, and we watched and waited. One hot morning on July 22nd, we were sitting on the shady stoop with my two babies. Soon we heard shouts and cheers and a band of soldiers was marching by on the street at the end of our block. Something about them looked familiar, and I remarked to Mother they looked like the Engineer boys. Just then an officer on horseback left the ranks and came galloping down the street. Georgie shrilled, "Why that's Snorter. That's my Papa's horse. Why that's my Papa," and out he rushed to meet him. We hardly knew E.M. He was in full dress uniform. The trappings of his horse were so gay, so unlike what George and I were accustomed to when he was on active duty. But the boys were all going in full dress marching uniforms to be mustered out. E.M. could not refrain from coming to us for a minute as he rode by, and greeted us all joyfully, then rejoined his men.

That evening my soldier came home to me, unbuckled his sword, laid off his uniform, his work for his country completed after four years of faithful service. He was just plain citizen Hill once more. The war was over and we were ready to begin life anew.

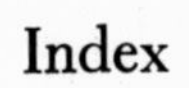

Index

INDEX

Anderson, Robert, Major 5n
Andersonville Prison, 330–1
Arsenal, St. Louis, xxxi, 10, 13
Atlanta, Georgia, 301, 303–4, 307
Augusta, Georgia, 312

Bates, Edward, Judge, 21, 21n
Battle of Belmont, 48, 48n
Battle of Bull Run, 25, 167n
Battle of Chancellorsville, 105, 105n
Battle of Chickamauga, 113n
Battle of Corinth, 92, 92n, 93, 97, 100, 107–8, 201
Battle of Fredericksburg, 105, 105n
Battle of Gaines Mills, 105
Battle of Gettysburg, 166, 166n, 167, 167n
Battle of Jonesboro, 302
Battle of Malvern Hill, 105, 105n
Battle of Shiloh (Pittsburg Landing) 92–3, 93n, 94, 97–8, 167n
Battle of Springfield, 52
Bell, John, xxvii, 4, 4n
Benton Barracks, 31, 33–4, 40, 331, 333
Benton, Jessie, 47n
Benton, Thomas Hart, 47n
Berkeley, Dr., 60, 63
Bissell, William H., 25, 25n, 26, 29, 32, 67–8, 84, 91–2, 125, 160, 168, 219, 220
Blair, Frank, Jr., xxxii, xxxiv, 10n, 18, 18n, 25, 31, 47n
Booth, John Wilkes, xxxv, xliii, 225, 230–1, 231n
Bragg, Braxton, General, 107n
Breckinridge, John, xxvii
Buell, Don Carlos, General, 107, 107n

Burnside, Ambrose E., General, 105n
Butler, Ben, General, 142n, 254, 254n

Cairo, Illinois, 44, 109, 114, 117, 120, 148–9, 168
Camp Jackson, xxxii, 9n, 10, 10n
Carondelet, Missouri, 9, 9n, 154, 180, 199
Centenary Methodist Church, St. Louis, 17
Chattanooga, Tennessee, 305
Churchill, Winston, 13
Cincinnati, Ohio, 116–7
Civil War, xxiii, xxxiii, 47n, 93n, 278n, 317n
Columbus, Kentucky, 64, 70, 120
Confederacy, xxiii, xxv, 22n, 93, 133, 164, 166
Connecticut, 104
Corps of Engineers, xxiii, xxviii, xxxv, 25, 43, 65–6, 70, 70n, 85, 91–2, 97, 158–62, 168, 171, 199, 291–2, 317–8, 327
Cozzens, Phebe, 51, 60, 93–4, 154
Crescent City, 109, 147
Cullom, George Washington, General, 66, 66n, 67–8
Cumberland River, 207, 278

Davis, Jefferson, xxxi
Dayton, Ohio, 98–103, 115–7, 126, 301
Douglas, Stephen, xxvi

Eads Bridge, St. Louis, 203, 203n, 278
Eighth Street M. E. Church, St. Louis, 21
England, xxiii
Everett, Edward, 4n

Flad, Lieutenant Colonel, 171; promoted to Colonel, 195; 197, 208, 278, 289
Foote, Commodore, 84–5
Forrest, Nathaniel B., General, xxxv, xxxix, xl, 127n, 128–9, 129n, 131, 134, 136–9, 266, 267n, 269, 272–3

Fort Donelson, xl, 51, 69, 69n, 77
Fort Henry, 69
Fort McAlllister, 315
Fort Sumter, xxxi, 3, 5n
Fort Thompson, 92
Fortress Monroe, 316
Frémont, John, General, xxvi, xxxiii, 25, 44, 47, 47n
Frost, D. M., Commander, xxxii, 10, 10n, 14
Full, Gina, 40

Galt House, 211–2, 301
Georgia, 167n, 307, 312
Germans, xxvii, xxviii, xxxiv, 6n, 17–8
Gettysburg, Pennsylvania, (See Battle of Gettysburg)
Gordon, Mr., 210–6
Grant, Ulysses S., General, xxxiii, xxxv, xxxvi, xxxviii, 48, 48n, 69, 92n, 93n, 115, 119, 125, 128, 137, 142, 161–5, 165n, 166, 167n, 213, 215–6, 219–22
Griffith, Captain, 29

Halleck, H. W., General, 66n
Hamburg, Tennessee, 97, 107
Harpeth Valley, 285
Highgate, Vermont, xxiii, xxviii, 104
Hill, Eben Marvin (E. M.), xxiii, xxviii, 3, 4; narrow escape, 14, 17; joins Union Army, xxviii, 22, 25, 26, 29; Captain, 30, 32; 34–5; in New Madrid, 70, 79, 83–4; 92, 97–8, 100, 102–3, 106–9, 113–5; illness, 116, 120–8; 146–7, 162–3, 167, 172, 177–8, 180, 187; promoted to Major, 196; 197, 207, 224–5, 245–7, 252, 256; at Waverly camp, 258–68; injured, 274–7, 288–9, 292–4; 317, 329
Hill, Elihu, xl, 116, 120, 120n, 121–3, 129–31, 134–6, 138, 143, 325
Hill, George (Georgie), xxiv, 103, 115–24, 126, 147, 171, 178, 180, 199, 209–10, 214–5, 221–4, 226, 249, 259, 262–4, 290, 296, 334

Hill, Sarah Jane Full, xxiii, xxiv, xxxiii; her personality, xlv, xlvi; on events in St. Louis, 9–18; works for sanitary commission, 50–6, 162; travels to Dayton, 98–100; meets Gen. Forrest, 136–8; meets Grant, 215–6, 219–22; at Waverly camp, 232–66; meets Andrew Johnson, 278–80, 280n, 283–4, 284n
Holly Springs, Mississippi, 125, 127, 127n, 142
Home Guards, xxxi, 6, 10n, 14, 18
Hood, John B., General, 273, 273n, 287, 303, 308
Hooker, Joseph, General, 105n
Howard, O. O., General, 302, 302n, 320–3
Howard University, 302n
Hunter, David, General, 47n

Illinois, 47, 55, 113, 203
Island No. 10, 70, 70n, 79n, 84, 91, 98, 106–9, 113, 160, 320

Jackson, Claiborne, Governor, xxvii, xxxiii, 6n
Jackson, Tennessee, 109, 113–4, 117, 128, 142, 144
Jim Crow Laws, xliv, 314n
Johnson, Andrew, Governor, xxxv, xlii, xliii, 278, 278n, 279–80, 280n, 283–4, 284n
Johnson City, Tennessee, xliii, 277–8, 278n, 289, 292

Kansas, xxv
Keeling, William, Captain, 102
Kempin, Mrs., 13
Kentucky, xxv, xxvi
Kingston Springs, Tennessee, xlv, 289, 292, 294, 300
Knower, Dr., 109, 191, 250–1, 274, 283, 289, 295, 323–5
Ku Klux Klan, xxxix, xli, 129n

Lafayette Park, St. Louis, 26, 31
Lamine, Missouri, 34, 43, 49, 68, 70
Lee, Robert E., General, xxxv, 69, 166

Lincoln, Abraham, xxv, xxvi, xxxi, 4, 6n, 47n, 113n, 159n, 165n, 166, 254n, 280, 284
Little Egypt, Illinois, xxv
Louisville and Nashville Railroad, xxxv, 207
Louisville, Kentucky, 211, 300-1, 330
Lyon, Nathaniel, Captain, xxxi, xxxii, 10, 10n, 13, 13n, 18, 52, 52n

Maryland, xxv
Mason, Chaplain, 211-6, 219, 222-5
McMurray, Captain, 147-8
McPherson, James B., General, 177, 191, 191n, 192, 304
Medical Corps, 50
Memphis, Tennessee, 106, 109, 117, 143-4, 146, 202
Mercantile Library Hall, St. Louis, 60, 63
Miami River, 101
Millikens Bend, 175
Mississippi River, xxv, 44, 70, 79, 92, 106, 108, 153, 161, 164, 203, 278
Missouri, xxv, xxvi, xxviii, 4n, 5-6, 10, 44, 59, 77, 272
Missouri Republican, xxvii
Morris, Frank, Reverend, 64, 219
Morris, J. N., xxxix
Mower, John, General, 198, 198n

Nashville and Northwestern Railroad 291n, 292
Nashville, Tennessee, xxxv, xliii, 115, 202, 207-10, 214, 222, 225, 251, 269, 277, 290, 297, 299, 300
Negroes, 78, 158, 182, 230, 251, 254, 254n, 265, 279-80, 288, 314, 314n
Nevins, Allan, xxxii, 5n
New England, 106
New Madrid, Missouri, 70, 78-9, 79n, 83-5, 98, 100, 108, 287
New Orleans, Louisiana, 142n, 172, 175, 181, 192

New York, 115
North Carolina, 326

Ohio River, 92
Otterville, Missouri, 43–4

Palmer, John M., Colonel, xxxvi, 109, 113, 113n, 211, 213–4
Parker, Lieutenant, 108–9
Parker, Mrs., 109
Pemberton, John, General, 163, 163n, 331
Pittsburg Landing, (See Battle of Shiloh)
Polk, Leonidas, General, xxxiii
Pope, John, General, 70n, 78, 79n, 84–5, 91–3, 107, 113, 119, 125
Price, Sterling, General, 22, 22n, 33–4, 44, 77
Pulaski, Tennessee, xxxix, 129n

Queen of the West, 172, 175, 177

Richmond, Virginia, 326
Rosecrans, General, 287

St. Cloud Hotel, Nashville, 221, 270
St. George Episcopal Church, St. Louis, 60
St. Louis and Cincinnati Railroad, 148
St. Louis, Missouri, xxiii, xxiv, xxv, xxvi, xxviii, xxxi, 18, 29, 34, 48, 59, 63, 93, 97, 99, 114, 116, 128, 148–9, 151, 171, 188–9, 198–9, 203, 301, 325, 329
Sam Young, 161
Sanitary Commission, St. Louis, 50, 93, 152–4, 162
Savannah, Georgia, 317, 319
Schurz, Carl, General, xxxi, 9, 9n
Sedalia, Missouri, 44
Sherman, William Tecumseh, General, xxxiii, 162, 167, 167n, 177, 184, 196, 213, 303–4, 307–9, 314–5, 327

Sickles, Daniel, General, 278, 279n
Sigel, Franz, General, xxxi, xxxiv, 9, 9n
Soldiers' Aid Society, St. Louis, 49–50, 59, 93, 98, 151–3, 330
South Carolina, 317, 317n, 318, 323
Springfield, Illinois, xxxii
Stanton, Edwin, 165n, 254n

Tennessee, 93n
Tennessee River, 207–8
Texas, 198
Thomas, George H., General, 287, 287n, 308
Thompson, Charles, Lieutenant, 29–30, 33, 79, 83
Trenton, Tennessee, xxiv, xxxix, xl, 116–7, 119–20, 267n, 269
Turnervereinen, xxxi
Twain, Mark, xxxix
Tweedale, Major, 168, 195, 208, 307, 320

Vermont, xxiii, 70, 102, 104, 115
Vicksburg, Mississippi, 128, 143–4, 158, 159n, 160–1, 165, 165n, 166–8, 171–2, 175–6, 186, 189, 222, 331
Virginia, 179, 314

War Department, 165, 165n
Washington, D.C., 327, 329
Waverly, Tennessee, 232, 249, 258, 285, 294
West Point, New York, 48, 85, 107n, 167n, 198, 302n
Wheeler, General, 313

Yates, Richard, Governor, xxxii, xxxiii
Yeatman, Mr., 152
Young's Point, Louisiana, 158–60, 176

Zagonyi, Charles, Colonel, 52n

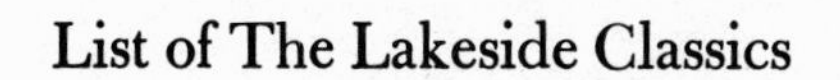

List of The Lakeside Classics

The Lakeside Classics

Number	*Title*	*Year*
1.	The Autobiography of Benjamin Franklin . . .	1903
2.	Inaugural Addresses of the Presidents of the United States from Washington to Lincoln . .	1904
3.	Inaugural Addresses of the Presidents of the United States from A. Johnson to T. Roosevelt	1905
4.	Fruits of Solitude by William Penn	1906
5.	Memorable American Speeches I. The Colonial Period	1907
6.	Memorable American Speeches II. Democracy and Nationality	1908
7.	Memorable American Speeches III. Slavery	1909
8.	Memorable American Speeches IV. Secession, War, Reconstruction	1910
9.	The Autobiography of Gurdon Saltonstall Hubbard	1911
10.	Reminiscences of Early Chicago	1912
11.	Reminiscences of Chicago During the Forties and Fifties	1913
12.	Reminiscences of Chicago During the Civil War .	1914
13.	Reminiscences of Chicago During the Great Fire .	1915
14.	Life of Black Hawk	1916
15.	The Indian Captivity of O. M. Spencer	1917
16.	Pictures of Illinois One Hundred Years Ago . .	1918
17.	A Woman's Story of Pioneer Illinois by Christiana Holmes Tillson	1919
18.	The Conquest of the Illinois by George Rogers Clark	1920

Number	*Title*	*Year*
19.	Alexander Henry's Travels and Adventures in the Years 1760–1776	1921
20.	John Long's Voyages and Travels in the Years 1768–1788	1922
21.	Adventures of the First Settlers on the Oregon or Columbia River by Alexander Ross	1923
22.	The Fur Hunters of the Far West by Alexander Ross	1924
23.	The Southwestern Expedition of Zebulon M. Pike	1925
24.	Commerce of the Prairies by Josiah Gregg	1926
25.	Death Valley in '49 by William L. Manly	1927
26.	Bidwell's Echoes of the Past—Steele's In Camp and Cabin	1928
27.	Kendall's Texan Santa Fe Expedition	1929
28.	Pattie's Personal Narrative	1930
29.	Alexander Mackenzie's Voyage to the Pacific Ocean in 1793	1931
30.	Wau-Bun, The "Early Day" in the North-West by Mrs. John H. Kinzie	1932
31.	Forty Years a Fur Trader by Charles Larpenteur	1933
32.	Narrative of the Adventures of Zenas Leonard	1934
33.	Kit Carson's Autobiography	1935
34.	A True Picture of Emigration by Rebecca Burlend	1936
35.	The Bark Covered House by William Nowlin	1937
36.	The Border and the Buffalo by John R. Cook	1938
37.	Vanished Arizona by Martha Summerhayes	1939
38.	War on the Detroit by Thomas Verchères de Boucherville and James Foster	1940
39.	Army Life in Dakota by De Trobriand	1941

Number	*Title*	*Year*
40.	The Early Day of Rock Island and Davenport by J. W. Spencer and J. M. D. Burrows	1942
41.	Six Years with the Texas Rangers by James B. Gillett	1943
42.	Growing Up with Southern Illinois by Daniel Harmon Brush	1944
43.	A History of Illinois, Vol. I, by Gov. Thomas Ford	1945
44.	A History of Illinois, Vol. II, by Gov. Thomas Ford	1946
45.	The Western Country in the 17th Century by Lamothe Cadillac and Pierre Liette	1947
46.	Across the Plains in Forty-nine by Reuben Cole Shaw	1948
47.	Pictures of Gold Rush California by various authors	1949
48.	Absaraka, Home of the Crows by Mrs. Margaret I. Carrington	1950
49.	The Truth about Geronimo by Britton Davis	1951
50.	My Life on the Plains by General George A. Custer	1952
51.	Three Years Among the Indians and Mexicans by General Thomas James	1953
52.	A Voyage to the Northwest Coast of America by Gabriel Franchère	1954
53.	War-Path and Bivouac by John F. Finerty	1955
54.	Milford's Memoir by Louis Leclerc de Milford	1956
55.	Uncle Dick Wootton by Howard Louis Conard	1957
56.	The Siege of Detroit in 1763	1958
57.	Among the Indians by Henry A. Boller	1959
58.	Hardtack and Coffee by John D. Billings	1960

Number	*Title*	*Year*
59.	Outlines from the Outpost by John Esten Cooke	1961
60.	Colorado Volunteers in New Mexico, 1862 by Ovando J. Hollister	1962
61.	Private Smith's Journal	1963
62.	Two Views of Gettysburg by Sir A. J. L. Fremantle and Frank Haskell	1964
63.	Dakota War Whoop by Harriet E. Bishop McConkey	1965
64.	Honolulu by Laura Fish Judd	1966
65.	Three Years in the Klondike by Jeremiah Lynch	1967
66.	Two Years' Residence on the English Prairie of Illinois by John Woods	1968
67.	John D. Young and the Colorado Gold Rush	1969
68.	My Experiences in the West by John S. Collins	1970
69.	Narratives of Colonial America, 1704–1765 by various authors	1971
70.	Pioneers by Noah Harris Letts and Thomas Allen Banning, 1825–1865	1972
71.	Excursion Through America by Nicolaus Mohr	1973
72.	A Frenchman in Lincoln's America, Volume I, by Ernest Duvergier de Hauranne	1974
73.	A Frenchman in Lincoln's America, Volume II, by Ernest Duvergier de Hauranne	1975
74.	Narratives of the American Revolution by various authors	1976
75.	Advocates and Adversaries by Robert R. Rose	1977
76.	Hell among the Yearlings by Edmund Randolph	1978
77.	A Frontier Doctor by Henry F. Hoyt	1979
78.	Mrs. Hill's Journal – Civil War Reminiscences by Sarah Jane Full Hill	1980

HERMANN HESSE

Modern Literature Monographs

HERMANN HESSE

Franz Baumer

Translated by JOHN CONWAY

Frederick Ungar Publishing Co.
New York

Published by special arrangement with Colloquium Verlag, Berlin, publishers of the original German *Hermann Hesse*.

Second Printing, 1970

Printed in the United States of America
Library of Congress Catalog Number: 68–31446
Standard Book Number: 8044–2027–0

With Hesse what is moderate is not the emotion or the thought, but solely its expression. And the thing that moderates the expression is an exquisite feeling for the seemly, the reserved, the harmonious and, in cosmic terms, the interdependence of things. It is a restrained irony which I believe very few Germans capable of. The absolute lack of this irony so often spoils for me the works of many of their authors who take themselves so terribly seriously.

—André Gide

Contents

1	*Meeting in Montagnola*	1
2	*Origins and Youth*	17
3	*Beginnings*	35
4	*A Look into Chaos*	47
5	*Magic Garden in Ticino*	61
6	*The Romantic and the Realist*	89
7	*The New Consciousness*	105
	Bibliography	115

1

Meeting in Montagnola

Let us suppose that about a decade ago, when Hermann Hesse was in his eighties, somebody who was curious had not let himself be intimidated by Hesse's aversion to visitors. By inquiry he has made his way through the Ticino mountain village of Montagnola to the almost hidden path that is supposed to lead him to the object of his curiosity. After a short distance, beyond the last rows of village houses, he is in the midst of a meadowy slope high above the Lake of Lugano when he halts perplexed. Without having achieved his purpose, he thinks of turning back. Then, from the stone post of an unmarked garden entrance, the glaring white of a freshly limed surface catches his eye. As he draws closer, the power of the black hand-painted letters increases, and our curious visitor, close to his goal, encounters his last—let us hope he finds it insurmountable—obstacle: NO VISITS, PLEASE.

He can console himself with the thought that many others before him have looked at this sign and respected the wish of the invisible house's invisible owner. Perhaps he would tread the return path with less disappointment if he knew that even a colleague and friend of Hesse had had the same experience. It was after the war, and the imperative request was at that time on a plain wooden board. The visiting colleague, seeing it, is supposed to have written beneath, "Well, some other time. Yours, Thomas Mann." So at least goes the rumor, but we need not believe it. Thomas Mann often visited Hesse in Montagnola.

If the intruder is thick-skinned and disinclined to understand the inscription on the gate, another solemn admonition awaits him on the door of the carmine-red house, the Casa Rossa. It is a yellowed sheet of paper on which are typed the words of Meng Hsieh:

When one has grown old and his work is done, it is his right in stillness to make friends with death.

He does not need men. He knows them; he has seen enough of them. What he needs is quiet.

It is not becoming to seek out such a man, to accost him, to plague him with chatter.

The seemly thing is to pass by the gate of his dwelling, as if no one lived there.

The words of the old Chinese sage pertain to someone who has done his share in life, and Hesse in all modesty may claim them for himself. His extraordinarily copious work, which includes all forms of prose—novels and stories, fairy tales, letters, critical essays on literature and culture, book reviews, articles, diaries, and dialogues as well as lyric poetry—has exerted on three generations of readers an attraction that does not age. The man with the narrow birdlike face and clear blue eyes whose diagnostic look in 1959 was as sharp as ever—this man has also made his contribution as editor and collaborator on various periodicals, as editor of numerous works of literature, as adviser for prisoners of war in World War I, and, not least, as one who constantly spoke out for peace, a warner, seismograph, and critic of

his time. As such he has again and again been reviled or systematically ignored by the official German world.

And yet it was not the bitterness of one who is aggrieved that led Hesse since 1945 to withdraw still more than before and to barricade himself behind such solemn phrases. The words of Meng Hsieh conceal irony and a deeper meaning. Irony always hovers between the call of life and the knowledge of transiency and death. So Hesse engaged in his mockery of those who were too importunate, whom he evaded in the role of "nobody." But he also practiced a concealed mockery of himself by making features of his own life interchangeable with those of the Chinese sage. He thereby gained the spiritual detachment that is the only way to accomplish the earnest task of "making friends with death."

Thomas Mann—if indeed it was he who complied with the request (surely not meant to include him) that was posted at the garden gate—certainly did not write his reply only because he succumbed to the unconquerable urge of the man of irony who enjoyed the opportunity to slip into the role of an intimidated stranger. This metaphysician of exchanging roles, for whom irony was the pathos of the middle ground between the command to live and sympathy with death, had—with those few words of his—merely proclaimed in his own way a colleague's respect for the friend's life law that consists of self-realization and need for solitude.

One person who got to see the author more

easily than any stranger was an old woman of the village with whom he conversed across the fence at the hawthorn hedge. What they talked about, of course, was not the great world's affairs or its literary problems, but the art of growing old. They exchanged complaints great and small, and perhaps relished the fact that at eighty—in spite of sparse white hair, a gaunt neck, and a painful gait—one could hardly be counted old in a village that proudly numbered among its inhabitants a centenarian.

Sometimes in autumn a plume of smoke rising from the large garden of the Casa Rossa was seen. Then one knew that the dweller was building a fire with leaves and dry twigs. Perhaps the old master of the bead game sat meditating before it, and his thoughts may have been of travel, perhaps of the journey to the East that transported him beyond space and time. Or perhaps he was busying himself somewhere else in the garden. Then no one but his wife could succeed in calling him back into the house. This was Ninon, and it is said of her in one of Hesse's fairy tales that she had proved to be a skilled tamer of birds.

But let us beware of seeing in Hesse only a man who was living an idyll. This life of his enclosed in quiet was reached by an arduous road through suffering and chasms of despair.

Hesse had lived in the carmine-red house since 1931. It was placed at his disposal for life by his prosperous friend H. C. Bodmer. But Hesse had lived in Montagnola since the spring of 1919, when after a

period of violent crises he came to the Ticino mountain village to begin a new life. For twelve years he lived in the Casa Camuzzi, the many-cornered, ingenious, idiosyncratic building that a Montagnola builder of that name had erected in the previous century in a baroque-playful mood for himself and his family. From the balcony of this house that played a significant role in Hesse's work and for a time became his "Saint Jerome's study," he observed in those years life and its doings:

> I see the world down there and think, "They can have it." I have no luck in this world, I have not fitted well with it, and it has answered and repaid my aversion abundantly. But it has not killed me. I still live, I have defied it and held my ground, and if I have not become a successful manufacturer or boxer or movie star, I have become the thing that as a boy of twelve I set myself to be—a poet. And I have learned, among other things, that if one desires nothing of the world and simply observes it quietly and attentively, the world has much to offer of which the world's successful darlings know nothing.

The tiny stone balcony—only a pace across and a half-pace front to back—is the balcony of Klingsor, the expressionistic painter who wrestles with death and despair, and in whom Hesse created a powerfully moving self-portrait soon after his arrival in Ticino. When we step out on this balcony, we see that the steeply falling terrace garden below—with its tall, fan-crowned palms, its cedars, chestnut trees, fig trees, rhododendrons, its black-red copper beech, and its yew trees, lianas, spiraeae, wistarias, and creepers—is Klingsor's magic garden. We recall the picture of Klingsor with its many faces, all of which

reflect Hesse's own features, as the man of forty-two then saw them: the remembered faces of childhood and youth, of a drunkard and wastrel, of a man thirsting and suffering, of a man persecuted and seeking. Klingsor-Hesse, with death in his eyes, hears the music of decline and fall. Whoever is able to interpret his self-portrait will say that what Hesse drew in the summer of 1919 is "the tired, greedy, wild, childlike and sophisticated man of our late time, the dying, death-willing man of Europe."

If from the little Casa Camuzzi we then look at the lake ringed by mountains, a second picture arises, one Hesse conceived earlier than that of Klingsor, a picture from the spring of that same year. Far out into the lake at night glides a boat; slowly a figure bends over the boat's edge, drops into the water, and sinks. It is Friedrich Klein of the story "Klein and Wagner" ("Klein und Wagner"), whose road likewise leads through distress and despair until the drowning man finds life's meaning and salvation.

The figure of Siddhartha also had its origin in the Casa Camuzzi. Once again, it is a bitter road that leads from the defiant readiness to hurl life "at the feet of mocking gods," to the smiling wisdom that hears in the sound of the river the consoling voice of the unity of all being. Between the book's two parts lies a pause of almost a year and a half, a period during which the dwelling in the Casa Camuzzi became a hermitage. Hesse was making up for the time he had not spent in ascetic meditation, so as to steep himself entirely in the kindred world of

the Indian spirit. More sharply than ever before did he experience the truth "that it is nonsense to set out to write something that one has not lived."

But the peace of Hesse-Siddhartha, too, was short-lived. *Siddhartha* is followed—with *The Spa Visitor (Kurgast)*, *Picture Book (Bilderbuch)*, and *Nuremberg Journey (Die Nürnberger Reise)* in the interval—by *Steppenwolf (Der Steppenwolf)*, which once again shows a life that comes up to the brink of suicide. "Why should I not be a wolf of the steppe and a coarse hermit in the midst of a world none of whose goals I share and none of whose joys appeal to me!" The words appear in this book written in 1927, which tells of days of "soul death" and days of

> inner emptiness and despair, when amid an earth that has been destroyed and sucked empty by big corporations, humanity in general, and so-called culture, with its lying, common, tinny, and meretricious glitter, grin into our faces at every step of the way.

All these figures and many others come to life when we step onto the little stone balcony of the Casa Camuzzi. All of them have features of their creator, features that the biographer has to scrutinize, because Hesse's inner dramatic tension played a more important part in his life than the events of his external life did. In December 1928, during his work on *Narcissus and Goldmund, (Narziß und Goldmund)* Hesse described his manner of work:

> A new literary creation begins to come into existence for me at the moment when a figure becomes visible. For a while the figure can become the symbol and vehicle of my

experiences, my thoughts, and my problems. The appearance of this mythic person (Peter Camenzind, Knulp, Siddhartha, Henry Haller, *et al.*) is the creative moment out of which everything comes into being. Nearly all the prose works I have written are biographies of the soul; not one of them is concerned with stories, involvements, and tensions. On the contrary, each of them is basically a discourse, in which a single person—just that mythic figure—is observed in his relations to the world and to his own ego.

After Hesse's move into the new house, the music of decline and fall was no longer heard. Klingsor and the wolf of the steppe had been transformed. But no transformation is possible unless the germ of the new is already in the old. Thus Hesse took with him into the new house and into his new life Klingsor's love for the stars and his magical knowledge of man's brain as the home of all illusions, of which the worst is "time." And he was prepared to pursue further that "divine trace" that, in the starry clear laughter of the immortals and in the gaiety of Mozart and his music, already accompanied the wolf of the steppe as the countermelody to despair.

Much had happened since 1931 and the entry into the new house. But since the voices of chaos, amidst the barbarity of National Socialism and World War II, were now shaking the world more powerfully than ever, Hesse answered them with the timeless cosmos of *The Journey to the East (Die Morgenlandfahrt)* and *Magister Ludi (Das Glasperlenspiel)*.

Remarkable is the way the structure of the new house accorded with the transformed artist and his

spiritual world. Casa Camuzzi is comic, expressive, and romantic; with columned balustrades, little towers, and weather vane, it lies dreamily and meditatively above the melancholy secret of its exotic garden, the luxuriating vegetation of which reminds one of procreation and birth, primordial mother and death. The Casa Rossa, on the contrary, has clearly articulated classic forms. The large, parklike garden —which was long tended by Hesse himself and had grown to be a part of his life—does have secrets of its own such as its fireplaces, in which Hesse liked to build a smoking charcoal pile. (For Hesse, fire signified "a chemical-symbolic service to divinity," a "retransformation of the manifold into the One.") But this garden, which was much less exotic, was without demonic quality. It had beds of flowers and of vegetables. Its growth had limit and moderation. There were in it neither creepers nor palms nor the spectrally bizarre lianas. Instead, there was the small square of a bamboo forest, the fresh green of its lance-shaped leaf tips waving high above the slender yellow stalks. This is the bamboo copse of the Elder Brother in *Magister Ludi*, the hermitage and stage for Hesse's *I Ching* studies. The wolf of the steppe had become a pupil of the Chinese sage.

There was still another difference between the old house and the new. The latter lies outside and above the village, whose crowded roofs with the Camuzzi facade extending above them can be seen only far below Hesse's broad, pulpitlike studio window. Here the author without himself being seen had a distant view. Farther from the water, yet overlooking

a large surface of the lake, he was closer in this house to the clouds, yet when he looked beyond the clear outlines of the mountains of the Ticino, he had a still more open view of the sky than before. Thus he continued to be bound to the sealike, mirroring, self-concealing, and yet again revealing, elements of moisture, the ever-changing nature of the water and the clouds to which he was constantly drawn. But now he viewed them from a greater distance, with his eyes on what stood firmly outlined behind them.

Expanse of lake and sky, scent of water and weeds, swaying sedge as I stride on the damp sandy shore, above me the clouds and a few birds in the infinite heavens—how I once loved these things! Since then, without being rightly aware of it, I have always lived in a spot somewhat farther from a lake and closer to high mountains, the character of which was something firm and precisely outlined, and which did not consist chiefly of sky, air, haze, wind and motion.

It is not only the small change of dwelling within the Ticino mountain village that is significant. All spheres of Hesse's life had a relationship to his inner world and to his forms of expression at various times. We shall confine ourselves at this point to Montagnola. Looking out from the Casa Rossa, we recall the words that the bead-game master Josef Knecht once addressed to his worldly friend Designori:

"Look at this cloudscape with its ribbons of sky. At first glance, one might think that depth is where the picture is darkest. But one immediately perceives that this something dark and soft is only the clouds, and that the depth and vastness of space begins only at the edges and fjords of these cloud-mountains, and sinks into the infinity where the stars,

solemn and majestic, stand for us humans as supreme symbols of clarity and order. The world's profundity and its secrets are not where the clouds and blackness are; depth is where it is clear and serene."

We have now successfully made our way—as invited guests, not as intruders—to the author's carmine-red house. Our next task is to describe this meeting and to attempt a portrait of Hesse. But this is very difficult. All of the many faces that he has worn during his more than eighty years of life have engraved their traces on him. For weeks the painter Ernst Morgenthaler made sketch after sketch and picture after picture, persistently struggling to unite if possible all the facets of his subject in one portrait. Hesse always had to snatch the picture from him just as one essential, valid expression that had just been captured on paper was about to be destroyed by continuous new overlays of expression. We too must confine ourselves to a formula. We cannot copy all the many features that reveal themselves in constant change behind the live kinetic folds and wrinkles of this face. The formula to which we shall adhere is: kindness, bravery, modesty, humor.

With surprising elasticity Hesse opens the door of his atelier. There is something musical in the rhythm of the movement with which he is suddenly standing there in the room. He is a very fragile and slender yet energetic man, who looks immediately and freely into your eyes, and his greeting radiates a kindness that places him above and beyond anything like a gruff-mannered recluse. Humor often hovers behind his voice and his words. He is by no means

prepared to talk only about literature. Ruefully he shakes his head over those who "read only Hesse."

"What does Augustine say?" he smiles. " 'Beware of the man who has read only one book.' "

Willing to reminisce, he often relates very small scenes from the rich picture album of his life. His memory works with extraordinary precision; often he can recollect "the almost glassy brightness and transparency of the feelings" out of which he shapes his creations.

With amusement he speaks of the textbook interpretations that always begin with the words, "By this passage the author means to say . . ."

"No," he says. "The author did not mean to say anything. He meant only to find an apt expression for capturing the flight of a bird or the movement of a butterfly. People constantly forget the artist's sensual components." What Hesse means by this is expressed in his fairy tale of Han Fook and the "master of the perfect word."

Finally the conversation does turn to things literary, to Thomas Mann, Bertolt Brecht, and others. Hesse is very well informed on recent literature. Stacked everywhere are books by younger contemporaries, which are sent to him in copious quantities by the authors themselves or their publishers. From these, among other books, his wife reads to him daily. His judgments are always cordial and considerate. His sympathies are touched when someone recognizes in his work features that are revolutionary and diagnostic of the age, and desists from labeling him the backward-looking romanticist

that he by no means is. In all these conversations it is evident that Hesse has long since passed beyond the stage of "exaggerated seriousness about self." He notes with equanimity and humor the grossly one-sided interpretations—among which are the psychoanalytical as well as the sociological—that are applied to him. "In the West I am interpreted psychologically, in the East sociologically," he says with a smile. "In the East when they see a poem by me that is somewhat depressive, they say at once, 'Here you can see how he suffers under the Western system.' "

Then he tells of the manifold threads of intellectual kinship. Mostly the exchange has taken place only in letters, but in the course of his life, the correspondents have formed a network of relationships that it is a joy for him to survey.

And then Hesse speaks of old age. Not of its tribulations, which he gallantly and quickly dismisses, but of the advantages of newly gained perspectives:

> It is almost a new dimension. In hearing Mozart's *Figaro* today, for example, I experience all the *Figaro* performances that I have ever heard, from my first when I was very young up to now; and everything that is connected with this opera, with Mozart's music generally, and with all other composers that I knew and felt akin to, at once and simultaneously takes on life. It is a greater polyphony than one achieves in one's youth.

At evening he points from his study window to the mighty chestnut trees below, which are just in bloom. When he speaks of nature and his garden,

he does it tenderly, as if he understood its mute secrets and were himself an organic part of its silent growth and its eternal law of dying and becoming. Then he says something about which we can only hope that this time he may be wrong: "This year everything is blooming with special force. It is as if nature wanted to give its all once more, one last time before a catastrophe."

Indescribable is the combination of Italianate *grandezza* and a melancholy suffused with courageous serenity—its source is a profound knowledge that comes with age, the knowledge of the inexorability of farewell, of all farewells—with which Hesse calls out his *addio* and then, turning once more in front of the door of his study, his singsong *ciao*.

2

Origins and Youth

The classical landscape of the Ticino has been described by Hesse again and again, and has been captured in many of the watercolors that he was so fond of making. But just as often it is the romantic towers and gabled houses, the trout streams, meadows, and chestnut trees of his birthplace, Calw, that we encounter in his books. In Calw on the Nagold, a little Black Forest town with a typically Swabian atmosphere, Hermann Hesse was born on July 2, 1877.

Two years younger than Thomas Mann and Rilke, he was, like them, born into a seemingly secure world. But beneath the surface of that world, the idyllic life of which was being poetically invoked one more time by Mörike and Keller, the forces of sickness and decay were already at work. Scarcely a quarter-century later they will be revealed in *Buddenbrooks*. Psychoanalysis, the relativity theory, and atomic physics will be determinants of a new age. In the year of Hesse's birth Sigmund Freud was already twenty-one years of age. Two years after Hesse's birth Albert Einstein was born.

In literature Hesse's generation includes—besides Rilke and Mann—Rudolf Borchardt (born 1877), Hugo von Hofmannsthal (1874), Marcel Proust (1871), Paul Valéry (1871), Paul Claudel (1870), André Gide (1869), Maxim Gorky (1868), Stefan George (1868), Romain Rolland (1866). Among the younger members were Virginia Woolf (born 1881), James Joyce (1882), Gottfried Benn (1886), and T. S. Eliot (1888).

In these names is expressed all the tension of

an age of transition. Hesse, always an individualist, had assimilated this tension into himself. But in terms of his family origins, too, there were tensions for him to overcome. The elements of his family history range from Baltic and Hanseatic to Swabian and French Swiss. His father was a Balt; his mother half Swabian, half French Swiss. Both, as strict Pietists, had devoted their life to missionary work. The road takes us to India, where Marie Gundert Dubois, Hesse's mother, was born in Talachari on October 18, 1842. Her father was the renowned Swabian missionary and Indologist Dr. Hermann Gundert; her mother was Julie Dubois, who came of a Calvinist vintner family from the region around Neuchâtel.

In particular, the heritage of this Swabian grandfather (the names of his ancestors—"Bible Gundert," and "Schoolmaster Gundert"—were well known in Swabia) exerted lasting influence on Hesse. Grandfather Gundert must have been a very wise man of great learning and with great understanding of people and their ways. His study room was enveloped with a secret, magic quality. From many lands he received visitors, with whom he conversed in English, French, Indian, Italian, Malayan, or another of the thirty languages he had at his command. With his broad white beard and his eyes full of the world's sadness and of serene wisdom, he was for young Hesse the venerable, omniscient patriarch, who was more powerful than father and mother. But he also transmitted to the young boy another heritage, which was still much alive in him though some-

what concealed beneath piety and service to the Kingdom of God.

It was the heritage of the Swabian world, a wonderful mixture of material narrowness and spiritual grandeur, which in the Swabian Latin schools, the evangelical cloister seminaries, and the famous Tübingen *Stift*, had for close to two centuries preserved, enriched, and enlarged itself. This was the Pietist world of the Swabian parsonages and schools, to which belonged such men as Johann Albrecht Bengel, Johann Christoph Blumhardt, and Friedrich Christoph Oetinger. They developed a spirituality and religious sensibility that were clarified by the rationalist critique, one that made them capable of "seeing into the heart of things." Extending from Pietism to radical "free thought," it was constantly oriented toward the "central knowledge" of being. This we read in Oetinger, who lived in the first half of the eighteenth century; as pastor of Hirsau, he was also in regular contact with neighboring Calw. He and Bengel received overdue homage in Hesse's *Magister Ludi.* In conversation Hesse liked to refer to this Swabian Pietism, and he retained in his desk drawer an unfinished manuscript on its history that he originally intended to include in *Magister Ludi.* But it is not Pietism alone that had its echo in Grandfather Gundert. In the Swabian world and Swabian tradition that he embodied, others—Hölderlin, Hegel, Mörike—had also grown up.

The paternal line was quite different. Hesse's great-grandfather, Barthold Joachim Hesse, came from Lübeck. As was proper for a native of a Han-

seatic city, distant travel attracted him at the early age of sixteen. Thus it was that he came to the southern coast of the Gulf of Finland and settled in Reval as a merchant. Later he moved to Dorpat, where we find him as a brother member of the Great Guild and choirmaster of the German Congregation. Christina Elisabeth Sengbusch, a Balt, became his wife. One of the children of this prolific marriage was Hesse's grandfather, Dr. Carl Hermann Hesse, later district physician and state councillor in Weissenstein in Estonia. Like the Swabian grandfather, he too was a Pietist. But he was a very practical and merry man who was not drawn to scholarly study and painstaking research. He no more attempted to conceal his Hanseatic nature in performing his services to the Russian crown than Hesse's maternal grandfather attempted to conceal his Swabian nature in carrying on the pioneering work of the Pietist mission in India and on the Malabar coast.

In Weißenstein, Estonia, in the humble old doctor's house with its high slate roof, yellow walls, and white shutters—a house that became a place of help for many seeking counsel—Hermann Hesse's father, Carl Otto Johannes Hesse, came into the world on June 2, 1847. His parents sent him to the venerable Knights' and Cathedral School in Reval, which was then the capital of Estonia. Until he became a Swiss citizen, Johannes Hesse traveled on a Russian passport. Since 1710 the government of Estonia had belonged to the empire of the czar as the northernmost of its three Baltic provinces.

At eighteen Hesse's father is to be found among

the pupils of the Basle Mission House. In the summer of 1868 he was ordained a missionary in Heilbronn, and a year later he began his journey to the region of the Blue Mountains, where he was introduced to the missionary work that he was to perform on the Malabar coast. But the tropical climate was too much for him. Because neither his head ailment nor his intestinal ailment were responding to treatment, he left India at twenty-five with a heavy heart. After a brief stay in his Estonian homeland, he followed a summons to the Basle Mission in Calw on the Nagold, where Dr. Hermann Gundert needed an assistant to work on the mission's magazine. Dr. Gundert had been living there since the spring of 1859; he, too, because of the climate, could not return to India.

In the old gray house, built close against the mountain, that is now the home of the Calwer Publishing House, Johannes Hesse got to know Marie Gundert Dubois, his future wife. Later Hesse wrote of his parents that "in blood they were strangers, in spirit brother and sister." Marie too had in her early years put all of her energies into mission work. As the widow of the missionary Charles Isenberg, she moved back to her father's house in Calw. Of Johannes Hesse, the new assistant living in the house with them, she noted, just after his arrival:

> One must esteem and love him, this fine, pious, intellectual man. But for me his aspect always has something melancholy. He looks as if he had been made for a better world. . . . To the people of Calw he has a very important look about him, in his foreign attire.

Scarcely a year later she wrote: "So I am again a happy wife at the side of a faithful husband, who will help me on the way to our Heavenly home and who is especially a great support in the rearing of my sons." The wedding took place on November 22, 1874. The boys who would become Hesse's half-brothers were eight-year-old Theodor and five-year-old Carl. Two years before Hesse's birth, in 1875, his favorite sister Adele was born.

Hesse has again and again occupied himself with his origins and his family tradition. From an early age two traits made a strong impression on him: his parents' almost monklike piety and the iridescent colorfulness of the Oriental world. The exotic magic of the East lived above all in the figure of his grandfather, who was always deep in his Indological work, and who kept in his cabinets strange clothing, figures, and Buddha images, cups and bowls from India and Ceylon, strings of wooden beads, palm-leaf scrolls, turtles of green soapstone, and idols of wood, glass, quartz, or clay. It all "smelled of the sea, and spices, and faraway lands, and cinnamon and sandalwood. It had all passed through brown hands and yellow hands, had been moistened by tropic rain and Ganges water, dried in the equatorial sun, shaded by the primeval forest."

But behind all the knowledge of Mohammedan and Buddhist prayer exercises, behind all the Malayan words and prayer songs (which Hesse's mother also spoke and sang) stood the Christian faith in the Holy Trinity. The history of Hesse's criticism of and doubts about this inherited faith, and his grad-

ual arrival at a piety nourished (as he himself tells us) from Greek, Jewish, Indian, and Chinese sources as well as from Christian ones—the history of this is the aspect of his life drama that lends the tense excitement to his work. It was not only the Swabian world of his grandfather or only the world of his mother (which also embodied the "secret, primeval" quality) that lived in him. The paternal inheritance had also contributed to Hesse's makeup.

This Johannes Hesse was a man of great kindness and great strength in suffering, whose "bequest of a discipline and a faith" in one's calling and an obligation to follow it had a lasting effect on his son. Admired with shy reverence, he was "a stranger, a noble and rare butterfly or bird that had flown to us from other zones, distinguished and isolated by his delicacy and his sufferings and not less by his silent longing for home." A good storyteller, he knew how to evoke for the children a little Estonia and at times to awaken in them the passionate desire to see one day this Estonia and Latvia, where one was invited to remote estates, could travel across country by horse carriage, and everywhere found tables richly laden with foods as if the Land of Cockaigne. At home there was also a picture of Czar Alexander, a samovar, and Estonian toys, and the youngest sister was called Marulla.

Until his death Hesse's father adopted nothing of the Swabian world which surrounded him in the dialect of his wife and children. He always spoke the pure, cultivated High German with the melodious Baltic accent. The children were proud of this

usage even though their family thereby sacrificed a degree of familiarity with the native townspeople. This silent man (who chose for his epitaph the Psalm verse "The string is torn, the bird is free") wrote to the Basle Mission Society, when he was still an eighteen-year-old *Primaner*,* a letter that was very characteristic of him and showed his unusual singularity and his consciousness of goal. In this letter he called himself a "servant and vassal" of the Lord and wrote that for him, theology was the means to a "great, holy purpose." His wish was directed "to a corporate community in which my own Self would disappear—for it had long since grown too strong for me."

These two feelings were significant in the spiritual inheritance of the son. The wish of the Pietist father to become a Christian servant and vassal found in the poet a further stage of realization as a "servant of the spirit," crowned in the figure of the bead-game master Josef Knecht. And the community to which self would be subordinated—which Johannes Hesse sought—has been realized in parable by Hermann Hesse in the League of Travelers to the East as that space- and time-spanning "society of the spirit" which he belonged to as a poet and which he served. With Hermann Hesse too membership in this society is preceded by a turning away from the "exaggerated seriousness about Self" and by adopting the road of renunciation that leads to

* A student in one of the two highest classes in a German *Gymnasium* of that day. The American equivalent would be a college freshman or sophomore.

become a magician, so as to be able to heighten and transform the reality which, now anxiously, now mockingly, he was rejecting.

The experience of childhood was so important for Hesse because it summoned him again and again to be precise in the portrayal of this memory, and it was primarily out of this storehouse that he shaped his literary creations. Constantly drawing upon prototypes, and by this same act reflecting in the microcosm of his inner world an entire macrocosm, he could afford to do without a modern montage principle that has to rely on the inclusion of external tension elements as well as the interweaving and assimilation of foreign sources. Out of the well of childhood and memory grew Hesse's art of the simple, which he was continually at pains to perfect and in which the Chinese later became his masters. It is "that secret art of seeming to say only the simple and plain, while thereby agitating the listener's soul as the wind does a sheet of water."

From the age of four to the age of nine, Basle was the second home of Hesse's childhood. In the spring of 1881 his father was sent there to be the editor of the mission magazine and teacher in the mission house for German language and literature. These years in the cheerful and calm neighborhood of the outer Spalenquartier on what was then the edge of the city were happy years for the Hesse family. In his early work *Hermann Lauscher*, and again in 1948 in an essay in the volume *Late Prose (Späte Prosa)*, Hesse has described his childhood years in Basle. For this period, the first and original

experience was the wide meadow behind the house, with all its countless details and secrets. There were also his mother's stories, compared with which the tales of later storytellers and raconteurs of world repute were to seem awkward and tasteless. But another occurrence in this period was the transition from dreaming to thinking. Into the child's world the invasion of school had come—the first division of one's time into work time and free time, the division of the child's garden-world into home and school, into two spheres, in which love was to be offered to the master of one and fear to the master of the other. And now happiness for the young Hesse began to be mixed with bitterness. As he became accustomed to a strict teacher's frequent blows and detention, he gradually lost his ingenuous feeling toward the parents who were unable to protect him from the superior alien power. The school system of that day, which has its prototype in Heinrich Mann's *Professor Unrat,* is well known. In 1906, about the same time as that book and a few years later than Emil Strauß's *Freund Hein,* there appeared Hesse's own reckoning with the school in his story *The Prodigy (Unterm Rad),* which has since been translated widely, even into Japanese.

If when playing at robber captain, general, or Indian chief, the young Hesse, as compensation for his early suffering, soon exceeded all his comrades in wildness, still he was different from them. As a boy he already had his *daimonion.* It appeared to him in the form of "the little man." This magical phenomenon—which in the terms of modern de-

velopmental psychology can be roughly equated with the "picture vision" of the child in the mythic stage—

> was a tiny shadowy gray being, a dwarf, a spirit or a cobold, an angel or a demon, who sometimes was there, in my waking as in my sleeping moments. He went before me and I had to follow him, more than I did my father, my mother, my reason, indeed often more than my fear. . . . The little man had no name. But the most impossible thing in the world, once he was standing before me, would be not to follow him. Where he went, I followed—even into water and fire.

A remarkable projection of archaic layers of the mind. In the dangerously awake sensibility of the child there already lay the possibilities of an artist.

At the beginning of July 1886 the family moved back to Calw. To give up the life in Basle, the stimulating and and like-minded company of the mission people, and not least their beautiful home, was a great sacrifice that Hesse's parents made for Dr. Gundert's sake. The old man had requested that his son-in-law be appointed his assistant and successor on the mission committee. The family returned to live for more than three years in the damp and unhealthy Calwer Publishing House.

Again and again one is struck by the piety, renunciation, and self-sacrifice with which Hesse's parents accepted their life. "We let ourselves be guided, and are quiet," wrote Hesse's mother. Hesse's own questing spirit, his obstinacy, his criticism and his doubts, were linked to this influence of his parents, just as were his sense of responsibility, his unreserved honesty, and his readiness for personal sacrifice.

Young Hesse was very musical; at an early age he learned *Lieder* melodies and chorales by heart, and sang everywhere—on the way to school, in the garden, often even after he had gone to bed. For his ninth birthday he received a small violin, which for many years went with him on all his travels. He found in it, besides the countless agitations, joys, and sorrows that were not long in coming, "a secluded retreat, an inner home, a refuge." Not by chance was it that the instrument that meant all this to him was the violin—the most feminine of all instruments, the one with the most subtle variations, the one that gives a pure sound only when it and the musician are in perfect unity. Lenau also played the violin; so did Hölderlin and Paul Klee. As late as 1932, in *The Journey to the East*, the question is asked, "What are you going to do now when you no longer have your violin?" The sale of the violin in that book becomes a symbol of forgetting a valuable part of the inner life.

The musical exhilaration and reverie of Hesse's early years were antipodal to what he was undergoing at school, which, until his fourteenth year, had for Hesse "the close atmosphere of a penal institution." At twelve he was already clear in his own mind that he wanted "to become either a poet or nothing at all." But this astonishingly early clarity of purpose was soon followed by the painful realization that, although there is a road, a school, a course of study by which one can become a teacher, a pastor, a physician, an artisan, a merchant, a postal official, and even a musician, a painter or an architect, there is

no road, school, or course of study by which one becomes a poet. Out of the child's question—whether his goal could be realized—grew criticism of the school's authority. Leading to serious conflict, this precipitated the first real crisis in Hesse's young life. The child had perceived lucidly the equivocal nature of a pedagogy—indeed, of the adult world in general—that, because of its own mediocrity and lack of existential courage, allows greatness only as a distant idea in remote historical perspective.

> It was the very same with the poet as with the hero and with all strong or beautiful, sanguine, and out-of-the-ordinary people and movements: If they lived in the past they were glorious and every schoolbook was full of their praises; but if they lived in the real world of the present day they were hated. Presumably the teachers were specifically trained and hired for the purpose of preventing as far as possible the growth of magnificent free men and the committing of great, splendid deeds.

Thus the young Hesse soon saw nothing but abysses between him and his goal. Everything seemed devalued and uncertain. But he adhered stubbornly to his plan to become a poet. At thirteen the conflict began. Hesse's conduct at school and at home left so much to be desired that he was sent "into exile" to the Latin school in Göppingen. His stay there lasted only a year. Hesse was supposed to be studying to become a theologian. In 1891 he passed the difficult Württemberg state examination and entered the monastery school at Maulbronn with a scholarship.

Hesse often evoked the atmosphere of that

famous seminary: its romanticism, the closeness of its monastic atmosphere, the three-basined fountain and the quiet monotony of its singing waters, the cloister and the well with its Gothic roof, the romanesque columns and arches, the chestnut trees, the humanistic names of its lecture halls (Forum, Athens, Sparta, Hellas), the teachers and boyhood friendships, and the whole student life. He even brought out the special kind of neurosis that the place induced in the people who lived there. (Something that Hölderlin too had experienced within these walls).

Hesse, struggling for self-determination, was not quite fifteen when, suddenly overwhelmed by the tempests within him, he fled from the cloister. His absence was reported to the police, and for a day the woods were searched for him. He spent a night in the open field when the temperature was 10 degrees centigrade, and almost died from the exposure. After his release from the infirmary, he was sent to the detention room and then home on vacation. Not everyone received him as understandingly as his grandfather did—"So, it's you, Hermann? I hear you made everybody here red in the face recently."

What the boy suffered from most was the mildness and embarrassed anxiety with which people, acting as if he were afflicted with some weird malady, hovered around him. He went to Bad Boll to the famous social theologian and exorcist Blumhardt (the son of the miracle doctor-exorcist whose patient Mörike had been), but the exorcist failed. For the next four years everything went wrong. At the *Gym-*

nasium in Cannstatt, Hesse endeavored to continue his studies, but the result again was the detention room and dismissal after one year. For three days he was an apprentice in an Esslingen bookshop. Running away again, he was missing for several days and nights—to the great worry of his parents. Then his father attempted to employ him as his assistant, but this too did not go well. A half year later, in the spring of 1894, he became an apprentice in the church-clock factory in Calw, where he learned how to hone and file clock wheels. Here he worked until the autumn of 1895. All that was needed was to understand him rightly; then he was "by nature a lamb and as docile as a soap bubble."

3

Beginnings

On October 17, 1895, Hesse began to work as an apprentice in the Heckenhauer bookstore in Tübingen. At last he had found a field of activity suited to him. In the old house opposite the college chapel, he passed his three-year apprenticeship successfully. His marked inclination for independent thought led him to pursue extensively personal studies on his own. Two great spirits above all inspired the eighteen-year-old.

In the corner of the attic room where I used to read—where no sounds could be heard other than the hourly strokes of the clock in the nearby belfry and the chattering of the storks that nested beside it—the men and women of Shakespeare and Goethe were my companions.

During this time Hesse himself was already productive. In September 1899, attention, for the first time, was directed to the twenty-two-year-old bookseller. In the publication *Boten für die deutsche Literatur* these words appear:

It may well be worthwhile to speak of a book that is reverent and pious and has a deep, prayerful voice. For this book is not far removed from being art. The beginning of art is piety: piety toward oneself, toward everything experienced, toward all things, toward some great model and one's own untested power. . . . In this feeling Hermann Hesse's book had its origin.

The reference was to Hesse's collection of sketches entitled *An Hour past Midnight (Eine Stunde hinter Mitternacht)*. The reviewer was Rainer Maria Rilke.

In this collection of sketches Hesse created a dream world sustained by a mood similar to that of

his *Romantic Songs (Romantische Lieder)*, which were also written in those early years in Tübingen. The verses are nostalgic and melancholy; again and again they sigh sadly at the transiency of things, including the passing of the poet's own youth. The tired summer sinks its head, and the wind moves faintly through the poplars. The young poet looks at his pale image reflected in the lake; behind him is a red sky, before him, evening fears, and twilight, and death.

Melancholy and fear of death are components of a dream world that is erected against workaday reality. Hesse's gaze had long been turned backward —to his origins, to childhood, to the fairy tale. It has always been a recollection of the oneness and entirety of being, as this makes itself felt not only as the heritage of romanticism, but also, by its nature, in modern psychology and in French symbolism from Baudelaire to Valéry, and on to Rilke, James Joyce, and André Gide.

When he was twenty-two, Hesse returned to Basle. He was still a bookseller. Following an old desire, he switched from new books to second-hand books. During the years that followed, he sought to clarify his relationship to the world and to himself. The result was a book that has been called his first credo—*Hermann Lauscher*.

This early work showed the special qualities of Hesse as a writer: the way in which a high degree of intellectual alertness related profoundly to the unconscious. This at first led to dissonance. The young man of twenty-two wrote in his diary:

What a night! Ten hours without sleep, every minute a struggle of my oppressed soul with cruel, tyrannical thought, a struggle accompanied by weeping and gnashing of teeth, a wrestling without weapons, breast to breast, one that employs all the tricks and cruelties of despair. All the boundaries and dikes that I had set in my inner life, all the seeds laboriously sown, all the foundation stones that I had placed, have in these hours been trampled to pieces and destroyed.

Here in Basle, on his way to self-realization, Hesse was already encountering the unconscious as a power whose pressure was shattering the values of the reasonable and the ordered, the entire world of his Pietist origins—"the white temples, the cool pictures of fond memory." Already "all that has been suppressed, put in chains, and half-subdued" was pulling at its fetters threateningly, and "the entire lower world" was being set free to reel upward in him. And yet he was not experiencing this as only a hostile invasion. He felt that "these desperate mutineers and image-destroyers" were also related to him, that they bore in them characteristics of his childhood days and dearest memories. But he was not yet able to subject these powers and give them literary form. More than one and a half decades were to pass before the artistic breakthrough to a redeeming symbol-world was successfully achieved. Still the predominant notes were twilight and dreaminess, estheticism, and an elegiac Narcissus-love for the lake that was visited again and again, whose thousand shades of color were felt as "the triumph of pure beauty over all movements of conscious and unconscious life"—the world of Arnold Böcklin, suffused with Chopin minor chords. All this was nonetheless very consciously experienced, and again

and again there was the play of irony. In *Hermann Lauscher*, Hesse also wrote of the "longing for a shrill, bacchantic passion, fatally woven of arrogance and insufficiency." The book expressed the antithesis between the Apollonian and the Dionysian principle as Nietzsche has described it. Behind *Lauscher* were the ardent studies of Nietzsche and the reading of Jakob Burckhardt that Hesse had been pursuing during his stay in Basle. Of these two, Jakob Burckhardt, whom Hesse memorialized as late as *Magister Ludi* (where he appears as Pater Jakobus), was to exert a more constant influence on Hesse's view of the world. But in this early period, Hesse took the antithesis that Nietzsche formulated about a phenomenon of cultural history (the intellectual world of ancient Greece) and, transposing it, applied it to himself. There he experienced the dual play of mind and instinct, the discipline of thought and the intoxication of feeling. Out of this tension grew artistic production.

But besides carrying on this credo-like disputation with himself, he also produced in this period works of literary art that have a quite magical quality of language, such as the poem to Elisabeth. Perhaps this unattainable loved one whose praises he often sang in verse was the daughter of Pastor Laroche, in whose house Hesse was staying at that time. Through his connection with the family of Rudolf Wackernagel, official archivist and historian of the city of Basle, he became acquainted with Karl Joël and Heinrich Wölfflin. In Basle he also acquired a living relationship to the fine arts.

Hermann Lauscher appeared in 1901. In the

same year Hesse made his first Italian journey. Already showing himself a critic of his times, he became conscious for the first time in Florence of "the whole shabby ludicrousness of modern culture." At every step in Italy he rejoiced in the naturalness and candor of a life "over which lay the ennobling and refining influence of a tradition of classical culture and history." It awakened in him the desire to lead his life outside contemporary society, to which he would always be a stranger.

The novelist Paul Ilg, who did not know the young Hesse personally, called the attention of the Fischer publishing house to the just-published *Hermann Lauscher*. Samuel Fischer cordially invited the young author to submit new work to him. Hesse wrote that this was the first literary recognition and encouragement he had received in his life. "At that time I had begun *Camenzind*, and Fischer's invitation greatly spurred me on. I finished it; it was accepted at once. I had 'arrived.' "

Peter Camenzind, with which Hesse became famous overnight, appeared in 1904. Two studies, on Boccaccio and Francis of Assisi, also belong to this period, in which echoes of the Italian experience still linger. The first volume of poetry had already been published in 1902. It was supposed to be for Hesse's mother, but never reached her; on April 24, 1902, she had succumbed to a severe kidney ailment.

In the summer of 1904, after the success of *Camenzind*, Hesse married Marie Bernoulli, daughter of an old Basle family of mathematicians. Now that he could relinquish bookselling, he decided to

live in the country. A major reason for this decision was that Marie Bernoulli shared Hesse's wish to live simply and to be close to nature. Her fondness for a half-peasant, half-manorial country house with a mossy roof and a murmuring spring beneath ancient trees was in accord with Hesse's own taste. Later he was to become more realistic in these matters. In September 1904 the couple rented, for one hundred and fifty marks a year, an old farmhouse with abundant timbering in the rustic style. It was in Gaienhofen, an out-of-the-way village on the Lake of Constance. The nails that the master of the house hammered in the little room were taken from old crates and had first to be hammered straight on the stone threshold. The young Stefan Zweig went to visit and made such an unpleasant acquaintance with the low-lying door jamb of the old house, which in his enthusiastic entry he failed to notice, that he had to lie down for a quarter of an hour before he was able to speak again. The whole enterprise was a youthfully passionate attempt to lead a life in accordance with the ideals of Ruskin, William Morris, and Tolstoy.

Hesse was at first content. After all the tempests, he had reached his goal. He was a self-supporting writer and could enjoy the balmy breeze of recognition.

The bitterness of the years of growth and school, when I was often very close to ruin, was now smiled at and forgotten. Even the relatives and friends who had hitherto been in despair over me, now gave me friendly smiles. I was victorious, and if I did the most stupid and worthless

thing, people thought it delightful. I too was very much delighted with myself.

He wrote books and was regarded as an amiable author who lived in peace with the world. In 1905, together with Ludwig Thoma and Conrad Haußmann, he founded the periodical *März*, published by Albert Langen, which was mainly directed against the personal rule of Kaiser Wilhelm. But he did not as yet take these political activities too seriously.

Following *The Prodigy* there appeared in 1907 and 1908, under the titles *In This World (Diesseits)* and *Neighbors (Nachbarn)*, a series of stories in which an idyllic world was given form with the precision of a Gottfried Keller. These were followed in 1910 by *Gertrud*, a novel about a musician. Hesse received the following telegram from Olaf Gulbransson:

Dear Hermann Hesse: You are a fine fellow. This evening your *Gertrud* passed through my skin and veins in great fiery waves, and I often had to grip the table. I had to make a drawing while Grete read it aloud. Here—I must thank you. Yours, Olaf.

Gertrud is not only the story of an unhappy love and marriage but also a panegyric to music as the consolation and justification of all life. In it the fragrant and romantic sounds of the Gaienhofen period predominate.

Marie Bernoulli, who was a very individual and exceedingly sensitive pianist, played much Schumann and Chopin for Hesse during this time. Older than he, she loved quiet solitude and, most of all, flowers and song. In the fairy tale *Iris*, which Hesse

dedicated to her even after the marriage had ended in separation, he wrote:

> Sometimes she was so tender and sensitive that everything alien pained her and easily brought her to tears. Then she was again quietly, finely radiant in a solitary happiness, and whoever saw her felt how hard it would be to give this beautiful, strange woman something and to mean something to her.

Hesse traveled in Switzerland, Germany, Austria, and Italy. In the years before World War I, he went to Italy for a few days every spring. On many of these excursions, which were usually to small cities in Tuscany and northern Italy, he was accompanied by Othmar Schoeck, the composer and pupil of Max Reger who has set many of his poems to music. Hesse told us in a memorial written in 1936 that he had Schoeck to thank for a very great part of what he learned about good music in the Gaienhofen period. In the first years of his friendship with Schoeck, "out of the recipient's need to give effect to his thanks," he even wrote the libretto for a romantic opera, which, however, could not be used.

In 1907 Hesse built a house of his own outside the village of Gaienhofen. It had its own garden and afforded a distant prospect across the Lower Lake of Constance, the Swiss shore, Reichenau, the Cathedral of Constance, and the mountains. But even in the old farmhouse he has already felt as if he were "in the land of the Philistines"—the title of one of the sketches in the *Picture Book*—when he regarded his little cask of wine in the cellar and confessed to himself, "So I am doing well, very well. Even

my cat is getting plump; she gets as much milk as she likes." While he was still building his own house, he sang in another sketch the praises of wandering. He gazed after every vagabond "as if the fellow were a king, with esteem, admiration and envy." Soon he had become a stranger in his own house.

Hesse's three sons were born in Gaienhofen. They too live today in Switzerland, where Bruno the oldest is a painter, Heiner a decorator, and Martin a photographer.

In the summer of 1911, the year of Martin's birth, Hesse, tired of Europe and "out of sheer inner need," went to India. But unable to find what he was seeking, he returned disappointed from Sumatra, southeast Asia, and Ceylon. The land of the temples and the Upanishads had been too much profaned by commercial efficiency, which had crept in even in places that once served only the gods. And, rather than bringing him closer to the Indian spirit (with which he was already closely occupying himself), the charm of the exotic separated him from it. In Kandi, in the midst of Buddhist priests, he felt the same homesickness for the true India as he had previously felt in Europe. At odds with himself, he had fled from Europe in an attempt to achieve detachment and a vantage point of vision. But he was soon forced to recognize that the peace he was seeking and the India he was seeking were not to be reached by ship or by train.

. . . I had to find all the magic bridges myself. I had also to cease being hostile to Europe in my heart, and instead, in heart and mind, make the true Europe and the true East my

own. This took years and years, and they were years of suffering, years of unrest, years of war, years of despair.

After this journey, Hesse was finished "with the quest for India and the flight from Europe." What he found confirmed, however, was the knowledge that

> in Europe, as in Asia, there was a timeless subterranean world of values and of the spirit that had not been killed by the invention of the locomotive or by Bismarck, and that it was right and good to live in this timeless world, in this peaceful spiritual world in which Europe and Asia, the Veda and the Bible, Buddha and Goethe, had an equal share.

At the end of the year he returned from India. Internal and external causes of discontent with the Gaienhofen life led him in 1912 to sell his house and move to Ostermundingen near Bern. There he rented the house of his friend, the painter Albert Welti, who had died a few months before. Situated on the Melchenbühlweg above the Wittigkofen castle, this pretty seventeenth-century estate in the Bern style had a half-primitive, half-patrician quality that was quite in harmony with what Hesse and his wife desired at that time. In the 1914 fragment of a novel, *The House of Dreams (Das Haus der Träume)*, it is portrayed with reasonable fidelity.

But it was still too redolent of death. From the beginning, life in the new house was darkened and unhappy. There Hesse wrote the novel about a painter, *Roßhalde*, which appeared in 1914, and in it we have little difficulty in recognizing problems and tensions of his own marriage. But the approach of World War I was also casting its shadows before it.

4

A Look into Chaos

With the advent of World War I there began for Hesse a time of which he later said that "Job had become his brother." What made him different from the others when "the so-called time of greatness" had come was—as he says himself—not that it found him more prepared, more dignified, or better. The difference was that he lacked the compensation of enthusiasm.

No, I could not share the joy over the time of greatness, and thus it was that I suffered miserably under the war from the very start, for years desperately resisting a disaster that seemingly had burst out of a clear sky, while all around me the world behaved as if full of joyful enthusiasm over this same disaster. When I read poets' and novelists' newspaper articles, in which they discovered the blessings the war had brought, and the professors' rallying calls, and all the war poems from professorial study rooms, I felt more miserable still.

At the beginning of the war Hesse offered his services to the Swiss consulate, which assigned him, as a half-Swiss, to civilian duty with the legation in Bern. Together with the zoologist Professor Woltereck, he established a department for supplying German prisoners-of-war with literature, and became co-editor of the periodical *Vivos Voco*. He was director of the biweekly *Sonntagsbote für deutsche Kriegsgefangene* ("Sunday Courier for German Prisoners-of-war") and ran a prisoner-of-war library of his own.

For Hesse the war meant not only the destruction of his freedom and independence. Rather it proved to be "the great moral crisis" that forced him to justify anew his entire thinking and his entire

work. From the start he was in sharp opposition to the war. His antiwar writings were collected and published by him in 1946 under the title *War and Peace (Krieg und Frieden)* and were dedicated to the memory of his friend Romain Rolland.

With an appeal entitled "Friends, Do Not Speak in These Tones!" (*"O Freunde, nicht diese Töne!"*) he addressed himself in September 1914 to the poets and writers of the world, asking them to deny their voices to the war's hymns of hate. But his call that "love is higher than hate, understanding is higher than anger, and peace is nobler than war" failed to echo. In the German press he was reviled as a traitor to the fatherland. In addition to numerous abusive letters from unknown people, letters soon also came from booksellers, letting him know that an author such as he no longer existed for them. Many an old friend informed "[me] that he had been nursing a viper in his bosom, and that in future that bosom would beat only for *Kaiser* and *Reich* and not for a degenerate such as me."

The only positive reaction to Hesse's appeal was a letter he received from Romain Rolland. In him he found a like-minded traveler on life's road, and a friendship began that lasted until Rolland's death. In a letter of February 1915 Rolland expressed his wish and hope for a *"union sacrée de l'esprit européen,"* and Hesse in his reply also expressed the belief that recognition of the need for such a union of the European spirit "will soon grow mightily."

Exactly two years later Hesse published in the *Neue Zürcher Zeitung* his appeal, "To a Minister

of State" ("An einen Staatsminister"), reminding him of the words of the Sermon on the Mount, "Thou shalt not kill."

> I was full of uneasiness and anxiety, [he wrote] and while I thought and wondered where the cause lay, I suddenly remembered a few sentences by you, Mr. Minister, that I had read in the past few days. Your speech was polished; for the rest, it was not particularly new, important, or thought-provoking. Reduced to its essentials, it said pretty much the same thing that all rulers have for quite some time been accustomed to say: that in general one desires nothing more ardently than peace and a new unity and fruitful labor for the future of nations; that one wants neither to enrich oneself nor to gratify murderous appetites; but that "the moment for negotiations" has not yet come, so that for the present one must go on waging war valiantly. This, more or less, is a speech that every minister of every belligerent nation could have made, and perhaps will make tomorrow, or the day after.

Hesse's suffering over the hatred that was continuing unabated had by then reached a stage where it completely isolated him from the world. He had hardly any contact with the circle of German republican emigrants who were living in his vicinity. Even Hugo Ball, the cofounder of dadaism, who at that time belonged to a small radical antiwar group and lived in the environs of Bern, did not know that Hesse was living there too. Not until 1919 did the two become acquainted.

So preoccupied was Hesse with the question of whence came the disaster of war that he did not even notice that he was receiving another kind of attention. Overnight, Bern had become crowded with agents, spies, military personnel, diplomats, journal-

ists, speculators, and black marketeers. In this new center of international espionage and intrigue, Hesse himself was spied upon, his sentiments were sounded out, and he appeared suspect now to one camp, now to another, now even to his own countrymen. Even his friend Fritz Brun, conductor of the city orchestra of Bern, felt offended because Hesse was refusing all invitations to concerts. The theme of Hesse's first appeal against war had still been one of hope in the victory of reason and goodness, and its title, taken from Beethoven's Ninth Symphony, referred to the consolations that are to be found in music. Two years later, he had grown so sensitive that music itself had become something he could hardly endure. A few bars, he told us, were enough to "cause the whole makeshift order and discipline in which I held myself to collapse, and to awaken an intolerable yearning to flee from this world and this war."

Anyone who so identifies himself with the fate of his times becomes skeptical of all ideals. In a letter to Romain Rolland dated August 4, 1917—written about the same time as the appeal "To a Minister of State"—Hesse wrote that even "Europe" was no longer an ideal for him, so long as under its aegis people were killing one another. The war placed him before the abyss. It led him to an "awakening," to a recognition of the reality that lies beyond all the consolations sought in the appearance of things, beyond all separation and exclusion of the realm of evil from our consciousness. He felt ill for quite some time. In 1916 his father died, and he

visited his home town of Calw once more. That same year, on his doctor's advice, he put himself under the care of the psychoanalyst I. B. Lang, a disciple of C. G. Jung, visiting him frequently in Sonnenmatt near Lucerne. About seventy sessions took place between then and November 1917. The young physician won Hesse's confidence. He understood how to help him achieve the breakthrough of a symbol world that had long been latent in him.

Hesse's experience with psychoanalysis found its literary expression in *Demian*, which had an electrifying effect on German youth immediately after the war. Greeted with stormy applause, the book, written under the pseudonym Emil Sinclair, was at first taken for the work of a young man who was showing his own generation new roads to follow. It was only later that a style analysis by Eduard Korrodi established Hesse's authorship. In this book Hesse, now forty, touched the nerve of the time with uncanny precision. *Demian*, which prophesies the downfall of the old Europe, is a profession of faith in man. "People know less today than ever what a really living human being is. They shoot them dead in batches, and in every one they kill a precious, unique experiment of nature." Every human being

> is not only himself. He is also the unique, quite special, altogether important, and remarkable point where the phenomena of the world intersect just once and never again in precisely this way. Therefore, every human being's history is important, everlasting, divine; therefore, every human being, as long as he lives and carries out nature's will, is something wonderful and worthy of every attention. In

every human being the spirit has become form; in every one a creature suffers; in every one a redeemer is crucified.

In words such as these Hesse revealed himself as an existentialist. Not in the sense of a trend in philosophy, but in the original meaning of the word, as one who—unconcerned with systems of thought, dogmas, abstractions, and philosophies—always takes as his starting point the individual, the concrete uniqueness of the person. *Demian* is closely bound up with the fate of the war and of Europe. In it there are hard words of criticism for a Europe that has grown old and rigid. But who understood, two decades before World War II, the warning about the beast whose soul had been fettered too long? And who believed the prediction that "something great and terrible" was coming? For its author, too, this book that evolved in time of war was, first of all, a self-liberation.

Psychoanalysis meant for Hesse a decisive encounter with the powers of the unconscious, which he experienced as operative realities. For him to appear before them amounted to "looking into chaos." It included risking his existence as a person and as an artist. Psychoanalysis revealed to him, on the "road to the inner self," new dimensions he had previously only surmised. Yet he did not fall into its power; it was only a transitional stage. As often as he made reference in later years to its value, he also called attention to its dangers.

Psychoanalysis came to meet Hesse's hyperactive conscience halfway. Great as was the role that it played as Hesse was finally breaking through the last

the dangerous, touching, irresponsible yet tender of conscience, soft, dreaming, cruel, profoundly childlike "Russian man," as we are still fond of calling him even today, although I believe he has long since been at the point of becoming European man. For it is precisely this that is the "downfall of Europe."

And again:

The "Russian man" (which we have long since had in Germany also) is not signified by the single word "hysteric," neither is it by the word drunkard, or criminal, or poet, or saint—but by all these characteristics simultaneously coexisting. Russian man—Karamazov—is at once murderer and judge, ruffian and creature of most tender soul. He is the most perfect egoist, just as he is the hero of the most perfect self-sacrifice. Together in this man are exterior and interior, good and evil, God and Satan.

The profound shock of the war had clarified Hesse's vision. Need we remind ourselves that analyses such as this can be confined neither to an imaginary magic-mythic sphere nor to a romanticizing *gnosis*, but that they press forward, as this one did, to the center of an approaching reality? In the National Socialist concentration camps we have seen perverse varieties of the human type that Hesse described. The brute of "tenderest soul," the mass-murderer, esthetically inclined, who is a family man, are types that have appeared in many postwar trials.

During the war years then, there took place in Hesse a breakthrough to his own unconscious that forced him to "look at chaos." What was also happening was that his own experience was enlarging into the suprapersonal, so that his work now was

becoming a fateful parable. It is in this sense that the closing words of the article on Karamazov are to be understood. The passage illuminates, in the figure of Dostoyevsky, the relationship of the poet to the seer:

In the soul of Dostoyevsky, that which elsewhere we call hysteria—a certain sickness and capability for suffering—has served humanity as an organ, pointer, and barometer. Humanity is about to notice this. Already half of Europe, at least half of eastern Europe, is on the road to chaos, moving drunkenly in a holy madness along the edge of the abyss, and singing—singing hymns of intoxication as Dmitri Karamazov sang. The ordinary citizen laughs at these songs, offended by them; the saint and seer hears them and weeps.

But Hesse's experience with psychoanalysis, as well as his thorough study of the world of Buddha and Lao Tse, had revealed to him the knowledge of the vital unity of opposites and the law of the countermovement. For him there was, hence, no such thing as absolute ruin. In September 1914 he wrote verses on the Bhagavad Gita, in which he renounced war, "the blind god of senseless sorrows," though he knew that war and peace are equally valid in the realm of the spirit, which death does not touch. Downfall means for him transition. But a new cosmos can come into being only where chaos in all its abysmal totality is recognized and suffered through (even by the self, through the "journey to hell"). This insight meant a far-reaching transformation not only in Hesse's life but also in his creative activity. Many of his friends now turned away from him, some because he did not adopt the role of a leader with definite prescription and program, others be-

cause he no longer wrote books without moral commitment that edified and entertained.

> My friends were right when they told me that my writings had lost their beauty and harmony. Such words only made me laugh. What do beauty and harmony mean to a man condemned to death who is running for his life between walls that are caving in?

From then on he divested himself of all remnants of the interest in writing idyllic works that entertained. He made his final departure from the seeming security of the middle-class world. At the centennial celebration of Gottfried Keller's birth, on July 10, 1919, he also parted from the writer who had at times been his model. His tribute was entitled "Sunset over Seldwyla" ("Seldwyla im Abendrot"), and sunset indeed lay over the sinking world of the Swiss master. Times have changed, he said. Our problems are different from those of Gottfried Keller's men and women. Fate has since come to pass. Amid the scorched earth of Europe, Seldwyla had become an amiable curiosity.

It was not only his external world that crashed with World War I. The war period also saw the beginning of the breakup of his family. Besides his son's illness of several years, the first warning signs of his wife's melancholia began to manifest themselves. When after difficult years the malady fully erupted and Marie Hesse had to spend a long time in sanatoriums, even the framework of family life dissolved. Hesse had to place the children in other homes. For long months toward the end of the war he sat alone in the neglected and desolate home.

The money had been spent, and the house was now much too large. It had no electric light, and often there was no kerosene. The pretty estate had become the residence of demons. Its bare walls reflected the chaos of the external world.

The poems written at that time contain all the suffering of those years. In them we hear the nightly rustling of the elm trees, and the garden full of the laughter of ghosts. The candle has burned low, his glass is empty, and Hesse sits and hears the straining of the wind at the shutters and the anxious voice of the cobwebbed clock on the wall. Shadows and fear come creeping out of every corner. But again and again his gaze wandered out to the world in flames. "Ministers, Excellencies, and Generals, the devil take you!" "Dear Brother Death" had become a cool star of longing. *Steppenwolf* visions were already flickering upward. "What are we doing here on earth? Poets, children, and fools are strangers in the world. Let us become officials and professors, or lunatics, or wild beasts of the field!"

It was a time of transformations, of trials and ordeals. At the end these grew to the point where they no longer had anything to do with the war and the fate of the world. Hesse was entirely submissive to his own fate, "though at times with the feeling that it was a question having to do with all inhumanity in general."

Through gazing into chaos he had, however, gained a new standard by which to measure his own life. He would have left the house in Ostermundingen long before, had his work for the German

prisoner-of-war welfare permitted it. Not until the spring of 1919 was he free. In this same year his marriage ended in divorce. Hesse had lived in Albert Welti's house for almost seven years. More than half were years of chaos. The departure from Ostermundingen was not difficult.

5

Magic Garden in Ticino

On May 2, 1919, Hesse wrote to Romain Rolland: "I have had to bear a very heavy burden in my personal life in recent years. Now I am about to go to Ticino and once again live a while as a hermit of nature and of my work."

Hesse had already visited Ticino a few times during the war and liked it very much. Here exoticism and classical proportion are united; here are subtropical vegetation and the secure garden-world; here is an adventurous kind of beauty that is combined with reminiscences of childhood. Here are the splendor of colors, gray skies full of longing and sadness, and palm-fringed sunsets over glittering waters, bordered by the clear lines of steeply rising mountains. More than elsewhere, life in Ticino is in the present; and yet, more than elsewhere, it also recalls the transiency of things. Passion and reflective meditation are intertwined. High above blue lakes stand flaming van Gogh cypresses; before the houses are rose arbors in silent fire. In a singsong speech that is still tart and precise, *un bicchiere di vino* is ordered, and the girls who live there have melodious names such as Ersilia and Rosita.

This small land on the south slope of the Gotthard agreed with Hesse. It was as if just beyond the tunnel the fairy tales began. But they would have to be told in a new language. A language more glowing, so as to capture the land's expressive quality; more restrained, to satisfy the classical proportion of the south; and, finally, a language very diaphanous, to express both of the foregoing qualities simultaneously. This is the road from the expressionistic

Klingsor-style to the ascetically restrained language mastery of *Siddhartha* and on to the many-layered filigreed style of *Magister Ludi* and the late prose of Hesse.

Ticino had an effect like a magic garden on Hesse, who in the last years of the war had almost lost his faith in the value of his creative work. When he arrived in Lugano in the spring of 1919, however, he was again clear in his mind that morally there remained only one possibility of existence for him. That was to put his literary work "before everything else, henceforth to live for that alone, and not to take seriously from now on the collapse of my family, or the severe money problem, or any other consideration. If this did not succeed, I was lost."

He remained a few weeks in Sorengo and sought a suitable dwelling. In Montagnola he found the Casa Camuzzi, into which he moved in May 1919. From Ostermundingen he had sent only his books and the great desk that had been made for him at the time he moved into the Gaienhofen farmhouse, and which he used until his death. Otherwise, he lived with rented furniture for twelve years in the Casa Camuzzi. Just after making the move he wrote "Klein and Wagner" ("Klein und Wagner"), which appeared that same year. In its psychic structure, though not in the externals of its plot, it too is strongly autobiographical. The hero of the story sees the most ardent wishes of his life fulfilled; he becomes aware of "the long-forgotten yearning for the south, and a desire—that had never become clear and free—for flight and freedom from the dusty ser-

vitude of his marriage." But the south meets him at first with that implacable quality of the beautiful that Rilke in his elegies has recognized as "the beginning of the terrible." It meets him with that excess and that heat that, pitilessly as the sun, reaches into the most hidden depths.

So it was that in this first span of time in Ticino, when chaos was still echoing, there again appeared (as counterpart to the classical dimension, which had not yet been wholly recognized) Dostoyevsky and his geographically and spiritually boundless world. Like him, Hesse too now portrayed with understanding complicity the fate of a criminal whose guilt is comprised not only of deeds but equally of thoughts. This is the official Friedrich Klein, who breaks out of the worthy middle-class world to make his way through distress and crime to become himself. "Klein and Wagner" was followed immediately by "Klingsor's Last Summer" ("Klingsors letzter Sommer"), which came into being in a few ecstatic weeks of summer. With these two works, Hesse relaxed to the extent that by the following winter he was able to begin *Siddhartha.*

In "Klingsor's Last Summer" the old sorcerer and fairy-tale king of the saga, the poet with the magic power of words of whom Novalis had written, comes again to life. But Hesse spanned the arc from romanticism to expressionism. His Klingsor is not a poet but a painter. In Ticino how could he be anything else? Like the Klingsor of the saga, however, he strayed along the paths of magic, which in Hesse always means "the road to the inner life" as well as

discernment of the unity behind the painful antitheses of existence.

But the voices of chaos were still loud. This Klingsor is still

> refined from every yearning, sick from every vice, inspired with enthusiasm by the knowledge that he is to perish, ready for every forward step, ripe for every step backward, all fervor and all fatigue, submissive to destiny and to pain as the morphine addict is to his poison, solitary, hollowed out, immeasurably old, at once Faust and Karamazov, beast and sage, wholly without ambition, wholly naked, full of the child's fear of death and full of tired readiness to die.

His life pulsates between passion and meditative reflection, between bacchantic intoxication with life and the ever-present knowledge of transitoriness and death. The poetic description of his being is a classic example of expressionist literary style.

Klingsor drains many beakers of wine and of love. But he knows it will not last much longer "else earth would fill one's hand and mouth and eyes!" Out of such a mood comes the poem on the transitory nature of things: "Leaf after leaf falls from my tree of life. . . ." But even when the wind someday blows cold around his grave, Klingsor will not be alone. The "eternal mother" will then bend over him.

Since *Demian*, an eruptive breakthrough of an interior world of images in Hesse had come to pass. One of these images was the figure of the primeval mother, and from this time forth it recurred often. Kindred to the Goethean mothers in *Faust*, it symbolized the element that is ever weaving at the loom

of life and ever in process of becoming, the element lasting and archetypal, the life that is forever renewing itself amid the transitoriness of the world.

But it is part of the drama of Hesse's life that he was never oriented only to one pole. Just as Klingsor is midway between Faust and Karamazov, so also Hesse's symbolism has its source in a polarity of tension. The archetype of the eternal mother is reminiscent not only of Goethe. She smiles at the bloom and decay and resurrection of things. It is a smile as *vegetatively* natural, and as enchanting, as the scent of flowers in the Ticino garden, a smile as remote and mysterious as the starry Ticino sky above the San Salvatore and the dusky lake. Radiating all the luxuriant prodigality of nature, such a smile still comes, after all, mainly from an acquiescence to one's own destiny. And now into the magic world of Ticino another voice sounded. It came from the lonely mountain world of the Upper Engadine, from Sils Maria—the voice of Nietzsche-Zarathustra.

In "Zarathustra's Return" ("Zarathustras Wiederkehr") Hesse called upon his readers to acknowledge destiny, elevate it to be their god, and become one with it. This "Address to German Youth" ("Wort an die deutsche Jugend") written in 1919 has justly been called the most laudable political achievement of any literary figure of that time. He who has recognized destiny will never want to change it, Hesse called down from his mountain to his youthful readers. It is childish to try or even want to alter fate. Everyone gets embroiled in a fight and beats each other to death. To alter fate was what

was being strived for by the Kaiser and the generals and all those who did not yet recognize that fate tasted bitter only so long as one regarded it as something intruding from without, something hostile, and not as a power that, being part of the self, had to be mastered from within.

The theme was not new. It was the shifting of accent—which had begun with the advent of symbolism—from the exterior to the interior world, a shifting of consciousness that in the more recent intellectual history of the West had its beginning in romanticism, while it drew upon the ancient doctrines of the East. Rilke, the typical heir of symbolism, called to his loved one that the world will be nowhere but within and that "the external dwindles and is ever smaller." He too knew that existence and fate, interior and exterior are names of *one* concept. But what in Rilke and the symbolists was often something esoteric and intelligible only to the initiate, was taken by Hesse and consciously confronted with reality. He transformed it into a new language of form and image that, in the preciseness of its delineation, henceforth was to prevail more and more over the romantic element that was to become more diffuse.

If "Klingsor" was still tempestuous excess, nonetheless there was in it the seed of *Siddhartha*, with its measured prose and its consoling world nourished by the wisdom of the East. The note was already heard in "Klein and Wagner." Friedrich Klein knows that every life is an exhalation and every death an inhalation of the breath of God, and that one

dies easily and that one is born easily once one has learned to let oneself fall and not to resist fate. This leads to the wisdom of Lao Tse, who teaches that the hardest of all things is overcome by the gentlest of all things. Expressed in Christian terms, it is the command not to resist evil with force.

The serene world of the East proved for Hesse more viable and enduring than the ecstatic world of Nietzsche, from which he later drew away even more. Yet Nietzsche did not disappear from his consciousness. Was it only for the mountain air that Hesse, year after year, spent a few weeks each summer in Sils Maria?

In ever-new parables Hesse now described the unity of all being. His invocation to this experience was always the comforting counterpart to the dissonant tones that were far from falling silent in him, sympathetic as he was to the misery of the times.

But even when he was still in Bern, and when writing was unable to satisfy him fully, Hesse discovered a new joy, which proved stronger than many a bottle of wine (which had not always successfully solaced him with forgetfulness). It was an activity of an almost meditative kind: painting. In Ticino it was to bloom. Already forty, he began suddenly to paint. It was not that he considered himself a painter. He painted because it made him more glad, more patient toward reality, for it gave him an additional means of transforming that reality. He can make houses laugh, dance, or weep, he can give faces to the trees and endow them with crowns

of fantasy that can just as easily be palm leaves as birds beating their wings or ascending. His small palette, whose colors have the power to illuminate, becomes for him an arsenal. "Klingsor" could not have been written without this intimate relationship to painting and color, which was wholly modern and existential. The accent is solely on color, not line. A few strokes with sepia—contours that become more and more sparing as time goes on, that achieve their effect through omission of the nonessential—suffice to give a picture its outline and external form. The color stood in direct relation to the psychic wave. Hesse in this learned much with the years. He preserved, even in the perfectionist world of the technical age, the courage to indulge in the luxury of dilettantism. Looking at many of his watercolors, one is reminded of August Macke and the Blauer Reiter circle, with which Hesse had in fact direct and personal connections. From his friend Louis Moillet he learned much about Paul Klee, whom he greatly admired. With Klee, Hesse's painter friend, Ernst Morgenthaler, long stood in a kind of pupil relationship. This is not to say that Hesse's painting was comparable with the work of these artists. But Hesse's drive to paint, and generally the work he did, was reminiscent of them. Anyone who wishes to know what the function of color in modern art is, and what is meant by Kandinsky's repeated requirement of "inner necessity," can learn this from reading *Klingsor,* in which the literary master has given form to that which the dilettante painter can only hint at. The expressionist painter effaces the

required white, substituting for it vermilion, with which it puts up a bleeding fight for permanence. Like catastrophes the colors discharge their tensions against each other; bright green and Naples yellow scream to the inexorable god; groaning, more blue is thrown into the insipid dusty gray. Painting is a dramatic happening that is made possible because the colors are independent living beings. It is entirely a question of their psychic effect: "Purple was denial of death, vermilion was mockery of decay." How does Kandinsky say it?

> Painting is a thundering collision of different worlds that in the struggle with each other, and out of that struggle are destined to create the new world that we call the resulting work of art. Every work comes into being . . . by catastrophes, which out of the chaotic roaring of the instruments finally form a symphony.

At times Hesse toyed with the thought "that I might perhaps still succeed in escaping literature entirely and making a living at the more appealing trade of painter."

The Ticino magic garden kept stimulating him to new studies. Ochre, Naples yellow, Venetian red, white, very light madder lake, Paris blue, vermilion—these were his favorite colors. A lovely selection of Hesse's watercolors of Ticino was published in 1955 by Woldemar Klein in Baden-Baden. In a 1920 book, *Travel (Wanderung)*, which was one of his favorite books, Hesse—in the synthesis of lyric poetry, prose, and painting—sounded a chord already fixed by the classical proportion of the south. More fantastic, more dreamlike, more glowing in

color were the somewhat later illustrations for the fairy tale "Piktor's Transformations" ("Piktors Verwandlungen"), which thematically recall in many characteristics Paul Klee.

Hesse's watercolors not only gave him joy but also helped him to surmount difficult years. But the help first began with others. Already during World War I he had begun, on the advice of a friend, to produce small handwritten booklets and portfolios, which he illustrated with tiny illustrations about seven-by-seven centimeters in size. The proceeds belonged to the prisoners-of-war. Then came years in which Hesse himself was glad to have such commissions. But even in the bad time following World War II, when, though his paintings had grown more varied, his powers had grown weaker, it gave him amusement "to transform a handful of white sheets into an illuminated manuscript, and to know that the handwriting will become further transformed, first into money, then into parcels containing coffee, rice, sugar, cooking oil, and chocolate."

One may think what one likes of Hesse's painting—he himself never claimed to be anything more than a dilettante—but it proved fruitful and important for his life and literary work. Painting stimulated him and compelled him to temper the musical rhythm of his nature and his creative art and to set bounds to his romantic self-release. The southern landscape was conducive to this development toward the classical.

All the incandescence of the south, excess and passion, enthusiasm for life and enthusiasm for

death found their liberating expression in *Klingsor.* Then Klingsor's magic garden was transformed. It became a grove of contemplation, a shadowy mango forest of India. "In the shade of the Sal Forest, in the shade of the fig tree," Siddhartha grows up. For almost three years he too was the symbol and vehicle of his author's experience, thoughts, and problems. In this work, which in the very rhythm of its language and the precisely balanced melody of its sentences affords the proper garment for the Indian scenery, Hesse's idea of the "three stages of becoming man" is integrated. It states that the road of every separate individual leads from innocence and childhood, by way of guilt and despair, either to ruin or to knowledge, spirit, and faith. Siddhartha travels this latter road. After he breaks through despair—which is not only Oriental but also Kierkegaardian—he perceives the sacred *om,* the *om mani padme hum,* the Brahmans' religious formula for the unity of all being. It can be experienced only by gaining in one's conscious life the victory over time, which Klingsor had already recognized to be deception. Here we have the addition of the fourth dimension, which in connection with Einstein's theory of relativity plays a role again in *Steppenwolf.* Hesse-Siddhartha asks:

Was all suffering not time? Was all torture of self and fear of self not time? Was not everything difficult and everything hostile in the world vanquished and gone as soon as one had vanquished time, as soon as one could think time out of existence?

This book with its Oriental metaphorical language has since received wide distribution and high recognition in India and Japan. Lectures on the author are held at the Zen Buddhist Komazawa University. An Indian scholar wrote to Hesse about the book:

> I feel it as the great tribute to the sons of this country from one of the great minds of our time. . . . Frankly, it is your thirty-year-long meditation and studies (*tapasya*) which have taken the form of *Siddhartha*.

Today the work has been translated into nine Indian dialects. In Japan Hesse stands at the head of the list of all German authors translated into Japanese.

Hesse wrote nothing that he had not personally experienced. *Siddhartha*, too, is the fruit of submergence in his own self and in nature. This is why there lies, between its two parts, a pause for meditation lasting approximately a year and a half.

On August 10, 1922, just as the book was finished, Hesse wrote again to Romain Rolland, to whom Part One is dedicated:

> Your kind letter begins with the question whether I am still "in Lugano." That is hard to answer. I do so by saying that I still live in Montagnola, but that for about a year I have not been in Lugano, although it is only an hour's walk from here. You see from this the kind of life I lead—Saint Jerome in his study.

Was he just a dreamer, ignorant of the ways of the world? The same letter (written in 1922!) contains the sentence: "Over in Germany the spiritual atmosphere has something of anarchy but also re-

ligious fanaticism. It is a mood of the end of the world and the coming of the thousand-year *Reich*."

To arrive at knowledge Hesse required the medium of solitude. In 1923, for the first time in five years, he wintered in a city. But he no longer knew what to do with its attractions. From Basle he wrote to Romain Rolland, in whom he was glad to confide. "I do not find the way back to a social life here either. And this has got nothing to do with the fact that I shall soon remarry. At heart I am a *samana* and belong in the forest."

He spent Christmas of that year in Delsberg in the Jura, at the home of his fiancée's parents. In 1924 he married Ruth Wenger, the daughter of the Swiss author (little known in Germany) Lisa Wenger. But three years later this marriage too ended in divorce.

The peace of Siddhartha had long since melted away. In southern summers passion and sorrow again rose to the point of agonized tension. "Red blooms the flower of delight. . . ./Many women have I known,/Many have I loved with sorrow,/To many have I given pain—." But all intensified living in the present is also intensified knowledge that all things pass away: "Fragrantly wilts in my hand, the irretrievable rose."

In 1925–1926 for a few months Hesse was again traveling. It was already the "loping gait" of the wolf of the steppe for whom none of the inhabited places can become permanent home. "I am having hard times. With aversion I begin each day of my life anew"—Romain Rolland read these words in

January 1926. In the spring Hesse was again back in Montagnola. In the following year *Nuremberg Journey* and *Steppenwolf* were published. In the little travel book Hesse told of Blaubeuren and its saga of the beautiful Laux. He recalled his youth, the Swabian world which he still very much loved, and Mörike and Gottfried Keller. But especially he recalled Hölderlin and his poetic fragment "Night," which even as a boy, when he first discovered it in his schoolbook, enchanted him as no other poem later could. This encounter, as he told us, "perhaps made me become a writer." In this book there was much talk about humor, one of the better products of mankind, a crystal "which grows only in deep and lasting sorrows." Thus in this period the ground was being tested for its load capacity.

Yes, with humor it would be borne—even the railroad stations, even the barracks, even the literary readings. With laughter, with not taking reality seriously, with the constant knowledge of its destructibility, it could be borne. One day the machines would run berserk against each other, the arsenals would discharge their junk, and, where today a large city stands, one day grass again would grow and the weasel and the marten prowl. No, one does not need to do this funny world the honor of taking it seriously.

Here is already the prelude to *Steppenwolf*. How very much identical Harry Haller too is with Hermann Hesse is impressively shown by a photo of the author taken in 1927. The wolf of the steppe too is a critic of his time. In the midst of "this so very contented, so very bourgeois, so very spiritless world" he no longer finds a home, and must declare

himself a lunatic, a wild beast astray. Exactly five years later, in Aldous Huxley's utopian novel *Brave New World*, again the hero who has remained a human being appears as "the wild man" in the eyes of his contemporaries. But Harry Haller's suffering goes deeper. It comes not only from the painful gift of being the antenna and barometer of an epoch. The wolf of the steppe's look:

> went to the heart of all human nature. In a single second he expressed eloquently the doubts felt by a thinker, perhaps a knower, concerning the dignity and the very meaning of human life. This look said: "Look, such apes are we! Look, such is man!" And all renown, all cleverness, all achievements of the intellect, all beginnings of sublimity, grandeur, and permanence in human nature collapsed and were so much buffoonery!

Harry Haller's despair, which leads him to the verge of suicide and on which he delivers a classic psychological treatise in his book of confessions, does not come solely from the isolation of the outsider Hesse who in this period was "so horribly alone." It comes from the suffering over the *principium individuationis* generally. Harry Haller is a highly individual personality whose differentness has reached the culminating point, from which it yearns again toward simplicity, toward dissolution in a world beyond the world of phenomena, toward origin. Hesse-Haller was affected "by the guilt feeling that comes of individuation"; quite in the Schopenhauer sense, he felt guilt by his mere existence. Be it recalled that Schopenhauer's thought too has strongly Oriental characteristics. What fun-

damentally distinguished Hesse from the Oriental world, however, was the active nature of his life and thought, which in the existential sphere never contented itself with passive resignation. What was profoundly sympathetic and familiar to him—as he once said in a letter to Thomas Mann—was "to undertake the impossible though knowing it is that, to take the tragic actively upon oneself." This attitude led him to reject someone like Heidegger.

In the summer of 1952 he wrote from Sils Maria:

> *Geworfensein*—the state of being thrown—the term which the philosophy of our day uses to characterize man's life, does not satisfy me. It is a nervous, hysterical draping of something inadequate in the grander garment of the seeming-tragic. In the process even an elevated term such as "tragic" loses all value, and man—simply by having been born and by being unable to make out of that fact anything right—becomes a kind of hero.

The wolf of the steppe, too, with all his mood of suicide, is sustained by his humor and faith in the "trace of divinity" in his life. A breakthrough to humor was also the sense of the "magic theater," which Hesse-Haller "needs for the liberation of his neglected soul." Now a magic began to work its effect. It seemed first to lead out of the Ticino magic garden, its vegetative intricacies and its classic dimensions, into the mirrorlike brightness of a consciousness that transcended space and time. The "magic theater" was a passage through the inner world, which first of all is equivalent also to a passage through hell. Once again the self became a model of

historical events, for the book paints on the wall threateningly the new war that was approaching. Many of Hesse's readers, intent on harmony, were not pleased with this look at hidden realities. For them *Steppenwolf* marked a retrogression from *Siddhartha*. Transfixed by the "look into chaos," they failed to notice that in the center of this book was the "magic theater," and in its center, in turn, was the *Tat twam asi*—the perpetual self-discovery and self-encounter in the Promethean depths of one's own being, which embraces not only the realms of light but also those of evil and guilt. It is from just this that the altruistic moral of this dogma from the Upanishads was derived. The ripeness of humor, too, grew out of the courage to find total knowledge of self, which includes the demonic. Hesse-Haller, between jazz and *The Magic Flute*, was on his way to this goal. The "magic theater" showed him the laughter of the immortals, Mozart and Goethe in their unchanging and eternal state of being.

Long after *Steppenwolf*, but not uninfluenced by it, the experience of the *Tat twam asi* reappears in works by Hermann Kasack and Ernst Jünger. Hesse in his novel had essayed to describe border regions of what was still hardly expressible. This many-layered novel is, nevertheless, structured like a fugue. "Is it necessary to say that *Steppenwolf* is a novel that in experimental daring is not inferior to *Ulysses* and *The Counterfeiters?*" asked Thomas Mann. As a friend of Hesse he still had many an occasion later to get to know the "wolf of the steppe" from another

side as well. Montagnola was an important destination on all of Thomas Mann's European travels after 1945. Occasionally the two also met in Sils Maria. There was a meeting there as recently as 1954, when Thomas Mann was reading the proofs of *Felix Krull*, that picaresque novel that Hesse especially loved for its tone and atmosphere and the high-altitude freshness of its art. Erika Mann wrote of this meeting:

> Exceedingly genial and chatty, companionable, indeed gallant—this is how we know the "wolf of the steppe" whose world-shyness and need for solitude vanish as soon as he sits around the table with friends. And they were friends, Hesse and my father, brothers in the spirit who would hear no ill spoken of each other, and who manfully resisted as soon as anyone tried to play the one against the other.

Present at these meetings was Ninon Ausländer. The archeologist, philologist of ancient languages, and scholar of fairy tales was more than twenty years younger than Hesse, to whom she had been married since November 1931, with whom she had lived since 1927. In the summer of 1929 Hesse wrote verses of thanks—"For Ninon" ("Für Ninon"). Two years earlier, the poems "Crisis" ("Krisis") were his bitter reply to the good wishes expressed at his fiftieth birthday. What did the friends who wanted to see just the charming and significant side of his nature know of how things really were with him at this time? "Red eyelids stared in the mirror/ And gray hair that withers and dies." Some of these verses, because of their private character, have not been included in the published edition of his col-

lected poems. Some have such titles as "To John the Baptist Spoke Hermann the Drunkard" ("Zu Johannes dem Täufer sprach Hermann der Säufer"). Others take us into the world of nightclubs, perhaps down on the quay at Lugano, where Hesse would have liked so much to break through his solitude and be a saxophone-player in a jazz band: "Merrily I blew into my curved blowpipe. . . . And sacrificed with dance to the god Baal." But to him, the "poor idiot," this happiness was not allowed. Again and again "Hölderlin's deep music" rose in his memory.

A year later he was again working on the story *Narcissus and Goldmund*, which appeared in 1930, before his marriage and move to the new house. He had overcome another crisis. His own subjective sphere was objectivized in the figures of the ascetic monk and the sensuous artist. Instead of the landscape of the south, the German world and the Swabian atmosphere of the cloister of Maulbronn are forcefully invoked. Martin Buber, in the official speech he made in 1957 in Stuttgart on the occasion of his friend's eightieth birthday, summed up Hesse's life and work with the formula, "service to the spirit," and made reference to the great dialectic relationship between the two characters in this story, in whom Hesse for the first time had "given corporeal form to the conflict of the spirit."

In all his changes Hesse remained true to himself and his ideal. This constantly led him into a sphere beyond the reality that is subject to the laws of causation. So in 1932 there appeared the abstractionist book, *The Journey to the East*, a work that

is both fairy tale and symbol of the interior world. It was paralleled by a dimension of consciousness which, in the coincidence of the remotest past with the remotest future, yielded a new, transparent omnipresence. The League of Travelers to the East is above space and time; it is that transcendental "order of the spirit" in whose membership Hesse counts all those spirits—be they Lao Tse and Goethe, or Novalis and Paul Klee—who have penetrated through to "the heroic and the magical." Be it noted that the heroic is placed on a par with the magical. On their journey to the unity of all places and times, the Travelers to the East do not indulge in passively "letting themselves go" into vast mystic depths of uncontrolled thoughts and feelings. Rather they undertake the impossible, although they know it to be such, and they actively take upon themselves the tragedy of being yoked between wish and causation-determined reality.

The result is the liberating irony that sparkles again and again from the lines of this book. In his foreword to the French edition, André Gide said of this:

> The gladdening irony of Hesse seems to me dependent on his ability to step out of himself, to see himself without observing himself, and without complacency to judge himself. . . . This kind of unassuming modesty becomes all the more perfect, the more that talent and virtue are combined with it.

From then on Hesse's life became quite withdrawn, which does not mean that he took no interest in the events of his time. But his protest "against the

brutal, bloodthirsty stupidity of men" changed more and more into the conviction that pure artistic production, as a spiritual reality, was another form of counterforce against chaos. He continued to hold himself apart during the Third Reich. From the beginning of the new regime he was on the list of unwelcome literature. His books did not fall victim to the burnings, but, later, paper was no longer authorized for the publication of his writing.

Again he wrote, on January 26, 1936, to his friend Rolland:

> The experiences that we had then in the world war are all being repeated today, and again being repeated is the temptation to doubt the very value of the mind and the word. That now, in the midst of quite nasty experiences, I am able to resist this doubt, is largely thanks to you and your example.

Ten days later:

> My life in Montagnola is not quite so calm as it appears to you. At present, for example, I am again the target of stubborn harassment in the press, with slanders, falsified biographic data, etc. . . . Let us hope that death one day will really bring us the great peace for which one sometimes longs.

After the notorious SS organ *Das Schwarze Korps* "occupied itself" with Hesse's personality, Will Vesper's *Neue Literatur*, which had expressed itself once before on the same theme, in November 1935, began a new inflammatory article. On November 3 Hesse had his answer delivered to its editorial offices through the *Société des Ecrivains Suisses*. In it he energetically denounced the use of such abusive language as "The German writer H. Hesse assumes

the role of national traitor," or "To please the Jews etc., he assists in disseminating abroad false notions that are injurious to the fatherland." He requested the editorial office, "in future contributions in which a hitherto esteemed colleague is dragged in the dirt, the trouble at least be taken to eliminate blatant lies and slander." He also pointed out that he was not a Reich German but a Swiss citizen. If, amid the rather hostile sentiment prevailing abroad, he continued to champion and propagate German literature "despite its present state," he did it (he said) not as a "national traitor" but because he had full right to.

It is a question of what one understands by the terms Germany and German literature. Thomas Mann too had given unmistakable expression to this in 1937, in his famous New Year's letter to the Rector of the University of Bonn on the occasion of his refusal of a doctoral degree.

Hesse had been a Swiss citizen since 1923. His reply to the slanders in Will Vesper's periodical was quoted in German newspapers under the heading "Letter from a Strange Foreigner" ("Brief eines merkwürdigen Ausländers) and commented on accordingly. In the process it became plain that after World War I Hesse's antinationalist and antimilitarist attitude had not been forgiven.

The speeches of Hitler and his ministers, their newspapers and pamphlets, had an effect on Hesse like that of poison gas. It penetrated up to his Ticino mountain village.

It did not require the mass atrocities, which only became known years later—sufficient was this poison gas, this dese-

cration of the language and dethronement of truth to bring me again (as during the years of the first world war) to the edge of the abyss. The air was again poisonous; life was again put in question. This was the moment in which I had to summon up all redeeming powers in me to examine and make secure all I possessed of faith. Something had arisen that was far worse than the vain Kaiser and his demigod-like generals had been, and would probably lead to something worse than that kind of war we had come to know. In the midst of these threats and dangers to the physical and spiritual existence of a writer in the German language, I turned to the salvation of every artist—work.

The work that now comes into being—plans for it had already been formed—was *Magister Ludi*. In the middle of the war, in 1943, it was published in Switzerland. It bears the dedication "To the Travelers to the East." Three years later Hesse received for it the Nobel Prize. In 1947 he received an honorary doctor's degree from the University of Bern.

In Josef Knecht, the hero of this voluminous novel, we may once again see an incarnation of Hesse, no doubt his most sublime one. But he has also created a self-portrait, interwoven with fine irony, in the figure of the Elder Brother, the great scholar learned in Lao Tse and Dschuang Dsi and *amateur* of the Book of Changes (the *I Ching*).

Knecht's spiritual home is Castalia, a pedagogic province similar to the Goethean one. The name is a reference to the spring Castalia, sacred to the muses, on the southern slope of Mount Parnassus. In *Magister Ludi* occidental tradition and Oriental wisdom are united. Just as it links the realms of the

unconscious with those of the intellect, and those of the intuitively creative artist with those of the abstract thinker, so also it combines the ideas of romanticism, pythagoreanism, the Platonic academy, ancient China and India with the speculations of Nicholas Cusanus, Abelard, Bolzano, Leibnitz, and Hegel, to achieve a synthesis encompassing many countries and times. The two main pillars of the "bead game" are mathematics and music, two disciplines seemingly opposed though, in fact, they are recognizable to the ordering mind as mutually corresponding symbols. In these two symbols Hesse tallied the sum of his own life. It is a metamorphosis in which all preceding stages of crisis and despair have been transformed into clarity, and all clown-laughter into the courageous serenity of one who has attained to knowledge.

When in 1944 the two volumes of this work arrived from Switzerland in Pasadena, California, Thomas Mann—who was working on his own *Doctor Faustus*—spent days occupied with them "in the most personal way." Till then he knew only the introduction as published in advance in the *Neue Rundschau*.

> Now that I could see the entire work, I was almost frightened at its kinship with that which was so urgently occupying me. The same idea of a fictitious biography, with the touches of parody that this form brings with it. The same connection with music. Cultural and epoch critique likewise. . . .

Mann finds "startlingly great" similarity, and in his diary gives blunt expression to his feelings: "To be

reminded that one is not alone in the world is always unpleasant."

But in the character of Magister Thomas of Trave Hesse has erected to Thomas Mann a beautiful monument of friendship. In it is also expressed—by means of Magister Thomas's manner of treating the bead game—the difference between Magister Thomas and Josef Knecht.

Magister Ludi and *Doctor Faustus* cannot be compared only in terms of their criticism of the age. (This is present in abundance in Hesse's novel, which indeed he had written "in despite of the grinning present.") The likeness between *Magister Ludi* and *Doctor Faustus* lies even more in the larger relationships, which Thomas Mann found "staggering." *Magister Ludi* is characterized by a linking of mathematics, music, and theology and by the bead game's resemblance to the capacity of mathematics "for using figures and axioms of Euclidean geometry as parables to elucidate concepts in philosophy or theology." This is actually very much akin to the intentions of the *Doctor Faustus* of Thomas Mann. Because Mann saw music as "always a magical union of theology and the so-entertaining subject mathematics," he was convinced that the magical nature of music can be dissolved in reason. Reason and magic met in Thomas Mann also in "what one calls wisdom, initiation, in belief in the stars and in numerals."

Even though *Magister Ludi* is an art *sui generis*, its fundamental symbols in mathematics and music rest principally on geometric-magical configurations

that lead from Plato's Academy, one of its guiding models, to the geometric symbolism of German romanticism as well as to that generalized mathematics of nonmathematical objects that marked the age of *mathesis universalis*, for which the names of Descartes, Pascal, and Leibnitz are characteristic. All these stations in the history of Western thought are interwoven with the traditions of the Orient in the filigree-like thought and style of this late work, which represents a "*unio mystica* of all separated members of the *universitas litterarum*." The mathematical tradition might be traced from Bolzano—who is also included in *Magister Ludi*—through Schröder, Hilbert, and Scholz up to the present, and thus be placed in relation also to the mathematical constructions of Schönbergian music, which form the material for the tonal creations of *Doctor Faustus*.

But precisely in the fact that this does not happen, though Hesse knew these roads too, lies the fundamental difference between his book and that of his friend. Thomas Mann's novel is the expression of lamentation, a scream out of the time's chaos, a cry about a world that is dialectically hovering between damnation and hope of redemption. Hesse's book is an alternative—defiantly, chaos is opposed by a cosmos newly erected on classical proportions and traditions. The Castalia that he projects into the future is a realm of the spirit. It exists in the state of having become one with all times in history, that heroic-magical goal of the Travelers to the East for whom Castalia is intended. As for the "music of the universe" that the Magister Ludi Josef Knecht per-

ceives, what the Chinese Lü Bu We said two thousand years before about the nature of music is still valid: It originates in measure and has its root in the great Unity. Therefore this music is not lamentation, but gaiety. And this kind of Castalian gaiety

is neither a trifling attitude nor is it complacency. It is the highest knowledge and love, the affirmation of all reality, it is awakeness at the edge of all depths and abysses, it is a virtue of saints and knights, it is imperturbable—and old age and the nearness of death only serve to make it grow.

To perceive it required many years of meditation, many hours in the bamboo grove reading *I Ching* and Lao Tse.

And yet this bamboo grove was in Montagnola, and when the Elder Brother emerged from it, it was again the Ticino magic garden, blue and hazy, with its vine terraces, its lizards, and chestnut groves, and all its "fragrant mixture of southland and high mountains" that met his eye.

6

The Romantic and the Realist

In his biography, Hugo Ball calls Hermann Hesse the "last cavalier of the splendid train of romanticism." This dictum has very often been misunderstood. Conservative literary critics took it as grounds for classifying Hesse once and for all as "neoromantic." Critics moved by nationalistic resentment thus had the advantage of being more easily able to ignore Hesse's realistic diagnoses of his own time by relegating him to the more innocuous role of the dreamer whose gaze is turned toward the past.

Hugo Ball's description of Hesse is not badly drawn, even though Ball, dying in 1927, did not know Hesse's later work. But the word romantic did not mean to Ball what it means to contemporary critics. Hesse himself was also occupied, often and thoroughly, with the question of what romanticism was. As early as the turn of the century, and again in the 1920's, he expressed clearly the view that for him romanticism was not something "that inspires teenage girls and causes sensible men to shake their heads," and that it was also not something without form and subject to no laws. For Hesse—"backward-gazing, romantic, infantile" as he occasionally described himself with irony—it is, he says, not a question of "progress or romanticism, of moving forward or moving backward, but of the exterior and the interior world."

The shift of consciousness from the external world to the internal (the historical origins and currents of which we have already mentioned) is of course a typical feature of romanticism. But it is the very feature that leads to the modern age. Thus

Hesse was one of the first to recognize the significance of not only Sigmund Freud, but also of Kafka and Marcel Proust, each of whom had, each in his own way, granted the powers of the subjective world the importance that was their due. It is the same with Hesse's evaluation of Paul Klee. Klee, too, was in this sense a romantic. He himself spoke of the "cool romanticism" of his pictures, and of the Greek dictum *Gnothi seauton* (Know thyself) as the only road to style.

Hesse's romanticism grew out of his protest against the flattened, two-dimensional reality of the civilization whose critic he was, a civilization intent on profit and material progress. His criticism can be bitter, ironic, or elegiac. In *Nuremberg Journey*, (1927) he prophesied the time when in the place "where today a large city stands, grass again would grow and the weasel and the marten prowl." The little parable "The City" ("Die Stadt"), written in 1910, has for its theme the final decay of a city after all its destinies and its epochs of flowering: man's perishable work is the prey of nature, which at the end leaves only "a tissue of rottenness." Modern painting, too, is not without the motif of the primeval landscape after the catastrophe of civilization.

Civilization and romanticism—an antagonism which goes through history. This early Hesse brings to mind Ortega y Gasset, who refers to the spectacle of sublime lasciviousness that romantics of all times have seen in ruins. Because they are the results of the decay of once rational systems that have been aban-

doned to the embraces of the vegetative element, they are symbols of all those scenes of ravishment in which instinctual nature triumphs over human moderation. Viewed psychologically, this romanticism is equivalent to the bursting loose of the entire lower world long held in chains, which the young Hesse describes in *Hermann Lauscher*. And yet it is not the same thing. Hermann Lauscher too strives for harmony of the conscious and the unconscious. Hesse did not subscribe to the romanticism of unbridled self-surrender to the vegetative element because of a quality that he opposed to this from an early age: the moderation of rationality and highly alert consciousness. Even in earlier works, in which he handled the theme of the opposition of culture and nature, he was drawn to the subject not out of sublime sensuality but out of a still-unmastered suffering at this antagonism. He never pledged himself to only one pole of this polarity. He viewed the interplay of life always with an intellectual detachment that extended even to his strong affinity for nature. Here too he was not just the traveler on foot, living out of his rucksack and going his way with frayed trousers and rumbling stomach, like the tramp in "Knulp" (written in 1915). Even the nature that he loved romantically he occasionally observed with realistic detachment. In 1910 he went on a zeppelin flight, and two years later he flew with the pioneering Swiss airman Oskar Pider in one of the primitive machines of that day, in order to be able to recognize and survey topographic structures in their broad outlines.

The realistic contemplation of reality from a distance, which constantly accompanies the poetic desire to transform it, made Hesse from the very beginning immune to all temptations of a superheated romanticism. Hesse always incorruptibly diagnosed that degeneration of romanticism, as we experienced it in the form of an hysterical reversion to barbarism. (The roots of it go back, however, to the *Vulgärpatriotismus* of the era of Kaiser Wilhelm and to many antecedent traditions of student fraternity life.) Thus in July 1933 he wrote to Thomas Mann:

> Very strange are the letters I have been getting from Germany, from adherents of the regime; they are all written at a temperature of about 42 degrees centigrade. . . . It is a mood of war and pogrom, joyous and heavily intoxicated. These are the tones of 1914, without the naiveté that was still possible then. It will cost blood and other things. It smells strongly of everything evil.

This is a point that a biography of Hesse cannot make too distinctly, for it helps to restore clarity to certain ideas that have become very clouded. One cannot speak of Hesse the romantic without also thinking of Hesse the realist, who, from the beginning, was the sharpest opponent of that romanticism that in the Third Reich, in the form of a distillation of half-truths, conducted itself as "German mysticism" and threw all reason overboard. Part of Hesse's realism is his high sensitivity to the political, to which he had been "awakened" since World War I. We have already mentioned that he was one of the founders of the anti Kaiser Wilhelm periodical *März* in 1905. The story "Friends" ("Freunde"),

which dates from 1908 and 1909, describes student life in the fraternities:

the comical uniforms, the speeches reminiscent of men's choral societies and color-guard ceremonies, the pledging of allegiance to the colors, the shabby and now-senseless romanticism of "Old Heidelberg" and "student freedoms," all the while paying homage to the crease in one's trousers.

Not quite ten years later the theme reappears in *Demian*. The drinking that was *de rigueur* among the university students reminds the narrator of dignified old civil servants

who clutched to the memories of the school terms spent in ceremonial drinking sessions as if they were mementos of a blessed paradise, and who made a cult of the vanished "freedom" of their student years such as poets or other romantics make about their childhood. They always sought "freedom" and "happiness" somewhere behind them, out of sheer dread that they might be reminded of the road of their duty and responsibility. A few years of boozing and celebrating, and then one knuckled under and became a serious gentleman in government service.

A theme, by the way, which was also present at this time in *Simplizissimus*, to which Hesse, beginning in 1905, was a contributor for decades.

Hesse the romantic, who tried again and again in his literary work to heighten "so-called reality" and to transform it into a fully realized, pure present, always nevertheless remained a very critical realist. As early as the time when Hitler was being "coddled and pampered in fortress confinement," Hesse found confirmation of what he had long feared—that nothing of the German Republic could be saved.

Soon afterward *Steppenwolf* appeared. And in 1930 he wrote to a female reader who, because of the "harmony" of the just-published *Narcissus and Goldmund*, preferred it to *Steppenwolf*: "It [*Steppenwolf*] recalls the war (which will again be here the day after tomorrow) and jazz music and movies and your entire life of today—and this hell you are unwilling to allow the writer to show."

Hesse's realistic perception of the perils of our time had its guiding counterpart in ancient, time-tested systems. In 1954 a Chinese applied to him for permission to translate Hesse's books and introduce them into China. "I wrote back that the China of today has banned Confucius and Lao Tse or declared them undesirable. I would not then like to see any book of mine in translation in a country that does not tolerate its own classics." Hesse's tradition-linked models however, because of his living relationship to them, are constantly divested of all encrusted conventionality, so that their contents, newly interpreted, can become effective as existential truths in the present. Many of his interpretations, even of biblical traditions, are existential and revolutionary. That he did not espouse any existential school was already established in the earlier discussion of Heidegger and Hesse. The farther Hesse's consciousness moved into the future, the more strongly he secured himself by old, time-tested traditions.

Gottfried Benn—another son of a family of pastors—the sovereign despiser of traditions and creator of new forms, once rated Hesse "as an average writer of novels of personal history, marriage,

lieved that Hesse, despite his declared opposition to the course Germany had taken, was one of the noblest witnesses to "the German soul," but that he could never succumb to its accompanying dangers —that of abandoning himself in passive, unconscious delight to a totalitarian madness—because he possessed

> this strange virtue whose praise he proclaims, which he declares that he loves more strongly and esteems more highly than all other virtues, the virtue which (as he laments) is so often and to such a regrettable degree lacking in the German soul—this virtue which he calls "self-will" [*Eigensinn*].

This self-will does indeed distinguish Hesse fundamentally from all negative romanticism. As a born protest against every kind of collectivization in life and thought, it is from the beginning an integral part of all his artistic and ideological utterances. This self-will was a component part of his unyielding individualism. It was part of the demand for self-realization as well as of the demand for self-identification with fate. In a reflective essay on self-will dating from the period after World War I, Hesse rectified his own interpretation of the concept of the heroic:

> The "hero" is not the good, obedient citizen who fulfills his duties. The only one who can be heroic is the individual who has made his "own mind," his noble, natural self-will,* into his fate. . . . Now I hear the authorities say: "You are preaching revolution." Again, an error that is possible only

* Hesse's statement in German has a word-play that becomes lost in translation. Hesse uses *eigenen Sinn* for "own mind" and *Eigensinn* for "self-will".—Tr.

among people who have the herd mentality. I preach self-will, not overthrow. Why should I desire revolution? Revolution is nothing but war. Just like war, it is a "continuation of politics by other means." . . . The man with the kind of self-will that I am talking about does not seek money or power. He does not scorn these things because he is some paragon of virtue and resigned altruist—on the contrary. But money and power and all the things for the sake of which men plague each other, and shoot and kill each other—these things are of small value to the man who has found himself, the man of self-will. He esteems only one thing highly—the secret force within himself that bids him live and helps him grow.

In a letter to André Gide in January 1951 Hesse addressed his French colleague as a lover and defender of freedom and a man of individual personality and self-will. Then he went on to lament that so many of their younger colleagues, as well as a good many of their own generation, were striving toward something quite other than individual responsibility—"namely, toward 'coordination,' be it the Roman Catholic, the Lutheran, the communist, or any other 'coordination.' "

Hesse and Gide had meanwhile become acquainted also personally. Gide visited Hesse in Montagnola in 1947.

This so very unromantic self-will of Hesse's does not stand in contrast to the secret league of the Travelers to the East and the community ethos of *Magister Ludi.* Rather it is what made both of these possible, because only from self-knowledge and unity with self can responsibility for the community and the necessity of service to the truth be recognized.

Since World War I, Hesse had been addressing himself above all to German youth, attempting to warn them against false pathos and ecstatic romanticism. As late as July 1958, at the request of a German youth organization, he addressed a statement on anti-Semitism to the youth of Germany. In it he unmasked hatred of Jews—and also the reaction to it, hatred of Germans, that has occurred since —as a disguised inferiority complex. And he set German youth the task of meeting hatred with a rational, dignified attitude and "an ever-watchful turning away from the faults of character and thought that marked that generation and its leaders" who were responsible for the anti-Semitism of their time.

He had not yet lost patience, although as early as 1932 he had written the following reply to an open letter by Dr. M. A. Jordan, entitled "The Writer's Mission," which appeared in the *Benediktinische Monatsschrift* of the Arch-Abbey of Beuron. The open letter had, for the sake of the confidence of so many of his readers, wanted to impose on him the obligation to leadership, to which Hesse replied: "I confess that I positively hate the word 'leader,' so much misused by German youth. Those who need and demand a leader are those who do not like to be responsible or to think themselves."

All these comments bespeak not romanticism but sober realism. Hesse's critically diagnostic glance was incorruptible. Where it was a question of perceiving reality, he never changed. As early as 1919 he addressed these words to the youth of Germany:

Our goal is not once more to become great and rich and powerful and have ships and armies again as soon as possible. Let our goal be no childish fantasy. Have we not seen what ships and armies, power and money mean? Has that already been forgotten?

Our goal, German youth, is not something that can be spoken of with names and numbers. Our goal is—like the goal of every being—to become one with destiny. If we are that, whether we be great or small, rich or poor, feared or smiled at, is of no consequence. Let the soldiers' councils and the intellectual workers make speeches on these matters! If in war and suffering you have not come to yourselves, not become one with yourselves, if you want now as before to alter fate, to flee suffering, to despise maturity, then perish!

But you understand me. I see it in your faces.

Yet thirteen years later, in January 1932, he was forced to say:

Germany is morally sicker even than in 1914. All has been forgotten that could have been learned through the war and its consequences.

Hesse's articles and reflective essays (which are frequently ironic), even when they are only journalistic pieces, had for him almost always one common theme—"the fight against that which, in speaking to our public, I call 'lying optimism.' "

Even as a spokesman for peace Hesse remained a realist, for there was for him no such thing as a lasting peace. Peace, says the monk Narcissus, must daily be fought for and won anew. This is a very occidental feature that belongs to the *vita activa*, which in Hesse always existed as a complement to the *vita contemplativa*. Therefore Hesse was also not a "Buddhist," as he was frequently labeled after *Siddhartha*.

"I could only laugh at this," Hesse commented, "for at bottom I knew that there was no profession of faith that I was farther from than this. Yet there was something right about it, a grain of truth concealed in it, that I did not recognize until somewhat later." This element of truth was the striving toward the opposite pole, the desire to pass beyond the continuous state of being moved, the wish of passing from the primacy of becoming and of reaching the state of rest and of being. But by his nature Hesse remained a Protestant. He remained unresting and critical, just as in his external appearance he belonged—as he once said himself—to the nomad type. In this connection it was precisely meditation that preserved him from emotional enthusiasm just as it did from the utopians' rationalistic belief in progress. The only "ism" that Hesse embraced was individualism or nonconformism. If we grant him a further "ism" and speak of him as an exponent of realism, this very term has an inner connection with the other two.

It is remarkable how *Peter Camenzind* (1904) already presaged the fact that Hesse was to become recognized not only as a writer but also as a diagnostician of his time. Peter Camenzind, who listens to the roaring of the rivers and storms, already stands beside dark abysses "like a seer full of premonition." The faculty of anticipation was strongly marked in Hesse, and frequently expressed itself in a realistic manner as the "glimpse into chaos." And yet this so realistic seer faculty that Hesse himself perceived in the figure of Dostoyevsky, is also linked to that

undying romanticism that is, he says, a movement involving not "forward" or "backward" but the exterior and the interior life, that is to say, their magical harmonizing. This is a romanticism that can be confused neither with *Biedermeier* nor with idyllicism. It is a romanticism that combines a crystalline consciousness with the subterranean realms of the unconscious. It was in this sense that Novalis said, "The man of perfect circumspection is the seer."

Another man of such circumspection was Jean Paul Friedrich Richter, who in his New Year's Eve fantasy of 1799–1800 predicted the great crowded cities of the future, the fleets of airships, the "conquest of Europe by the Americans," and flights to the moon. Not by chance he was one of Hesse's favorite writers, and was counted by him among the misunderstood but greatest talents of all time. Such preferences are biographically revealing. Many of Hesse's works—not only *The Spa Visitor*, which was inspired by *Dr. Katzenbergers Badreise*—have in them something of the world of Jean Paul Richter.

The secret of great personalities is that they elude all attempts at classification. Drawing from many sources and traditions, they still always remain themselves. One cannot speak of Hesse as the romantic without also being reminded of the great man of circumspection and realism.

7

The New Consciousness

Hesse's consciousness was existential. This assertion may amaze the reader as he thinks of the bead-game master in the magic garden in Ticino, the author of romantically musical lyrics in often traditional dress, and the invoker of venerable minds of gifted ages of history. But Hesse's law of living, summed up in the word "transcend!" (later he replaced this formula with the less moralizing, simpler word steps) meant, even in his late work, a resolutely cheerful striding across, fulfilling and leaving behind all that is spatial, all illusory security, a traversing of ever-new dimensions of consciousness.

Almost all Hesse's characters, not only Emil Sinclair in *Demian*, bear the sign of Cain on their forehead. All of them, even Josef Knecht, know the fate of the prodigal son whose inner needs make him break out of the shelter of his father's house and away from the security of fixed mores and traditions to face the naked reality of life. It is then in existential terms that this encounter with reality takes place. This theme—the motif of the "awakening"—extends through Hesse's entire work. It is an almost mortal adventure that can never last longer than some flashing seconds in duration. But these moments transform the human being and his consciousness. The reality that has been purified of "simplifications, systems, abstractions, and other lies or half-lies" extends from the most sublime heights of the beautiful to the deepest regions of terror. A magical reality, its law is paradox. Corresponding to it is a magic thinking and a magic consciousness. But the concept of the magical undergoes in Hesse that revo-

lutionary transformation and that interpretation that emerged in the great paintings of post-expressionism. It is the new, without-perspective consciousness of entirety, which emerges out of the three-dimensional spatially oriented system of thought to include also the factor of time as a simultaneity of all possibilities and phenomena of the world. The Maya experience of the Indian, the seeing through the deceptions of time and the illusory reality of our sensory impressions—what is this theme (which plays a major role in Hesse's life and thought even up to the Indian life story in *Magister Ludi*) but the negation of our merely spatial three-dimensional world? This experience too is one of the ways that lead to the fourth dimension, the *Diaphanik*, that which makes true being and true reality transparent.

The terrible beauty and the paradox of reality, endurable only for brief moments at a time, is something of which we become aware "only through some breaking of the dam or some terrible illumination." The dam-breaking and the "awakening" to this reality occurred in Hesse existentially—not on the level of speculative thought—through the experience of the war. "In my private life the war meant the rude awakening to the sight of reality, and to the tragedy of life and spirit." It was not for Hesse to philosophize about reality—that primeval forest of secrets—or about an incomprehensible divine power (whatever one may call it). Such speculations

are the work to which other people are called, for the human mind, that cannot be admired enough, has succeeded in

this too—in making out of the plainly unintelligible, out of the unique, demonic, and unendurable, a philosophy, with systems, professors, and authors.

Hesse's consciousness—which lay beyond all dogmas, systems, or collective consolations, which was oriented to the entirety of things, and which included also the demonic element of existence—appears throughout his work in poetic (not didactic) form. Only in this form does it communicate itself. It is a matter of experiencing, not of "interpreting." "Interpreting," he wrote recently in reference to the many writings about Kafka, is an often quite charming play of intellect, which is

> good for people who are clever but alien to art, who are able to read and write books on Negro sculpture or twelve-tone music, but who never gain access to the interior of a work of art because they stand at the gate, try a hundred keys, and fail to see that the door is already open.

He who goes through this gate finds in Hesse a consciousness that is unbroken in its humanity, one that extends into the abysses of despair and knows no reassurance, not even that of a traditional belief in God.

> I do not believe in any system of religious dogma. I do not believe, then, in a God who has created men and made it possible for them to perfect their progress from the stage of killing with stone hatchets to the stage of killing with atomic weapons—and has let them be proud of it. I do not believe, then, that this bloody world history has its "meaning" in the plan of a superior Divine regent, who has thereby devised for us something that, though we cannot discern it, is divine and glorious.

What a long road from the Pietist tradition of his father's house to this existentialist insight. And

yet Hesse's consciousness and his "knowledge or surmise—now become instinctive—that there is a meaning to life" sprang from a religious ground. The state of having been thrown into nothingness he rejected. The new consciousness that we find in Hesse was magical as well as existential. We have seen that Hesse's faith began on the other side of despair. His religion corresponded to the Taoist experience of the unity of all being. It was a faith that first became possible after the return of the prodigal son who has been enriched by suffering. In terms of consciousness, this faith means the integration of the paradoxical. Religion and faith as a cosmic experience constantly break through the confines of rationalist logic and causation-linked realities in the direction of the ultimate, absolute reality. Again and again Hesse undertook to describe this from all aspects, the last time being in *Magister Ludi.* This late work, which, in ever-new thinking and combinations, consolidates the microcosm and the macrocosm into a magic unity (in this respect it's comparable to Goethe's *Faust*) also shows, however, in its symbolism, strong relations to the consciousness and the total world picture (both decisively influenced by the natural sciences) of the modern age.

The exact, rational natural science of today largely confirms the intuitions of the poets, in that it shows, in the words of James Jeans, that the universe begins "to resemble more a great thought than a great machine." In Hesse we see the consciousness expanded to the point of integrating the paradoxical: "A good and a correct truth must be able to be reversed. The opposite of that which is true must also

be able to be true." Such an expansion of consciousness that can integrate the paradoxical into itself is the prerequisite for an understanding of the modern age's total world picture. The insight today into the structure of matter as an energy principle that many physicists no longer hesitate to declare is intellectual in nature, affords the reverse possibility of insight into the intellectual element as an energy which can at any time translate itself into reality. That intellectual content be translated into reality is the demand that is made again and again in *Magister Ludi*. The thoughts expressed in that book possessed for Hesse the quality of efficient realities.

Hesse's knowledge of the interchangeability of world and self, of subject and object, of interior and exterior, was akin to our contemporary consciousness. which has been determined partly by the natural sciences, just as it is also the heritage of old tradition. The natural sciences' total world view in our day is similarly marked by the fact that man more and more feels himself a partner in an interplay with nature; no longer does he see himself as the observer of nature who stands in an objective relationship to it. With his question that he puts to nature, with the fact that his methods are coming to grips with the problem, he simultaneously influences the kind of answer from nature that will appear in the results of his research. Werner Heisenberg is of the opinion that the "current divisions of the world into subject and object, interior world and exterior world, body and soul no longer rightly fit" and now lead to difficulties. In the natural sciences too "the subject of

research is no longer nature per se, but a nature that is exposed to human questioning, and to this extent man here again encounters himself."

It is the ancient *gnothi seauton* and the ancient *Tat twam asi.* The knowledge of self and the encountering of oneself behind all the phenomena of the world are basic experiences of a new, transparent consciousness, as it manifested itself in Hesse's life and work. As a writer, he can in this turn to old traditions. In 1919 he prefaced his Karamazov essay with the motto, "Nothing is without, nothing is within, for what is without is within." Here he is going back to Goethe: "You must always, in looking at nature,/Pay regard to one and all things;/Nothing is within, nothing is without,/For what is within is without."

New roads often lead to old truths. This is especially true of Hesse. Thus Harry Haller reflects about an amateur radio builder of the 1920's:

> There the industrious young man sat in his free time in the evenings and groped and fitted such an apparatus together, carried away by the idea of wireless communication, kneeling in pious adoration before the god of technology, who had managed, after thousands of years, to discover and to present most imperfectly things that every thinker had always known and made more clever use of.

He goes on to declare:

> The omnipresence of all forces and all deeds was something very well known in ancient India. Technology has simply brought a small portion of this fact into the general consciousness, in that it has constructed for this—that is, for the sound waves—a receiver and a sender, which for the

time being are dreadfully imperfect. The main point of that ancient insight—namely, the unreality of time—has not been noticed by technology up to now. . . . Men will discover, perhaps very soon, that not only pictures and events of the present and of the moment are in constant flow around us—such as music from Paris and Berlin that is now made audible in Frankfurt or Zurich—but also that everything that has ever happened is, in quite the same way, registered and extant, and that one day we shall doubtless, with or without wire, with or without atmospheric interference, hear King Solomon and Walther von der Vogelweide speak.

Here again is the consciousness of a space-time continuum. For Hesse, tradition and romanticism were also roads to a new consciousness. It is no accident that Novalis is one of the most frequently invoked spirits in *Magister Ludi*, which has so much to do with mathematics as well as with music. Novalis writes in the *Fragments*: "The life of the gods is mathematics. All divine emissaries must be mathematicians . . . a principal proof of the sympathy and identity of nature and feeling."

Let us play a moment longer this bead-game of stringing analogies together, and here there appears another relationship to the natural sciences' total world picture in our time. Again it is the natural scientist James Jeans who tells us that "nature and our conscious mathematical thinking work according to the same laws," and that there is sufficient justification "for our conceiving of the architect of the universe as a mathematician." Nor is it the dry mathematics of a nature-exploiting technocracy that Jeans has in mind. What he is thinking about is a mathe-

matics that is combined with the music of the universe, as it is pursued by the players of the bead game.

Even where Hesse listened to the "music of the universe" and invoked the "venerable minds of gifted ages of history," he did this out of that consciousness that accorded with the revolutionized foundations of the modern mind's conception of the world of today. He listened and he invoked with reverence, and always with a degree of irony. But the irony proceeded from knowledge of the problematic nature of human existence, and the transitoriness to which Castalia too is subject.

In courageous serenity Josef Knecht made his departure. Acting on an inner impulse, he left the secure traditions of Castalia's world. In this sense he, too, was a prodigal son who went out into naked reality. He ventured the hazard of encounter, and this time the hazard ended mortally. Yet as he departed, he knew that perhaps the hour of his death would send him young toward new spheres.

But anyone who would like to commit Josef Knecht and his creator to a schematic formula, or to force them behind the bars of categories, will find that Hesse eludes him today just as he escaped, many years earlier, from his fictional prison and its guards in *A Life in Brief*. Hesse goes into his own world of images as into a toy train; and if one is unable to board the train with him, one finds nothing left of Hesse the writer but a little fluffy smoke drifting out of the dark tunnel in the great mountain into which he has vanished.

Bibliography

Works by Hermann Hesse

Books and selected shorter publications. Published English translations are added in parentheses.

Romantische Lieder, poems. 1899

Eine Stunde hinter Mitternacht, vignettes. 1899

Hinterlassene Schriften und Gedichte von Hermann Lauscher, miscellany. 1901

Gedichte, poems. 1902

Peter Camenzind, novel. 1904 (Engl. 1961)

Boccaccio, monograph. 1904

Franz von Assisi, monograph. 1904

Unterm Rad, novel. 1906 (*The Prodigy*, 1957)

Diesseits, stories. 1907

Nachbarn, stories. 1908

Gertrud, novel. 1910 (*Gertrude and I*, 1915; new transl. *Gertrud*, 1955)

Unterwegs, poems. 1911

Umwege, stories. 1912

Aus Indien: Aufzeichnungen einer indischen Reise, notes and poems and the novella *Robert Aghion*. 1913

Roßhalde, novel. 1914

In der alten Sonne, story. 1914 (*In the Old Sun*, 1914; In *German Classics*, Ed. K. Francke. Vol. xix, 1914)

Knulp. Drei Geschichten aus dem Leben Knulps, novel. 1915

Musik des Einsamen, poems. 1915

Am Weg, miscellany. 1915

Schön ist die Jugend, stories. 1916 (*Youth, Beautiful Youth*. In *German Stories and Tales*, Ed. Robert Pick. 1955)

Alte Geschichten, tales. 1918

Zwei Märchen, tales. 1918.

Demian: Die Geschichte einer Jugend, novel. 1919 (*Demian*, 1933)

Kleiner Garten. Erlebnisse und Dichtungen, miscellany. 1919

Märchen, seven tales. 1919

Zarathustras Wiederkehr. Ein Wort an die deutsche Jugend, essay. 1919
Im Pressel'schen Gartenhaus, story. 1920
Klingsors letzter Sommer, tales. 1920
Gedichte des Malers, poems. 1920
Wanderung, notes. 1920
Blick ins Chaos, essays. 1921
Ausgewählte Gedichte, poems. 1921
Italien, poems. 1923
Sinclairs Notizbuch, miscellany. 1923
Bilderbuch, miscellany. 1926
Verse im Krankenbett, poems. 1927
Die Nürnberger Reise, tale. 1927.
Der Steppenwolf, novel. 1927 (*Steppenwolf,* 1927)
Betrachtungen, miscellany. 1928
Krisis. Ein Stück Tagebuch, poems. 1928
Eine Bibliothek der Weltliteratur, essays. 1929
Trost der Nacht. Neue Gedichte, poems. 1929
Der Zyklon und andere Erzählungen, stories. 1929
Zum Gedächtnis unseres Vaters, memorial by Hermann and Adele Hesse. 1930
Narziß und Goldmund, novel. 1930 (*Death and the Lover,* 1932; new transl. *Narcissus and Goldmund,* 1968)
Jahreszeiten. Zehn Gedichte mit Bildern, poems. 1931
Weg nach Innen, four short stories: *Kinderseele, Klein und Wagner, Klingsors letzter Sommer,* all written 1920, and *Siddharta,* 1922 (Engl. 1951) 1931
Die Morgenlandfahrt, novella. 1932. (*The Journey to the East,* 1957; new transl. 1968)
Kleine Welt, stories. 1933
Mahnung, stories and poems. 1933
Vom Baum des Lebens, selected poems. 1934
Fabulierbuch, stories. 1935
Das Haus der Träume, fragment. 1936
Stunden im Garten. Eine Idylle, poetry. 1936
Gedenkblätter, miscellany. 1937
Neue Gedichte, poems. 1937
Kleine Betrachtungen, essays. 1941
Die Gedichte, poems. 1942

Das Glasperlenspiel. Versuch einer Lebensbeschreibung des Magisters Ludi Josef Knecht, samt Knechts hinterlassenen Schriften, novel. 1943 (*Magister Ludi,* 1949)
Traumfährte, tales and fairy tales. 1945
Berthold, fragment. 1945
Der Pfirsichbaum und andere Erzählungen, stories. 1945
Krieg und Frieden. Betrachtungen zu Krieg und Politik seit dem Jahre 1914, essays. 1946
Der Europäer, five essays. 1946
Dank an Goethe, four essays about Goethe. 1946
Briefe, letters. 1951
Späte Prosa, miscellany. 1951
Eine Handvoll Briefe, letters. 1951
Gesammelte Dichtungen. 6 vols. 1952
Zwei Idyllen: Stunden im Garten, Der lahme Knabe, poetry. 1952
Hermann Hesse: Eine Auswahl, selections. Ed. Reinhard Buchwald. 1943
Hermann Hesse/Romain Rolland: Briefe, letters. 1954
Beschwörungen: Späte Prosa, miscellany. 1955
Gedichte und Prosa, poems and prose. 1956
Gesammelte Schriften. 7 vols. 1957

Books, Pamphlets, and Articles about Hermann Hesse

Ball, H., *Hermann Hesse: Sein Leben und Werk* (1927; rev. eds., 1947, 1956)
Beerman, H., "Hermann Hesse and the Bhagavad-Gita," *Midwest Quarterly,* I (1959), 27-40
Curtius, Ernst Robert, "Hermann Hesse," *Kritische Essays zur europäischen Literatur* (Bern, 1950), pp. 202-223
Fickert, J. J., "The Development of the Outsider Concept in H.'s Novels," *Monatshefte* LII (1960), 171-78
Freedman, R., *The Lyrical Novel: Studies in Hermann Hesse, André Gide, and Virginia Woolf* (1963)
Goes, A., *Rede auf Hermann Hesse* (1946)

Hafner, G., *Hermann Hesse: Werk und Leben* (1954)
Mileck, J., *Hermann Hesse and His Critics* (1958)
Peppard, M. B., "Notes on Hesse's Narrative Technique," *Kentucky Foreign Language Quarterly*, VI (1959), 169-78
Richter, Georg. *Hermann Hesse, der Dichter und Mensch* (Berlin, 1947), 48 pp.
Rose, E., *Faith from the Abyss: Hermann Hesse's Way from Romanticism to Modernity* (1965)
Schmid, H. R., *Hermann Hesse. Die Schweiz im deutschen Geistesleben*, Vol. 56/7 (1928)
Schmid, Karl, *Hermann Hesse und Thomas Mann. Zwei Möglichkeiten europäischer Humanität* (Olten, 1950), 48 pp.
Willson, A. L. "Hesse's Veil of Isis," *Monatshefte*, LV (1963), 313-21
Ziolkowski, T., *The Novels of Hermann Hesse: A Study in Theme and Structure* (1965)

W9-DIG-440

36:1 says the reason the ungodly do what they do is because there is no fear of God before their eyes. People need to know that hell is a real place, and there is only one way to avoid it.

At eight years of age, I had heard of hell and believed it existed, but I thought that only bad people went to hell. I didn't consider myself to be a bad person, so it just wasn't a concern to me.

Then in a Sunday morning service, our Baptist pastor preached a message titled, "A Tour of Hell." He completely disproved that good people went to heaven and bad people went to hell. He made it clear that only forgiven people go to heaven, and only those who don't accept the forgiveness that comes through faith in Jesus go to hell. He even named famous people I had heard of who had died; and he was bold enough to proclaim that they split hell wide open. That shook me.

I didn't respond during that Sunday morning invitation, but when I got home, I couldn't wait to ask my father about what this meant. Praise God, my father explained the whole plan of salvation to me. I realized I was a sinner, and the only way to heaven was through Jesus' sacrifice

(John 14:6). It was the revelation of hell's existence and my desire not to go there that got my attention and turned me towards the Lord.

Recommended teaching: *What Does the Bible Say about Hell?*

2. Salvation Is a Gift

Although the wages of sin were death, my dad shared with me that the gift of God was eternal life (Rom. 6:23). All I had to do to escape hell was receive what Jesus provided for me through His death and resurrection. I knelt and prayed with my dad right there in my bedroom.

I didn't have a "Damascus Road experience," where a light shone or an audible voice spoke, but I knew I was saved. Before I prayed with my father, I had no peace. I was under the conviction of the Holy Spirit and knew I needed God in my life. After prayer, all the turmoil was gone, and I had perfect peace. The Holy Spirit bore witness with my spirit that I was a child of God (Rom. 8:16). I just went out to play with total faith in the promise of God that if I would confess with my mouth that Jesus was my Lord, I would be saved (Rom. 10:9).

The very next day at school, my friends could tell a difference. They were telling off-color jokes and plotting things that eight-year-olds do, but I wouldn't participate. They asked me, "What happened to you?" I told them I got saved, and they laughed and made fun of me. But I wasn't ashamed of what happened. I knew I had changed. Praise God for the faith of a child!

Although I had accepted my salvation by faith in what Jesus did for me, I was soon misinformed through church that God's continued love for me was conditional upon my performance. I swallowed that lie, "hook, line, and sinker." That led to me trying to do everything they said so I could earn God's favor and blessings.

At my dad's funeral, when I was twelve years old, the pastor was singing my dad's favorite song, "How Great Thou Art." I was on the front row, just a few feet away from my dad's open casket and pondering the irony of what that song was saying to what I was experiencing. I had prayed and even fasted for my dad to be healed, and yet he died.

I remember praying, "Lord if You really are great, reveal Yourself to me." I didn't get any revelation right then, but I'm convinced my experience with the Lord, years later, on March 23, 1968, was a direct answer to that prayer.

By the time I was eighteen years old, I was a religious Pharisee. I didn't plan on that; it just happened through the performance-based teaching I was getting. I was living holier than anybody I knew. I'm not saying that in a prideful way, but it's just the way it was. I never said a word of profanity, never drank liquor, and never smoked a cigarette. And I still never have! I've never even tasted coffee—not that it's sin to do that. Mark 16:18 says you can drink any deadly thing and it won't harm you, so, I guess coffee is okay.

I'm just trying to communicate that I wanted to please the Lord with everything in me, but it never seemed to be enough. I had no confidence in my relationship with the Lord because I was so aware of my shortcomings. Once you start down that performance road, it's hard to find an exit ramp. So, I was just continuing in the same direction, even though it wasn't working.

Recommended teaching: *The New You & the Holy Spirit*

3. Living Sacrifice

I knew intuitively that the Lord had a purpose for my life from the time I was very young. I used to lie out in our backyard at night and look at the stars and ponder what life was all about... *What was my place in all of this?* But my life was pretty well-planned out through high school, so I didn't pursue the Lord's will purposefully.

In my senior year of high school, they had career days where they emphasized our need to make decisions about what we were going to do with the rest of our lives. That rekindled the desire to find out what God had planned for me. I didn't know where to start. I figured the Bible would be a good place to look, so I read through the whole Bible my senior year and even went through multiple commentaries.

Nothing specific popped out until Christmas 1967, during my first year of college. I was attending a church retreat in Cloudcroft, New Mexico, and a man was giving a devotional before we turned in for the night. He read Romans 12:1–2, and the latter part of verse two just jumped off the page at me. It said, "*...that [you] may prove what is that good, and acceptable, and perfect, will of God.*"

That was it! That was what I was looking for. The Holy Spirit had quickened the answer to my prayer to me. If I did what Romans 12:1–2 was telling me to do, I would manifest to my physical senses what His will for my life was.

I spent the next four months reading those verses nearly exclusively, asking the Lord what it meant to be a living sacrifice and how the renewing of my mind took place. I didn't fully understand it then, but the Lord began to show me that being a living sacrifice was God's will for my life, and the vocation He wanted for me was a by-product of that.

Then came March 23, 1968. I had an appointment with God that was put on His schedule that day I prayed at my father's funeral nearly seven years before. I was in a prayer meeting with my friends and some of the leaders of our church at 10 p.m. on a Saturday night.

Recommended teachings: *How to Find, Follow, and Fulfill God's Will* | *My Appointment with God*

4. My Relative Unworthiness

These prayer meetings, at least on my part, were very shallow at best. I would just pray a kind of standard prayer of repenting for my sins—even if I couldn't name a particular one—and asking God to send revival. My prayers were actually more for the benefit of my friends, not the Lord. I wanted to be perceived as being spiritual in their eyes. I wanted a little pat on the back.

But our youth leader prayed differently. He talked directly to the Lord, and the Lord actually talked back to him. I enjoyed listening to him, but after he prayed, there was nothing left to say. Therefore, I always tried to pray first and get my prayer out of the way so I could enjoy his.

However, that night he fell on his knees and started praying while my friends and I were still visiting. Instead of entering in with him, I was thinking, *What's everyone going to think of me? There is nothing left to be said after you pray. I won't look good compared to you.* I was actually mad.

That's when the Lord showed up. He interrupted our prayer meeting and showed me His pure holiness and my corrupt self-righteousness. I saw the glory of God, not with my physical eyes, but I got a revelation of God's purity and awesomeness. All my pride and arrogance burned up in the fire of His glory. Compared to most people, I might have looked all right; but I saw myself compared to God's awesome greatness, and I came up way short (Rom. 3:23).

The Lord showed me my hypocrisy and self-righteousness and that all my good works were like filthy rags in His sight (Isa. 64:6). My pride turned into utter contempt for my ungodliness and the realization that I didn't deserve anything but judgment. I turned myself inside out, repenting of everything I had ever or would ever do. I was afraid the Lord was going to kill me on the spot.

And remember, I hadn't committed a lot of sins outwardly, but Jesus said if you have committed sin in your heart, you're guilty (Matt. 5:21–28). I started confessing all my thoughts of lust and hatred, and I was naming names. Any reputation I had was destroyed. After an hour and a half of repenting of all I had ever done or ever would do, I was in tears on the floor, waiting to see what the Lord's response would be.

Recommended teachings: *Self-Centeredness: The Source of All Grief*

5. Unconditional Love

Instead of rejection, God's love overwhelmed me. For over four months, I was caught up in the love of God. I knew that God loved me like I had never known before; and for the first time in my life, I knew it had nothing to do with my performance. He loved me because He was (and is) love, not because I was lovely. That was a major revelation.

Although that experience was life changing, I didn't understand how a Holy God could love someone like me. For the first time in my life, I fully understood that I didn't deserve God's goodness. How could the Lord just overlook all my failures? I was confused.

As long as the emotional high lasted, I didn't let my confusion bother me. But as the feelings subsided, desperation set in. I didn't understand why I had experienced God's tangible love, and I didn't know what I had done to make it leave. I was desperate to get that feeling back. However, I was still passionate about God's love for me and lost interest in anything else.

Recommended teachings: *God's Kind of Love to You* | *Romans: Paul's Masterpiece on Grace*

6. The Peace of God

I was in my first year of college and loved being out on my own, but after tasting and seeing that the Lord was good, I lost my taste for anything else. I made the bold proclamation that I was going to quit college and just focus on the Lord. That didn't go over too well.

It was at the height of the Vietnam War, and I had a deferment from the draft as long as I stayed in school. I also was receiving money from my dad's social security, which I would lose if I dropped out of college. My family, friends, and church leaders all told me I was crazy. So, I stayed in college for a couple more months, but I was totally miserable. I somehow knew that being a math major wasn't what God had planned for me.

It all came to a head when I read in Romans 14:23 that whatever isn't of faith is sin. It dawned on me that I was in sin because I felt like the Lord was leading me to quit school and just seek the Lord with my whole heart, but I was staying in college because of people's reactions and the physical benefits for me.

I determined to decide one way or the other and not be in sin anymore. But what was the right decision? I was just a babe in seeking the Lord, and I didn't have any confidence that my opinion was better than everyone who had told me I was wrong.

That's when the Holy Spirit led me to Colossians 3:15, which says, *"Let the peace of God rule in your hearts...."* The Greek word from which *rule* was translated is the same root word that we get our word *umpire* from. The Holy Spirit was telling me to let peace call the shots—to just follow what gave me peace.

I didn't feel total peace in any direction. Quitting school meant losing money, possibly getting drafted and killed in Vietnam, and certainly criticized by a lot of people. But I had no peace whatsoever when I considered staying in school. So, I decided to quit school based on nothing but letting God's peace dominate me; and it was one of the best decisions I've ever made.

Looking back, I'm amazed that I was able to do this, but being led by the Lord really is as simple as letting the peace of God rule in your life. I've used this hundreds of times and have never regretted it. It is one of the greatest revelations the Holy Spirit ever gave me.

Recommended teachings: *Four Basics of Hearing God's Voice | How to Find, Follow, and Fulfill God's Will*

7. God's Word Is the Key

Sure enough, I was drafted and sent to Vietnam. I was assigned to a fire support base as a chaplain's assistant, but I was on my own eight months of the fourteen months there. My chaplain left about five into my tour, and he was never replaced. I had nothing to do.

The pull of every type of sin was greater than I had ever experienced in my short, sheltered life. The only thing I could think of to keep me from being sucked into the same ungodly acts of everyone around me was to stick my nose in the Bible and not come out. I started studying God's Word up to fifteen hours per day for fourteen months.

I've gotten much more revelation on the importance of God's Word since then, but I remember my first week in Vietnam: I was studying in Mark 4 about how the kingdom of God was like a mustard seed. It starts small but turns into the largest of all herb-bearing trees so that the fowls of the air come and lodge in its branches (Mark 4:30–32). I remember praying, "Lord, that's how I want to be. I want You to grow me so that I become this huge tree that gives shelter to people all over the world."

The Lord spoke so clearly to me and said, "If I granted you that kind of growth with the puny root system you have now, the first bird that landed in your branches would knock your whole tree over. One puff of wind would uproot you. You just need to focus on the roots below the ground, and the growth will come." He told me to quit praying, "God, use me" and to start praying, "God, make me useable."

That spoke to me so clearly that all I had to do was let God's Word take root in me, and it would do the rest. That became my focus. For over fifty years I've been studying the Word of God day and night, and it has truly transformed my life (Rom. 12:2).

Recommended teachings: *Plain As Dirt* | *Effortless Change* | *The Word Became Flesh*

8. Spirit, Soul, and Body

Although studying God's Word was laying a foundation in me, I was still perplexed by how such a holy, pure God could love someone like me. I didn't doubt His love. I had experienced it, but I just didn't understand it. How could He be just in His love and kindness to me when I knew I didn't deserve it?

Then I ran across 2 Corinthians 5:17, which says,

> *Therefore if any man* be *in Christ, he is a new creature: old things are passed away; behold, all things are become new.*

I just couldn't embrace that.

I knew I was in Christ, but it seemed like my old self was still in place, and there were many things that hadn't passed away. I was confused, fearful, and very unsure of myself. I was an introvert and found it very hard to talk to people I wasn't already friends with. It seemed like I failed God constantly. I just couldn't see this *"new creature"* when I looked at myself in the mirror.

Then the Holy Spirit led me to 1 Thessalonians 5:23, which says,

> *...and* I pray God *your whole spirit and soul and body be preserved blameless unto the coming of our Lord Jesus Christ.*

It dawned on me that I had only known myself in the body and the soulish realm. My body was obvious, and my soul was the inner personality part of me. But there was a third part of me that I wasn't aware of. That's the part of me that was like Christ. It was my spirit that was changed at salvation. In my born-again spirit, I was identical to Christ (1 John 4:17)!

I can see my body and feel my soul, but I can't see or feel my born-again spirit. I have to just take what God's Word says about who I am in the spirit and believe it. Jesus said,

> My word is spirit, and it is life. (John 6:63).

James said God's Word is like looking in a spiritual mirror (James 1:22–25). If I want to see my face, I have to look in a physical mirror. I can't see my face with my eyes directly. I have to look at the reflection in the mirror and act accordingly. I can't see my spirit with my eyes either, but I can believe what the spiritual mirror of God's Word says about me and act accordingly. This changed everything for me.

I now have dozens of teachings expounding on the spirit being the part of us where old things pass away and everything becomes new. In fact, this revelation of who I am in Christ was like a key that unlocked my heart to understand nearly every revelation the Holy Spirit brought to me after this. This is one of the greatest revelations I've ever received, and it came directly from the Holy Spirit. Man didn't teach this to me.

Recommended teachings: *Spirit, Soul & Body* | *Identity in Christ* | *You've Already Got It*

9. Speaking in Tongues

When I got back home from Vietnam, it was during the outpouring of the charismatic renewal. People everywhere and in every denomination were being filled with the Holy Spirit and praying in tongues.

It's a long story at how I arrived at this revelation; but I came to realize I was filled with the Holy Spirit that night in 1968 when God's love washed over me. I didn't speak in tongues at that time, but that's because I was a Baptist. We had been taught that speaking in tongues was of the devil, and I was afraid of it. I didn't want anything from the devil. Although I had come to the conclusion that the gift of speaking in tongues wasn't from the devil, I still had reservations that kept me from receiving that gift.

The Holy Spirit doesn't force you to speak in tongues. I had to speak in tongues in faith just like I had to believe it's the Lord speaking through me when I teach. If I just opened up my mouth, waiting on God to make me speak, nothing would come out. I had to talk and trust that the Lord was inspiring what I said. That's the way speaking in tongues works.

I began to pursue this gift of speaking in tongues, believing that it was a part of what I had received three years earlier in 1968. I needed the ability to by-pass my limited mind and pray directly to the Lord out of my spirit (1 Cor. 14:14). I had people lay hands on me to impart this gift until they nearly rubbed all the hair off my head, but nothing happened. I was getting desperate.

The Lord finally got through to me from Acts 2:4 that *they* spoke with tongues as the Spirit gave them utterance. The Holy Spirit didn't speak in tongues. They are the ones who spoke in tongues at the Holy Spirit's prompting or inspiration. I had been afraid that if I tried to force speaking in tongues, it would only be me speaking. It finally dawned on me that it would be me speaking, but not only me. It would be the Holy Spirit inspiring what I said. It had to be a step of faith.

So, late one night, in an empty field close to my home, I finally took that step of faith and started speaking syllables that made no sense to me. It was very awkward at first, and I was tempted to stop; but I had been searching for this for so long I wouldn't quit. I finally got freedom to continue and prayed in tongues for a long time.

It started raining, and I headed for home. It was dark, wet, and cold; and there were ditches between me and my house. I stumbled and fell a number of times, but I made it home. The Lord spoke to me that my life would be similar to what I was experiencing. I wouldn't do everything right, but if I didn't quit, I would accomplish what He wanted me to do and make it home. It was a powerful night, full of revelation knowledge.

Recommended teachings: *The New You & the Holy Spirit* | *10 Reasons It's Better to Have the Holy Spirit*

10. Faith

I had a close friend introduce me to faith teaching during this time. I remember going to hear Kenneth Copeland before he became well known. He was preaching on faith in a small Assembly of God church in Ft. Worth, Texas. It lit a fire on the inside of me.

I'm a very reserved guy and had never done this before or since, but during Kenneth's invitation, I got up and ran circles around the church, shouting. It struck a chord on the inside of me that had been just waiting to get strummed. I've never gotten over it.

Soon after that experience, Jamie and I got married. I decided that when we married on October 27, 1972, I would quit my job pouring concrete and go full time in the ministry. It was primarily the peace of God ruling in my heart that led me to do this as I've already described.

Jamie and I got bolder in our witness and ministry and eventually had to leave our Baptist church. Through a series of miraculous events, this led us to pastoring two small churches in Seagoville and Childress, Texas, and then a brief six-month stint in Pritchett, Colorado.

These were lean years in our ministry and finances. We never had over 100 people come to our churches, and Jamie and I would go weeks without food. One of my biggest mistakes was my belief that if I was called to the ministry, it would be sin on my part to work a secular job. While Jamie was eight months pregnant with our first child, we went for nearly two weeks with nothing but water. Praise God for Jamie! She never once complained to me. She treated me much better than I deserved and still does (Prov. 31:10).

Our poverty situation got better over the years, but it was much later—around 1996—when I finally began to get free from my wrong thinking about finances. I knew all the scriptures on God prospering us, but I was fearful of what man would say about us if we really took a stand on what I knew to be true. I was timid in my faith on prosperity, and it showed.

Recommended teachings: *Faith Builders* | *Faith Series* | *The Faith of God* | *Financial Stewardship*

11. It's Not All Spiritual

My faith had grown to the point where I had seen a number of miracles. I was gaining in my trust and confidence in the Lord and His anointing on my life, but we still weren't seeing many people respond. I felt impressed to go to Childress, Texas, and hold a meeting, but only a handful of people showed up. I was ready to leave and go to the next place in the morning, but during the night, the Lord spoke to me.

I had a dream about Moses and how things got worse, not better, when he first went to Egypt to deliver the Jews out of slavery. The Lord was telling me that just because the numbers weren't large didn't mean he didn't send me to Childress. I reasoned with Him that I held the meeting in obedience to Him, and He didn't bring the people. If He wanted me to stay, why didn't He bring more people to the meeting? That was a misunderstanding of John 12:32.

The Lord's answer changed my thinking and the whole course of my ministry.

He told me that if the people were spiritual enough to hear Him say, "'Go hear Andrew Wommack tonight at such and such a place,' then I wouldn't need you to minister to them. They aren't spiritual. They are mostly carnal, and you have to come across their path in some carnal way."

That totally changed my paradigm. As I thought on what the Lord had spoken to me, I began to ask, "How do I do that?" That's when the Lord led me to go on radio in

1976. I went out to the local country and western music station in Childress and talked to the manager. He was a Baptist preacher, and he allowed me to start a radio program that aired on his station five days a week.

I started making programs on a borrowed cassette player in a friend's closet. We didn't even have a house. We were living in motels—very cheap motels. That's how I started my media ministry, which has turned out to be God's way of enabling me to reach far and deep with the Gospel. I was on radio until 2019 and have been on TV since January 3, 2000, reaching (as of this writing) a potential of over five billion people per day. Praise the Lord! That was a great revelation.

Recommended teachings: *Excellence: How to Pursue an Excellent Spirit* | *How to Fulfill God's Will*

12. Grace and Faith

We started seeing a lot of miracles in Childress, Texas. My connection with faith was paying off big time, but it caused some questions in me. *If faith isn't understood properly, it leads to faith in what we do instead of faith in what Jesus did for us.* I knew many people who actually thought God was obligated to respond to their faith. It's like they were making God move with their faith.

Although I was benefiting greatly from the things I was learning about faith, my encounter with the Lord on March 23, 1968, caused me to know I didn't deserve God's intervention. I knew from that experience that it wasn't anything I had done that caused the Lord to use me. God used me because He was love (1 John 4:8, 16), not because I was lovely. Yet, God didn't move without me. As Ephesians 3:20 says,

> *Now unto him that is able to do exceeding abundantly above all that we ask or think, according to the power that worketh in us.*

Notice the last part of that verse says the Lord moves according to the power at work in us. No power working equals no miraculous results. What is the balance between what God has done (grace) and what I have to do (faith)? I found my answer in Ephesians 2:8–9, which says,

> *For by grace are ye saved through faith; and that not of yourselves:* it is *the gift of God: Not of works, lest any man should boast.*

The Lord showed me that faith doesn't move God. God moved by His grace two thousand years before I was born and provided everything I would ever need. His grace has come to everyone (Titus 2:11), but not everyone has received the benefit because not everyone has put faith in what He's already done (Rom. 5:2 and 11:6).

Grace is what God has already done, independent of me or my holiness. Faith is my positive response to what God's grace has already provided. My faith doesn't make God do anything. Faith only appropriates what grace has already provided.

Wow! This changed everything!

I quit doing things to get God to move and started resting in what He had already done (Heb. 4). This changed my life all over again.

The revelations from God's Word started coming even quicker and stronger. I finally began to understand just a little of what the true Gospel was (Rom. 1:16). That truly made everything Jesus provided, "nearly too good to be true news."

Recommended teaching: *Living in the Balance of Grace and Faith*

13. Healing

One of the areas I focused on early in my walk with the Lord was healing. I came to believe it was God's will to heal everyone every time. In fact, I found it was already done (1 Pet. 2:24). That knowledge alone caused me to start praying for anything that moved. I didn't see great results at first, but as I began to practice what the Lord was showing me, I learned; and to this day, I am still learning.

I don't claim to have arrived in this area, but I've left. I've seen blind eyes opened, deaf ears opened, the lame walk, and even the dead raised. Our own son was raised from the dead after being dead for over four hours. He was in a morgue, stripped naked, with a toe tag on. And yet he was raised up with no brain damage—no more than he had before.

As Kenneth Hagin said, "Healing is like the dinner bell God uses to bring people to Himself." Jesus said believers would lay their hands on the sick, and they would recover (Mark 16:18). I've laid my hands on tens of thousands of people and have seen wonderful results.

I'm now at a place where I would rather teach others to lay hands on the sick than to do it myself. It's not that

I don't want to see the sick healed, but I'm aware that I'm not going to be around forever. I've got to raise up disciples who can do what the Lord has taught me to do. That's what Jesus commissioned us to do.

Recommended teachings: *God Wants You Well* | *The Believer's Authority* | *You've Already Got It*

14. Discipleship

Jesus gave what is called the Great Commission in Matthew 28:19–20. He told us to make disciples not just converts. This has been one of the biggest failures of the body of Christ.

In an effort to get people to heaven, the Gospel message has been limited to just telling people that Jesus died for their sins so they could escape hell. That is better news than any of us deserve; and if that was all there was to salvation, I would certainly preach it. But Jesus purchased total redemption for us—spirit, soul, and body (1 Thess. 5:23).

It's true that our body and soul won't be perfected the way our born-again spirits are right now until we meet the Lord in the air, but Jesus told us to pray His will be done here on earth as it is in heaven (Matt. 6:10). Jesus not only forgave our sins but purchased our health and prosperity while we are still on earth (Gal. 1:4; 1 John 3:2). Jesus told us in John 14:12 that we would do the same works that He did, which included healing the sick.

This desire to make disciples led me to make all my revelations available free on cassettes at first, and ultimately on every available format. We quit counting after we had given away hundreds of millions of free books, videos, and audio teachings. That doesn't count the millions of free downloads of our materials from our website. This has turned out to be one of the best things the Lord ever led me to do. There are multitudes who have taken advantage of my teaching simply because it was free. And as we have given, the Lord has multiplied it back to us miraculously.

This desire to make disciples ultimately led to the Lord leading me to start Charis Bible College. In June 1992, while I was holding a conference in England, He spoke to me from 2 Timothy 2:2–4 about starting a Bible college. At that exact time, the Lord also spoke to a man in Woodland Park, Colorado, to dedicate his property for Christian education. He saw a vision of a building with glass all across the southern wall so people could see the beauty of Pike's Peak as they studied the Word. He only lived two weeks after seeing this vision, but twenty-two years later, it became a reality.

Without me knowing these things, I started the Bible college in 1994 and bought his property in 2009. Our first building was nearing completion in 2014 when his daughter saw our construction updates and realized we built the exact building her dad had seen. Psalm 118:23 became a reality:

> *This is the LORD's doing, and it* is *marvellous in our eyes.*

Recommended teachings: *Discipleship: The Path to Freedom* | *Eternal Life*

15. The Sovereignty of God

One of the most important revelations the Lord has given me concerns the sovereignty of God. I was brought up to believe that it was the Lord's will that my father died when I was twelve years old. We were taught that everything that happened was either caused by or allowed by the Lord. That is a faith killer.

Believing the Lord causes or allows everything leads to total passivity. After all, if the Lord is the One who brings sickness, why go to the doctor or take medicine and try to get healed? If God is the source of our sickness, then shouldn't we just submit like James 4:7 says? That kind of thinking gives Satan a free hand in our lives.

Jesus said it was the devil who came to steal, kill, and destroy; but He came to give us abundant life (John 10:10). If something is good, it's from God; and if it's bad, it's from the devil. God is not the source of rape, murder, lust, and all manner of ungodliness. We have an enemy who we have to resist (1 Pet. 5:9). If we don't resist the devil and what he is seeking to do in our lives, he won't flee (James 4:7).

We are the ones who give Satan free reign in our lives through our sins or our ignorance. It's the truth that makes us free (John 8:32). And it's only the truth we know that makes us free. What we don't know is killing us.

I think a wrong understanding and application of the sovereignty of God is one of the worst doctrines in the body of Christ. It misrepresents the true nature and character of God.

God is absolutely sovereign if you use that word the way dictionaries define it: "first in rank, order, or authority." The Lord is at the top of the "food chain." Nobody is above Him or controls Him. But that doesn't mean He controls everything. He gave authority to us.

Recommended teachings: *The Sovereignty of God* | *The Believer's Authority*

16. Authority

This led me to understand that the Lord won't do what He gave us authority to do. He told us to preach the Gospel (Matt. 10:7–8 and 28:19–20). Even an angel wouldn't tell Cornelius the centurion how to be saved. Instead, he told him to send to Joppa and have Peter come and share the Gospel (Acts 10:1–5). The angel had the knowledge but not the authority to preach to Cornelius.

The Lord told *us* to resist the devil and he (the devil) would flee from us (James 4:7). He told us to heal the sick, not to ask Him to do it (Matt. 10:7–8). This was demonstrated by Peter and John when they healed the lame man at the gate of the temple in Acts 3.

Then Peter said, Silver and gold have I none; but such as I have give I thee: In the name of Jesus Christ of Nazareth rise up and walk. And he took him by the right hand, and lifted him *up: and immediately his feet and ankle bones received strength. And he leaping up stood, and walked, and entered with them into the temple, walking, and leaping, and praising God.*

Acts 3:6–8

Peter didn't say, "Lord we are nothing and have nothing and can do nothing, but we know you can do all things. Please, if it is your will, heal this man." That's the way most Christians pray, but Peter said, "*Such as I have give I [unto you].*" Peter actually never prayed for this man. He just took the authority the Lord had given him and used it. That's radical, and that demonstrates the authority we have as believers.

We are not the source of God's power, but we do have authority to use His power. It's been committed to us; but if we don't use it, things won't get done.

It's like electricity. The power company generates electricity, but they put it at our command. If we don't flip the switch, the lights won't come on. It doesn't matter how desperate our need is; the power company won't flip the switch for us. We can plead, cry, beg, and even get others to plead with us; but if we don't do our part, the electricity won't flow.

Likewise, Jesus is the One who produces the power, but He has placed that power at our command. We aren't the power source, but we are the conduit through which the power flows. We could put a light bulb in our mouth, and it would never come on. We aren't the source, but the source has been placed under our command. That's what the Lord meant in Isaiah 45:11 when He told us to command Him.

We can't command the Lord in the sense that we are stronger than Him, and He has to do whatever we say. But He has given us power to be His sons (John 1:12), and His power is at our command. We have to take the authority He has given us and speak out His power.

Recommended teaching: *The Believer's Authority*

17. Faith Is Voice Activated

Proverbs 18:21 says,

> *Death and life* are *in the power of the tongue: and they that love it shall eat the fruit thereof.*

Most of us don't value the power of words the way we should. We would say that there are multitudes of words that don't matter. It's just idle talk. But that's not what Jesus said. He said in Matthew 12:36–37,

> *But I say unto you, That every idle word that men shall speak, they shall give account thereof in the day of judgment. For by thy words thou shalt be justified, and by thy words thou shalt be condemned.*

Every word that we speak and every word we hear is conveying either life or death. There is no middle ground. This is why Jesus was able to just speak to a fig tree and kill it without doing anything in the natural. One day he spoke to the tree (Mark 11:14), and the next day the fig tree was totally dead (Mark 11:20). His disciples were amazed, and His explanation of how He did it emphasized words three times.

For verily I say unto you, That whosoever shall say unto this mountain, Be thou removed, and be thou cast into the sea; and shall not doubt in his heart, but shall believe that those things which he saith shall come to pass; he shall have whatsoever he saith.

Mark 11:23

Jesus was able to kill a tree with just words because He believed that whatsoever He said would come to pass. Most of us say all kinds of things that we don't believe and certainly don't want to come to pass. That confuses our heart and keeps it from believing the things we do mean and want to come to pass.

For instance, we often tell people we will be someplace at a certain time, and we may or may not make it.

I once had a salesman come to an appointment thirty minutes late. He apologized but said now he was ready to deal. I saw he had a cell phone in a holster on his belt so I said, "You could have called." He admitted that but said it's all right now because he was there. I told him, "No, it's not all right. If this is how you treat me before you get my business, then how will you treat me once I sign up?" I told him he could leave.

He was as shocked as you probably are at what I said. But I've come to value my words and don't appreciate others not valuing their words. God is like that. We have to recognize that our words need to be *yes* or *no* (Matt. 5:37) so that we don't have to validate what we say with a vow or oath. If someone invites us to dinner at seven, they should be able to have the food on the table at that time, knowing we will not be late.

Our words are also important when we declare the tremendous promises of Psalm 91 about no plague coming nigh our dwelling and His angels having charge over us—they are all dependent on us speaking out our faith. Psalm 91:2 says,

> *I will say of the* LORD, He is *my refuge and my fortress: my God; in him will I trust.*

We have to speak our faith to release it. Faith is voice activated (Rom. 10:17). Failure to understand this has cheapened the value we place on words, and the evidence of this in our society is everywhere. People lie with impunity. A person's word used to be their bond, but today, even contracts don't mean much if you have a good lawyer that can manipulate words. In God's kingdom, words are everything. As Proverbs 18:21 says,

> *Death and life* are *in the power of the tongue: and they that love it shall eat the fruit thereof.*

Sadly, most people are "hung by their tongue."

Recommended teaching: *The Power of Faith Filled Words*

18. Don't Limit God

Probably the second most impactful revelation I received from the Lord, as far as shaping my ministry, was from Psalm 78:41:

> *Yea, they turned back and tempted God, and limited the Holy One of Israel.*

This revelation came to me on January 31, 2002. For months, we had been looking for new office facilities. We had totally outgrown the 14,600 square foot building we had been in for twelve years, and we were believing the Lord for larger facilities. In the process, the Lord spoke to me that I was limiting Him by my small thinking.

It's not like I didn't have a vision for increase. We had doubled the size of the ministry in the two previous years. We were searching for larger facilities to accommodate AWM and Charis. Compared to others and what we had done in the past, we were stretching ourselves, but we weren't stretching God.

The Lord clearly spoke to me that I was limiting what He wanted to do in my life. I was moving in the right direction but at a relative snail's pace compared to what He had planned for me. At the rate we were going, I wouldn't live long enough to fulfill His call on my life. I had to take the limits off. God is a BIG God, but we all can and often do limit Him.

There were a number of things on the inside of me that were limiting God. I was evaluating what I could do by the money I had. I was enjoying the relative anonymity I had and knew that increased exposure would bring increased criticism and persecution. I wasn't looking forward to that. I was secure where I was and didn't want to risk failure.

But the number one thing in me that was limiting God was the way I saw myself.

Don't misunderstand. I knew the Lord wanted me to have a worldwide ministry. I knew it was much bigger than the TV ministry I had at that time, which only reached 3 percent of the U.S. population. I knew what the Lord wanted me to do, and I was moving in that direction. I just wouldn't let myself see it. I could tell you what the Lord's will for my ministry was; I just hadn't let myself go there in my heart.

I think a fear of getting into pride was my biggest limiting factor. I knew that pride was the recipe for disaster (Prov. 16:18). Pride causes God to resist us (1 Pet. 5:5), and I certainly didn't want that.

I believe pride is actually the root of what happened to David (2 Sam. 11). As long as David was fleeing from his father-in-law and in desperate straits, he was humble and trusted God. There really wasn't much else he could do. But when he was a very successful king, who had subdued all his foes, he took his eyes off the Lord and became self-confident. He no longer had to depend upon the Lord as he had in the past. That self-reliance is pride.

Pride is not only arrogance. The middle letter of p-r-i-d-e is "I." At its core, pride is just being focused on and or reliant on self. You can be focused on self as being better than everyone else or worse than everyone else. Both of those extremes are pride.

I valued my intimate relationship with the Lord more than money, ministry, or anything else; and I just had not let my heart and mind go to the place where I saw myself having a worldwide impact. I was afraid it would go to my head. I knew that was where the Lord was leading me, but my fear of getting into pride kept me from really seeing it in my heart.

The Lord had to do a lot of work on me to overcome that fear of falling into pride. At that time, He assured me that he had been preparing me for thirty-four years, and He would continue the good work He had begun in me (Phil. 1:6) if I would just cooperate. I had to trust Him in this area just like I had learned to trust Him in so many other areas.

This led to me taking the limits off God and using my imagination in a way I hadn't done in the past.

Recommended teachings: *Don't Limit God* | *Don't Limit God X 10* | *Don't Limit God: Twenty Years Later*

19. Imagination

One of the main ways I began to start taking the limits off of what God could do in my life was to use my imagination.

Many people believe an imagination is just fantasy and child-like. They think we need to grow out of that and just deal in reality. But the reality is that our imagination is like our spiritual womb. Nothing in our physical life comes to birth without us first conceiving it in our hearts.

Isaiah 26:3 says,

Thou wilt keep him *in perfect peace,* whose *mind* is *stayed* on thee: *because he trusteth in thee.*

The Hebrew word that was translated "mind" in that verse is *yetser*, and it is the same word that is translated "imagination" or "imaginations" five times in the Old Testament. The meaning of that word is "conception, i.e., purpose."[1] Our imagination is where we conceive things.

If I were to ask you for directions, you would say, "Go down to the third light and make a left. There will be a

---

[1] *Strong's Definitions*, s.v. " יֵצֶר " ("*yēṣer*"), accessed June 13, 2023, https://www.blueletterbible.org/lexicon/h3336/kjv/wlc/0-1/.

convenience store on the corner," or something like that. You wouldn't be physically looking at any of those things, but you have a picture of them in your mind. That's your imagination. You couldn't find your way home or find your car in a parking lot without your imagination.

The point is, you can't function without your imagination.

How many windows or doors do you have in your house? Most of us haven't actually counted them, but you could tell me because you can see them all in your imagination. Your imagination is just your ability to see something on the inside that you can't see on the outside.

And when it comes to fulfilling God's vision for your life, you have to see it come to pass in your heart before you see it come to pass in the natural. Proverbs 23:7 reveals that as a man thinks in his heart, so is he. The way you see things on the inside becomes a self-fulfilling prophecy. Sadly, most of us use our imagination to see the worst-case scenarios or at best, to just keep the status quo.

In order for me to take the limits off what the Lord wanted to do in my life, I had to start dreaming big. I had to spend time seeing myself doing and being what He called me to do and be. I had to start using my imagination.

That's exactly what I did. I spent lots of time just day-dreaming about all the Lord wanted me to do. I started imagining what our Charis Bible College campus was going to look like. I spent many hours drawing crude pictures of the buildings, which our architects turned into beautiful renderings. I was actually eighteen months and $1.5 million into the architectural plans before I ever asked how much all of this was going to cost. I was not going to limit God by looking at my finances. The Lord was supplying my need according to His riches in glory (Phil. 4:19).

The results have been nothing short of miraculous. When the Lord spoke to me in 2002 about taking the limits off Him, we had twenty-eight employees. By mid-2023, we had over 1,100 employees worldwide and over 850 in Colorado. We started building buildings to handle the Charis growth, and we moved from just over one acre to 500+ acres. We had about $600,000 in assets back in 2002; and as of this writing, we now have over $130 million in assets and are growing exponentially. The best is yet to come!

We went from covering 3 percent of the U.S. population in 2002 to now covering over five billion people who are able to receive my TV broadcasts in ten languages. We now have twenty-two offices and fifty-two Bible colleges scattered all over the world. And on and on I could go with the comparisons. We've increased around two hundredfold in two decades.

When I took the limits off what I was dreaming of, it's like all restraints were removed; and what I knew to be God's will for my life started happening at an accelerated rate. I used to feel like I was pushing this huge boulder uphill with great effort. If I were to stop for a second, I was in danger of losing all my momentum, and it would roll back on top of me. Now I feel like that boulder is rolling downhill, and I'm running as fast as I can to keep up with it. We have moved into overdrive.

Recommended teaching: *The Power of Imagination*

20. Finances

Of course, everything in life and ministry takes finances to get it done. I struggled in the area of seeing my financial needs supplied probably more than any other area. As I've already shared in this booklet, Jamie and I were desperately poor for a long time, through my own misunderstanding about ministers not working a secular job.

But even after the ministry grew to a place where I had to be full time, I still struggled. We actually had collection agencies come after us, and we struggled to pay our bills. It was a major drain on Jamie and me.

Around 1994, I began to concentrate on improving in this area. I've always been a giver. I don't think I've ever had a dollar come through my hands that I didn't give off of. I knew what the Word of God said about giving, but it didn't seem to be working out very well for me.

I knew I was missing something, so I took about a hundred scriptures and began to meditate on them. After two years of doing that, I had a man come to Charis that was operating in a level of prosperity that I wasn't but desperately wanted to. I determined I was going to learn what he knew that caused him to prosper. I sat and listened to him for three hours each day for two days. He never said a thing I didn't already know and agree with. But the difference was, he believed it and was unapologetic about it.

I knew more than I was operating in because I had a fear of man (Prov. 29:25). I didn't want anyone to think I was talking about prosperity because I wanted their money. It was true I needed more money to accomplish what the Lord was leading me to do, but I wasn't looking to them as my source. I would gladly minister to people for nothing and had done so many times. My free cassette tapes were proof that I was willing to give anything I had to bless others. My heart was to give, not to receive.

But it truly became a revelation to me that receiving offerings wasn't about my need but about the people's need to give so *they* could receive (Luke 6:38). I was so concerned that people would think I was teaching about finances just because I wanted them to give to me that I wasn't sharing these truths with them. It was a subtle form of pride. I was just looking at things from my standpoint and concerned about what people would think about me.

Something broke loose on the inside of me with this revelation. I had a boldness come over me that set me free from the criticism that comes with prosperity. Jesus said that we would receive a hundredfold return on our giving in *this* life, with persecutions (Mark 10:29–30). The persecution He was speaking about was persecution associated with the prosperity that comes our way.

Fear of people's criticism and rejection over prosperity had made me timid when it came to receiving offerings. We were getting by. I would hold meetings with a budget of around $10,000, and typically get within $10 or $20 on either side of making that budget. But the week after I got that revelation, I held a meeting—just like the ones I had been doing for years—and our offerings were over $25,000! This was a major breakthrough.

Since that time, we have had over a hundred times as much money come through our ministry as before, and I'm seeing lots of other ministers set free in this area too. Prosperity isn't selfish if done the Lord's way. It's all about being a blessing to others. If the Lord can get it through you, He will get it to you. The Lord blessed Abram so he could be a blessing (Gen. 12:2). The Lord makes all grace abound to us so we can abound unto every good work (2 Cor. 9:8). He gives seed (money) to givers (2 Cor. 9:10).

I once had a Bible college graduate ask me to hold a meeting at his church. It was very small, so he had two other churches join him; and still, there were less than a hundred people at the meetings. He was afraid I wouldn't get much in offerings, so he asked me to receive my own offerings. I think the logic was that if I received the offerings, I wouldn't be able to complain.

So, the very first night, I got up and told the people I didn't need their money. I had just received a large offering at the last church I ministered in and was not a poor preacher that couldn't get out of town if they didn't give. The look on the minister's face said he thought I just killed the offering. That's because most ministers ask for offerings for their sake instead of for the people's sake.

I told the people that I was receiving the offerings so they could be blessed. It wasn't about what I needed. They needed to trust God in the area of finances. The minister told me later that the people gave the largest offerings for any guest minister they had ever had. And the following week after I left, the church broke out in revival.

The minister got in front of his twenty people on Sunday morning and apologized to his congregation for not telling them the truth about how they needed to give. He knew the things I shared, but like me, he was timid sharing those truths because he thought people might misjudge his motives. He got on his knees in front of the whole group and asked them to forgive him for not sharing these things with them.

The church people came forward to hug his neck and tell him they forgave him, and they started throwing money on the stage. They paid off all the church debt that morning. The preacher told me he didn't remember my sermons that week, but he would never forget the truths I said during the offerings.

Jesus said that trusting Him with money is the least use of our faith (Luke 16:9–13). If we can't do that which is least, then we certainly can't do the greater. Whether minister or lay person, we won't go far without money, and the Lord won't give us the financial increase we need if we can't handle it. The key is recognizing that money is our servant and not our master. It's just a tool that allows us to get more accomplished.

We now have a cash flow that enables us to do anything the Lord leads us to do. This wasn't always the case. This revelation on finances and how to receive them has transformed my personal life as well as my ministry. The Lord wants you to prosper more than you want to prosper, but this increase doesn't come by seeking money. We have to put the kingdom of God first, and then all of these other things will be added unto us (Matt. 6:33).

Recommended teachings: *Financial Stewardship* | *Finance Series*

Conclusion

There is much more that I could share. We actually have over 200,000 hours of free teaching on **awmi.net**. Some of this material is from our college instructors and conference speakers, but the bulk of it is all from revelation that the Lord has given me. If you were to listen to all of this teaching, twenty-four hours a day, it would take you twenty-two years to go through all of it. If you were only able to devote eight hours per day to it, it would take sixty-six years to go through it all.

I encourage you to use this booklet of just some of the revelations the Lord has given me to stir you up and make these truths your own. I know what the truth has done for me, and I know it will work for you. The Holy Spirit is sent to be our teacher (John 14:26), but we have to show up for class.

Receive Jesus as Your Savior

Choosing to receive Jesus Christ as your Lord and Savior is the most important decision you'll ever make!

God's Word promises, "*That if thou shalt confess with thy mouth the Lord Jesus, and shalt believe in thine heart that God hath raised him from the dead, thou shalt be saved. For with the heart man believeth unto righteousness; and with the mouth confession is made unto salvation*" (Rom. 10:9–10). "*For whosoever shall call upon the name of the Lord shall be saved*" (Rom. 10:13). By His grace, God has already done everything to provide salvation. Your part is simply to believe and receive.

Pray out loud: "Jesus, I confess that You are my Lord and Savior. I believe in my heart that God raised You from the dead. By faith in Your Word, I receive salvation now. Thank You for saving me."

The very moment you commit your life to Jesus Christ, the truth of His Word instantly comes to pass in your spirit. Now that you're born again, there's a brand-new you!

Please contact us and let us know that you've prayed to receive Jesus as your Savior. We'd like to send you some free materials to help you on your new journey. Call our Helpline: **719-635-1111** (available 24 hours a day, seven days a week) to speak to a staff member who is here to help you understand and grow in your new relationship with the Lord.

Welcome to your new life!

Receive the Holy Spirit

As His child, your loving heavenly Father wants to give you the supernatural power you need to live a new life. *"For every one that asketh receiveth; and he that seeketh findeth; and to him that knocketh it shall be opened…how much more shall* your *heavenly Father give the Holy Spirit to them that ask him?"* (Luke 11:10–13).

All you have to do is ask, believe, and receive!

Pray this: "Father, I recognize my need for Your power to live a new life. Please fill me with Your Holy Spirit. By faith, I receive it right now. Thank You for baptizing me. Holy Spirit, You are welcome in my life."

Some syllables from a language you don't recognize will rise up from your heart to your mouth (1 Cor. 14:14). As you speak them out loud by faith, you're releasing God's power from within and building yourself up in the spirit (1 Cor. 14:4). You can do this whenever and wherever you like.

It doesn't really matter whether you felt anything or not when you prayed to receive the Lord and His Spirit. If you believed in your heart that you received, then God's Word promises you did. "*Therefore I say unto you, What things soever ye desire, when ye pray, believe that ye receive* them, *and ye shall have* them" (Mark 11:24). God always honors His Word—believe it!

We would like to rejoice with you and help you understand more fully what has taken place in your life!

Please contact us to let us know that you've prayed to be filled with the Holy Spirit and to request the book *The New You & the Holy Spirit*. This book will explain in more detail about the benefits of being filled with the Holy Spirit and speaking in tongues. Call our Helpline: **719-635-1111** (available 24 hours a day, seven days a week).

Call for Prayer

If you need prayer for any reason, you can call our Helpline, 24 hours a day, seven days a week at **719-635-1111**. A trained prayer minister will answer your call and pray with you.

Every day, we receive testimonies of healings and other miracles from our Helpline, and we are ministering God's nearly-too-good-to-be-true message of the Gospel to more people than ever. So, I encourage you to call today!

About the Author

Andrew Wommack's life was forever changed the moment he encountered the supernatural love of God on March 23, 1968. As a renowned Bible teacher and author, Andrew has made it his mission to change the way the world sees God.

Andrew's vision is to go as far and deep with the Gospel as possible. His message goes far through the *Gospel Truth* television program, which is available to over half the world's population. The message goes deep through discipleship at Charis Bible College, headquartered in Woodland Park, Colorado. Founded in 1994, Charis has campuses across the United States and around the globe.

Andrew also has an extensive library of teaching materials in print, audio, and video. More than 200,000 hours of free teachings can be accessed at **awmi.net**.

Contact Information

Andrew Wommack Ministries, Inc.

PO Box 3333

Colorado Springs, CO 80934-3333

info@awmi.net

awmi.net

Helpline: 719-635-1111 (available 24/7)

Charis Bible College

info@charisbiblecollege.org

844-360-9577

CharisBibleCollege.org

For a complete list of our offices, visit
awmi.net/contact-us.

Connect with us on social media.

Andrew's LIVING COMMENTARY BIBLE SOFTWARE

Andrew Wommack's *Living Commentary* Bible study software is a user-friendly, downloadable program. It's like reading the Bible with Andrew at your side, sharing his revelation with you verse by verse.

Main features:

- Bible study software with a grace-and-faith perspective
- Over 26,000 notes by Andrew on verses from Genesis through Revelation
- *Matthew Henry's Concise Commentary*
- 12 Bible versions
- 2 concordances: *Englishman's Concordance* and *Strong's Concordance*
- 2 dictionaries: *Collaborative International Dictionary* and *Holman's Dictionary*
- Atlas with biblical maps
- Bible and *Living Commentary* statistics
- Quick navigation, including history of verses
- Robust search capabilities (for the Bible and Andrew's notes)
- "Living" (i.e., constantly updated and expanding)
- Ability to create personal notes

Whether you're new to studying the Bible or a seasoned Bible scholar, you'll gain a deeper revelation of the Word from a grace-and-faith perspective.

Purchase Andrew's *Living Commentary* today at **awmi.net/living**, and grow in the Word with Andrew.

Item code: 8350

ANDREW WOMMACK MINISTRIES